An Unplanned Life

For David Bardin

with all good
wishes,

George Elsey

at the Truman
Library
8. 14. 06

An Unplanned Life

A Memoir by George McKee Elsey

UNIVERSITY OF MISSOURI PRESS

COLUMBIA AND LONDON

Library of Congress Cataloging-in-Publication Data

Elsey, George M., 1918-
    An unplanned life : a memoir / by George McKee Elsey.
         p.   cm.
    Summary: "Memoir of the author's experiences working in the White House
during the Roosevelt and Truman administrations, including inside accounts of his
work on classified documents, U.S.-Soviet relations, and Truman's "Whistle-Stop
Campaign," and his long association with the American Red Cross"—Provided by
publisher.
    Includes index.
    ISBN-13: 978-0-8262-1622-9 (alk. paper)
    ISBN-10: 0-8262-1622-6 (alk. paper)
  1. Elsey, George M., 1918- 2. Political consultants—United States—Biography.
3. Presidents—United States—Staff—Biography. 4. Roosevelt, Franklin D. (Franklin
Delano), 1882-1945. 5. Truman, Harry S., 1884-1972. 6. United States—Politics and
government—1933-1945. 7. United States—Politics and government—1945-1989.
8. United States—Foreign relations—Soviet Union. 9. Soviet Union—Foreign relations—United States. 10. American Red Cross—History—20th century. I. Title.
    E840.8.E45A3 2005
    973.917'092—dc22

                                                                2005018186

∞ This paper meets the requirements of the
American National Standard for Permanence of Paper
for Printed Library Materials, Z39.48, 1984.

Designer: Stephanie Foley
Typesetter: Crane Composition, Inc.
Printer and binder: The Maple-Vail Book Manufacturing Group
Typefaces: Granjon and NeutraText

❦ In Loving Memory

Sally Phelps Bradley Elsey

February 15, 1921–November 19, 2004

Contents

A Few Words of Introduction

This is a memoir, not an autobiography. The Canadian writer Robertson Davies defined autobiography as a "pernicious form of fiction." I shall stay clear. This will not be a complete account of my life. Rather, it will be an easy flow of recollections—of people and events—as I remember and choose to record them. If some episodes are presented at greater length than their importance warrants, it is because they stand out so clearly in my mind. If the memoir must have a title, it will be *An Unplanned Life*. Why? This will become apparent as you read.

From time to time, fragments of conversation will appear as I noted them at the time, but this is not the place for an abundance of documents, letters, or photographs. Only a few of these will be included. Nor is this the place for descriptions of places where I worked or that I visited, no matter how fascinating they seemed to me at the time. Goethe, in his journal for May 7, 1786, wrote on reaching Taormina, Sicily, "Thank goodness, everything we saw today has been sufficiently described already." So it will be with the White House, the Pentagon, the "Marble Palace" of the American Red Cross. No descriptions of them or of Baghdad or Belgrade, Geneva or Jerusalem, Moscow or Manila, Seoul or Cetinje, or a score of other places well remembered but "sufficiently described already." Except for one place not well described—Oakmont, Pennsylvania.

So let the tale begin with Oakmont.

An Unplanned Life

Chapter One

From Oakmont to ONI

Mother, Dad, and I arrived in Oakmont by train in the early morning of September 15, 1925. Dad was on a year's sabbatical from teaching chemistry at the University of Kansas. We had been in Lawrence for seven years, moving from Palo Alto, California, where I was born on February 5, 1918, when Dad was teaching and completing his Ph.D. at Stanford. Rather than stay in Lawrence for research and writing, a common practice for faculty members in their free year, Dad opted for a change of scenery and mode of life. Welcomed at the research laboratory of Westinghouse Electric, where the director told him to look around and dig into anything he found interesting, Dad found the place fascinating. He was impressed by the brilliance of the physicists, chemists, and electrical engineers—among them several Russians who had fled the Bolshevik revolution. As the sabbatical year drew to a close, Dad decided that industrial research was more to his liking than teaching. He resigned his tenured post at the university and joined Westinghouse, then one of the country's best-known and most highly regarded industrial giants. His association with Westinghouse was to last fifty years.

Dad and Mother knew only one couple in the Pittsburgh area, Paul and Ida Faragher. Ida had been their high school classmate in Modesto, California, and they had become acquainted with Paul while he was earning his Ph.D. The Faraghers were settled in Oakmont, twelve miles north of Pittsburgh on the Allegheny River. Wishing to be near the only people they knew, Mother and Dad chose Oakmont too. It became my hometown then, and I still so regard it.

Oakmont in 1925 with a population approaching five thousand was an interesting community. It was a blend of city suburb, small industrial town, and business center for a countryside still dotted with family farms.

Some men commuted by train to the downtown offices in Pittsburgh of great corporations such as United States Steel, the Aluminum Company of America, and the Pennsylvania Railroad. Others, like Dad and Paul Faragher, drove to fringe areas where laboratories could sprawl over less expensive land—Dad to East Pittsburgh and Paul to the Aluminum Company's lab in nearby New Kensington. Founded in 1889, Oakmont had its own small industrial base. Two steel fabricating plants and a paint factory were among those alongside the railroad tracks. Their officials and blue-collar workers made up a good portion of the town's residents. The nearby hills and valleys were dotted with small dairy farms and truck gardens. Farmers came into Oakmont to sell their produce and to shop, some in cars so old they drew curious children—I among them. Many of the dairy farmers sold their milk to the Oakmont Dairy, but not "Old Jane." She brought her milk into Oakmont, delivering it to her faithful customers from a horse-drawn buggy—an object older and of even greater curiosity than the earliest Model T Ford. (It was on a small farm next to "Old Jane's," owned by the grandfather of one of my grade-school classmates, that I learned to milk a cow and handle a horse-drawn plow. Neither talent has been put to the test for more than seventy years.)

The population blend of this mixed economy was reflected in my grade school and high school classes. In Lawrence, my playmates had been cookie-cutter faculty children. Not so in Oakmont. My classmates, from third grade through high school, were racially, religiously, ethnically, and economically mixed. Their parents ranged from well-to-do to below the poverty line. Some spoke Italian, Greek, or a Slavic language at home. But we were all equal in the classroom and on the playground. A youngster accepts without reflection the environment he or she is in. Not until I entered college and once again found myself in a homogeneous group did I appreciate the value of growing up in a multicultural setting such as Oakmont's. (And that is why, as I write this, I am glad our grandsons are experiencing in their school years the blend of cultures that defines our nation.)

What was it like to grow up in Oakmont in the early years of the twentieth century? The main street, somewhat pompously named Allegheny River Boulevard, was a blend of houses and small shops along its one-mile length. Large shopping centers and supermarkets were decades in the future. A grocery store was likely to be a single room no larger—and frequently smaller—than a school classroom. Here one bought the staples—flour, sugar, canned fruits and vegetables, packaged baked goods, and so forth. (Frozen foods were in the future.) No one served himself. A clerk stood behind a counter. You gave your order, "Two cans of string beans, please." If you thought the clerk's memory was good enough, you might name three or four other items at the same time. She would move back and forth, pulling your items from the shelves and filling your market basket—if you brought one. Otherwise, she put everything in a "poke," western Pennsylvania talk for a large paper bag, penciling the price of each purchase on the bag and toting them all up at the end. No "scanners," just simple grade-school arithmetic, told you the amount owed.

We favored the A&P grocery store. Next to the A&P and in the same building was Ed Henke's butcher shop. If the cuts of meat you wanted were not in the display case, Ed would step into the big refrigerator, come out, and chop your lamb or pork chops as you wanted them. A door or two away, the Libertos dispensed seasonal fruits and vegetables from their own or their friends' farms. What wasn't grown locally came by train from the Pittsburgh wholesale produce markets. If you hungered for fish, you waited until Friday and then crossed the street to Volkwein's. In addition to groceries, Mr. Volkwein provided fish that came out from Pittsburgh in large insulated boxes on the first morning train on Fridays (and only that day). Frozen fish, like frozen vegetables, was in the future.

Oakmont had a family-owned bakery, but many—we among them— bought breads, cakes, and pies from a truck that came out from Haller's Bakery in Pittsburgh twice a week. The driver would knock on the kitchen door, and you took your pick from his large display basket. If you had ordered something special on his previous visit, that would be ready for you. My mother was not the best customer. She enjoyed baking pies and cakes herself. As for milk, unless you were a customer of "Old Jane's," the milkman left his glass bottle at the door early each morning, so early that in Pittsburgh's cold winters the paper cap that sealed the top was apt to be pushed right out of the bottle by the frozen cream. (In those days, before homogenized milk, the cream rose naturally to the top. The first thing one did on bringing the bottle into the house was to pour off the cream into its own pitcher—unless it was frozen!)

Oakmont had all the other necessary stores, all small and mostly family owned. The two drugstores had soda fountains, with the owner-pharmacist about as busy making ice cream sodas and milk shakes as filling the prescriptions of the town's physicians. Doctors and dentists practiced from their homes or from small offices above the stores on the Boulevard. The sole hardware store was owned by Mr. Bossert, who, when not advising on which tool was best for the task at hand, was likely attending to the town's business. He was our "burgess," the archaic term for mayor. Another one-room business was the First National Bank of Oakmont, across the street from the railroad station. It had outgrown its first home in the basement of the local Carnegie Library. (Almost every small town had its own bank until the Great Depression killed off thousands of them. Ours survived.)

Mr. Lenchner made men's suits from the front room of his house. Mr. Rodnok sold twenty-five-cent tickets to his movie theater (120 seats) and ran the projector himself. After the repeal of the Eighteenth Amendment, Oakmont had a state-owned liquor store—no private liquor stores were allowed in Pennsylvania. The conservatism reflected in the tight liquor laws was apparent in many other ways, not the least being rigid "blue laws." All businesses were closed on Sundays. The one exception in Oakmont was Pilgram's stationery and gift shop, where Fred Pilgram was allowed to sell the Sunday papers. My father was a faithful customer of Fred's, always buying the Sunday *New York Times,* which came out from Pittsburgh on a midmorning train.

When Oakmont's shops could not meet our needs, Pittsburgh's department stores were only twenty-five or thirty minutes away by train. But going "into town" wasn't necessary very often. We were content with our community, its businesses, churches, schools, and library—all within easy walking distance. Oakmont was, after all, only one mile square. It was a town where people knew one another, sometimes more about one another than you wished. When my father's sister Caryl was visiting one time from Chicago, she and I went for a long walk around Oakmont. I kept introducing her to other walkers. "You seem to know everybody," she remarked with surprise. "Sure, everybody knows everybody here," was my answer. An exaggeration, but not much of one.

There was one exception to this "small-town-ness." The Oakmont Country Club, perched on a hill above the town, overlooking the Allegheny River, had been founded in 1903, one of the nation's earliest golf clubs. It was Oakmont's one claim to fame. Many national tournaments had been held there and would continue to be. The club scarcely entered the consciousness of most of us. It was for "Rich Pittsburghers" who sped up the hill in their Cords, Franklins, Duesenbergs, and other luxury cars for afternoons of golf. Some members would arrive by train, to be met by the club's station wagon (whence the term). The club was several notches above most Oakmonters. The closest many of us came to it was as spectators at a tournament or, as was the case with some of my high school classmates, as caddies for the members. (There were no golf carts then; caddies carried the bags.)

Oakmont was a fine place to grow up. It was a happy place—until the Great Depression.

Historians mark the Stock Market Crash of October 1929 as the beginning of the most severe and longest lasting economic depression in the country's history. At the time, the Crash meant nothing to most youngsters, but my seventh-grade class was a bit different. Our arithmetic teacher was introducing us to business economics. We were learning how to write checks and balance an account, courtesy of the local bank, which provided the supplies. We learned how to compute interest on our imaginary savings accounts and what stocks and bonds were all about. We progressed to the point of making imaginary investments in stocks, most of us choosing stocks of Pittsburgh companies whose names were familiar to us. But instead of the paper profits our teacher expected, based on her experience of the Roaring Twenties, we watched with dismay as our fictitious stock portfolios fell through the floor. Our real-life education was beginning.

As the Crash turned into the Depression, Oakmonters began to suffer. Each year was worse than the one before. Some local businesses cut down on working hours, laid off workers, then shut down entirely. A few scraped along with just enough business to avoid bankruptcy. Many local merchants folded. Farmers came to the back door, begging housewives to buy at whatever price they could afford. Blue-collar workers fared the worst, but white-collar employees felt the pinch too. The fathers of some of my friends were fired outright. Dad was among the lucky ones. Westinghouse, like most big companies, began across-the-board salary cuts, 5 percent, then 10 percent, then another 10 percent. The checks were smaller, but they came every month. We felt ourselves among the fortunate.

One hundred and forty boys and girls were in my class entering Oakmont High School in September 1931. Only 103 graduated four years later. The families of some of the missing had left town in search of work elsewhere. Many had dropped out on reaching age sixteen, when compulsory schooling under state law ended. They sought work at whatever jobs they could find, even if only for a few cents per hour, to help their struggling families. Grim though the situation seemed to us in Oakmont, we knew that we were considerably better off than most of those in the Greater Pittsburgh area with its soup kitchens and thousands of homeless living in grim makeshift shelters.

By 1935, only 6 percent of the country's households earned as much as three thousand dollars a year. With the country in such dire straits, few youngsters fortunate enough to stay through high school could look ahead to higher education in any form. College was unthinkable for most. Even trade schools were out of reach. Unlike later years when "getting into college" was a tortuous challenge, in the midthirties anyone whose parents could scrape up the funds was likely to be welcomed at his or her school of first choice. Colleges ceased to be selective. They needed students. Twenty members of my graduating class were admitted to the schools they had chosen. Most economized by living at home and commuting to one of Pittsburgh's universities. A few attended schools, easily reached by a short drive, in nearby Ohio or western Pennsylvania. The other eighty-three? They looked for work.

Dad had hoped that I could go to Stanford as he, his brother, and two of his sisters had. In mid-Depression, the cost of four years of transcontinental train trips ruled that out. So where? It was up to me to find the answer. I had become intrigued by Princeton's recently established School of Public and International Affairs, which I had first read about in *Reader's Digest* at the onset of my senior year in high school. The SPIA (now renamed the Woodrow Wilson School) was intended to prepare young men (no women—they were thirty years in Princeton's future) for careers in government or foreign service. I wrote for a university catalog, read it through and through, and looked up everything I could find about Princeton in Pittsburgh's main library. Princeton seemed everything I could hope for. Mother and Dad were skeptical. Princeton was a long day's journey by car or train from Oakmont. However, one of Dad's closest friends, a fellow chemist, was on the Princeton faculty. Howell and Hannah Furman could be counted on to keep a watchful eye on me. Costs would be a problem. Princeton's tuition was a staggering $450 a year. Only the Massachusetts Institute of Technology was as high. Always the optimist, I applied for admission and a scholarship. I had done well in high school, graduating first in the class, but I realized how inadequate Oakmont High School's preparation had been when the college entrance exam scores came in. Mine were mediocre—and that's putting the best light on them. Nevertheless, I was admitted with a $400 a year scholarship, so hungry was Princeton for students in that Depression year, especially for students from public high schools to help soften its image as an elite place for eastern prep school graduates.

(Because the September 1934 issue of *Reader's Digest* was the origin of my interest in Princeton and attendance there was a major factor in shaping my career, I had the issue bound and have lovingly preserved it to this day.)

The first term at college was tough. Eighty-three percent of my classmates were from prep schools, mostly large, well-known eastern ones. They were far better prepared than I. However, by the second term I had learned how to study effectively, and by sophomore year all was going well. I made good friends, most of them in the 17 percent high school contingent and from families whose Depression era incomes kept us on modest budgets. No Philadelphia debutante parties for us, no weekends in New York nightclubs such as my short-lived classmate, John Fitzgerald Kennedy, enjoyed. Princeton's two movie houses sufficed.

Princeton had no fraternities. They had been abolished in the nineteenth century. All students lived in dorms on campus all four years. In the first two years, we ate in University Commons. Late in sophomore year, after a nerve-racking week of being called on in one's room by visitors from the eighteen "eating clubs," one hoped to be invited to join one of the clubs where he would take his meals in junior and senior years. My closest friends and I compared notes on the "bids" we had received and negotiated our group of seven into Court Club. Court was well down on the list as far as social standing was concerned, but it offered exactly what we wanted—a congenial group of hard-working students. So devoted to our studies were we that in our senior year Court Club was awarded an oversize silver cup called the Armstrong Trophy. This was an award to the club whose seniors had the best academic record of any club. In fact, we had the highest average any club had attained in the history of the trophy. Our noses had not been as close to the grindstone as that implies. Most of us were active in extracurricular activities. Emulating my namesake grandfather, George Elsey, who had been on the board of the yearbook at the University of the Pacific, I worked hard on Princeton's oddly named *Bric-a-Brac*. We on the board ran it as a moneymaking enterprise, splitting the take at year end. The healthy check went into my bank account along with proceeds from various other profitable activities. As a member of the Cashiers Squad, I was well paid for selling tickets, and I saw games for free.

In those pre–World War II years, newspapers such as the *New York Times* printed information about Ivy League schools in astonishing detail. The *Times,* for example, in March 1939, reported that 576 Princeton undergraduates were on the first term's honor roll, listing all their names with details on the extracurricular activities of many of them. When alumni reunions were held that June, the *Times* even gave details of reunion costumes—evidences, if you will, of social snobbery prevalent in that distant time.

Princeton alumni then and now are noted for their fierce loyalty to the university in general and to their class in particular. My class of 1939, year in and year out, has set records in the percentage of its members who contribute to annual giving. Classmates keep in touch—especially club-mates, but, alas, by 2000, I was the sole survivor of the seven who entered Court Club en bloc.

Although it was my interest in the School of Public and International Affairs that led me to Princeton, I grew increasingly interested in history—American history in particular. Senior year was devoted to writing a thesis and worrying about What Next? I decided on a career of teaching history at the college level, which meant graduate school. Harvard, Yale, and Princeton all offered generous fellowships. While I would have been happy to remain in Princeton, my faculty friends advised that Harvard had the best reputation for graduate work in American history—so Harvard it would be. Mother and Dad understood, although this was not the course Dad had followed, sticking with Stanford for his A.B., M.A., and Ph.D. The spring of my senior year was a good one for Dad. He had been awarded the company's highest honor, the Westinghouse Medal for Merit, for his skill in solving complex manufacturing problems with chemical implications. With it came a substantial salary increase. The family budget was no longer under the stress of the early thirties. My parents saw no problem in supplementing my fellowship to fund graduate school.

I left Princeton in June 1939 with warmest feelings, frequently remembering words that Harold Dodds, the university's president, had uttered in welcoming us as freshmen in September 1935: "If you give your best to Princeton, she will give her best to you, and both will profit by the transaction." I left the campus the afternoon of graduation day, somewhat tearfully, believing I had done my part and certain that the university had done its.

To repeat the oft-quoted opening words of Charles Dickens's *Tale of Two Cities,* "It was the best of times, it was the worst of times." So September 1939 seemed to me. Being a graduate student at Harvard on a fellowship, studying American history, made it the best of times. But just days before I arrived in Cambridge, the Second World War began. The worst of times had arrived.

Nazi Germany and the Soviet Union quickly overran Poland, bringing declarations of war from England and France. Not much happened, however, for some months in Western Europe, leading cynics to declare this was a "phony war." Isolationists led by such charismatic figures as Charles Lindbergh noisily argued that Europe was none of our business. All changed in April and May 1940. The German blitzkrieg raced through Holland and Belgium, drove a British army in northern France into the sea, smashed France's supposedly superior army, and forced a French surrender. Italy jumped in for the kill, threatening to sever England's "lifeline of the Empire." Taking the war to the north, Germany seized Denmark and occupied Norway. Nearly surrounded and pitifully weak, England stood alone. Japan had been flexing her military muscles for years, steadily encroaching into China and threatening American and European interests throughout the Pacific area. Jarred by all this, pressed by President Roosevelt, and strongly supported by a wide variety of public interest groups, Congress turned its back on the isolationists and began energetic programs to strengthen the army and the navy. In October 1940 came the Draft Act, which required all able-bodied young men to register for military service.

My Harvard roommate was Pitt Willand, a Princeton classmate and fellow Court Club member, also seeking a graduate degree in history. We were avid followers of world events, and we agreed we would probably be in uniform before we earned our Ph.D.s. We dug into our studies as though our lives depended on them (which, in a way, they did). Pitt's car provided relief from the grind. On pleasant weekends, we enjoyed scenic and historic surroundings—there was no shortage of either in an easy drive from Cambridge. Plymouth, Lexington, Concord, Salem, Portsmouth, Marblehead, the White Mountains, Boston itself—we enjoyed them all. But after each excursion, it was back to face the near certainty of war.

The history department faculty was concerned at the length of time it was taking its graduate students to complete their doctoral studies. With the prospects of military service intruding, it was likely that many might never get a degree. The department decided to select two or three students at the end of the first year and excuse them from the requirement to pass an onerous (and, to some, terrifying) oral "general examination," thus allowing them to start work on a doctoral dissertation at the end of the second year rather than two, three, or even four years later. I was thrilled to be one of those freed from the burden of preparing for "the general."

I had fallen under the spell of Samuel Eliot Morison, already well known for his books and soon to be even better known when he won the Pulitzer Prize for his biography of Christopher Columbus, based in part on his having traced Columbus's journeys across the Atlantic using navigational records of "the admiral of the ocean sea." Morison was generous with his time in a seminar on methods of historical research. Of pioneer New England stock, his family for generations had known other well-placed families, one being the Palfreys. The name meant nothing to me until, on one of my seminar assignments, I interviewed John Gorham Palfrey III, a prominent Boston attorney. I inquired about his family records. With his endorsement, over the next few months I extracted from attics of family members trunks, boxes, and cartons of correspondence, business papers, diaries, and documents from the mid-eighteenth century to the early twentieth century that had attracted no one's attention for decades. Generations of Palfreys had known generations of other worthy New Englanders. Letters of John Adams, John Quincy Adams, and Henry Adams, for example, were mixed with Palfrey family letters, as were letters from literary figures such as Henry Wadsworth Longfellow and Ralph Waldo Emerson. Not all Palfreys had stayed in Massachusetts. One had established a sugar plantation in Louisiana. Somehow, plantation records, complete with rosters of slaves, their prices, and their progeny, had found their way back to Boston. Out of all this, and much more, would there be a subject for a doctoral dissertation? Morison thought so.

In the summer of 1941, it was hard to concentrate on the past. Like every other healthy male, I was subject to the draft, being number 394 on the roster of the Oakmont Draft Board. A call-up in the next few months was probable. Determined to make as much progress in the Palfrey papers as possible before that occurred, I stayed in Cambridge working in the Treasure Room of Harvard's Widener Library, where I had arranged to store them and get them in order until their future could be decided. I shared working space with a graduate student from the English department. Richard Ballinger was a few years older than I. He was a Naval Academy alumnus who had not been commissioned on graduation because of an eye problem since corrected. Ballinger was now a Naval Reserve officer, expecting an early summons to active duty. "Why" he asked, "sit around and wait for the draft to suck you into the army? You ought to apply for a Naval Reserve commission. Naval Intelligence is actively recruiting guys like you."

The suggestion was as startling as it was unexpected. I took the subway to the headquarters of the First Naval District in Boston, was interviewed by the district intelligence officer, passed a physical examination, and left with an envelope bulging with forms to be filled out. Dick Ballinger, feeling himself godfather of the idea, began writing letters. One found its way to Lieutenant William C. Mott in Washington, whom I was soon to meet.

For the academic year beginning September 1, 1941, I had been granted one of Harvard's most prestigious and generous awards, a Sheldon Fellowship. It came with one condition—it was for travel and study away from Cambridge. Many Sheldon fellows in the past had gone to Europe, but the war ruled that out for me. I had chosen for my dissertation, from the mass of Palfrey archives, to write a biography of the first John Gorham Palfrey. He had had a multifaceted career: starting as a Unitarian minister, he had evolved into an editor of the country's leading literary magazine, antislavery spokesman, politician (serving one term in the House of Representatives with Abraham Lincoln, also a one-term congressman), and prolific historian. Since the Sheldon Fellowship prevented me from staying with my cache of papers in Widener Library, where should I go? I chose Washington, D.C. The Library of

Congress could provide almost everything I would need beyond the basics in the Palfrey papers, and those I could draw on as needed. The dissertation was not, however, the compelling reason for Washington. I wanted to be where I could press in person my application for a Naval Reserve commission.

I prepared to leave Cambridge in September 1941 with real affection for the university and the place, feeling—to my surprise—even more emotional than I had on departing Princeton two years earlier. Not only were there good friends among the students, the faculty, and the library staff, the Palfrey exercise had led to some fascinating Cambridge acquaintances. One of the most interesting was an elderly gentleman named Henry Wadsworth Longfellow Dana, whose grandfathers were the namesake poet and Richard Henry Dana, author of *Two Years before the Mast,* a favorite book of mine as a teenager. Mr. Dana lived in one of Cambridge's great eighteenth-century mansions, Craigie House. It had been George Washington's residence when he took command of the Continental Army early in the Revolution. In the mid-1800s, it had become Longfellow's home. Dana was so pleased at my showing him letters Longfellow had written to Palfrey, letters he had not known existed, that he invited me to visit Craigie House any time I wished. After one such visit, I wrote Tom Webb, my Princeton roommate, then teaching in California: "It is pleasant to sit in the poet's library at his writing table in the very chair that Washington sat in when that room was the General Headquarters of the American Army in 1775-1776." Cambridge had, indeed, offered many pleasant experiences, but it was time to move on.

While my Widener Library companion, Dick Ballinger, prompted my naval application, another Cambridge friend became its most enthusiastic advocate. James Risk had held a Naval Reserve commission since graduating from Dartmouth a few years earlier. Called to active duty in January 1941, he had given up his instructorship in American history at the Massachusetts Institute of Technology and had recommended me as his successor to fill out the school year. When an invitation to do so arrived, I turned it down, not wanting any interruption in my pursuit of a degree. When Jim learned of my naval application, he was eager to begin my education, urging me to visit his destroyer undergoing repairs at the Brooklyn Navy Yard. In late August, on my way back from a quick visit with Mother and Dad in Oakmont, and an all-important session with the Oakmont Draft Board, which agreed to defer my call-up until my naval status was determined, I had to change trains in New York. In those days, I occasionally wrote notes of events; this one has survived:

26 August 1941. Left Pittsburgh early morning, New York by late afternoon. In the 20 minutes between trains, I telephone Jim Risk, now on active duty as ensign, USNR. Instead of merely exchanging greetings, he invited me to come to the Navy Yard. This was too fine an opportunity to let escape, & I took a room, dressed & went to Brooklyn. In the heaviest rain of the year, I explored his destroyer, had dinner in the officers' mess & learned much. Later we saw the *Augusta,* flagship of the Atlantic fleet, returning to port for the first time since the Roosevelt-Churchill conference. Saw other cruisers in the Yard, also the two 45,000 ton battleships, the largest ever constructed, on the ways. The most thrilling experience was an hour or more going over the *Dido,* a year-old British cruiser badly bombed during the evacuation of Crete. I was astounded at the freedom we had. Jim, only a U.S. ensign, had the run of the ship. We saw the bomb damage, the bridge, the guns, etc—everything we wished. It was utterly amazing that our navies are in such close accord that this was possible. The two seem to be one. Met and talked with British officers. Then several good drinks at the officers' club, and back to NYC.

Jim had a few days' leave in early September and came up to Cambridge to visit friends. Determined to continue my naval education, he escorted me through the Boston Navy Yard, teeming with destroyers and other craft being readied as antisubmarine escorts for the convoys of merchant ships that were keeping England from collapse. Our historical bent led us to *Old Ironsides,* the 1794 frigate still on "active duty" as the flagship of the Atlantic Fleet although permanently moored in the yard. (I had first seen this oldest ship of our navy in 1927 on a New England visit with my parents. I bought then two desk ornaments made from ancient oak beams being replaced; they are preserved in my study.)

I left Boston for Washington on September 11, 1941, taking the overnight boat to New York. This pleasant, relaxed mode of travel ended in World War II, never to be resumed. In the ship's lounge after dinner with Harvard acquaintances, I listened to President Roosevelt's radio address telling the country that an American destroyer had been attacked by a German submarine in the Atlantic. Someone nervously wondered out loud if it wouldn't have been safer to take the train! Much of the next day I spent again with Jim Risk at the Brooklyn Yard. When he wasn't on required duty on his own destroyer, we checked out the many ships under construction. Still feeling a total novice, I boarded a train with Hanson Baldwin's *What the Citizen Should Know about the Navy* and read it all the way to Washington, arriving late on the afternoon of the thirteenth.

The city was crowded. The defense buildup had brought thousands of new federal employees to government departments. Fortunately, I had a convenient place awaiting me. One of Dad's Westinghouse colleagues had a brother-in-law on the staff of the Library of Congress, Tom Shaw. Shaw invited me to share his apartment just three blocks from the library, at 412 First Street, S.E. He helped me settle into a study carrel on the balcony of the library's great reading room and smoothed the path for research and writing. My heart, however, was not fully in a biography of a long-gone figure, interesting as he was. My work was desultory, interrupted by thoughts of the navy and by stirring events all about me. There were many college and graduate school friends in the city, some working for members of Congress, who alerted me to things I shouldn't miss. One such was the cliffhanger debate on the extension of the Draft Act, due to expire in October. It squeaked through the House of Representatives by a one-vote margin. More to the point for me was the status of my commission. Would it "squeak through" too? I asked for an appointment with Lieutenant Mott, recipient of one of Ballinger's notes. I found him on duty in the Office of Naval Intelligence in Main Navy, a World War I "temporary structure" still serving as naval headquarters on Constitution Avenue. (This "tempo" survived until the Nixon administration!) For security reasons, Mott could not be explicit as to his work, but he made it clear that he was in charge of a key small office that was certain to expand as the international situation heated up. He was on the lookout for new Reserve ensigns ("regular" officers were all being given sea duty). For whatever reason, soon after our first meeting, Mott said he was pushing my application and that I would be assigned to his group as soon as my commission came through.

On Saturday evening, December 6, 1941, some former Harvard graduate students and I had dinner. We speculated about how soon we would be at war with Germany, eager as Hitler was to wage all-out submarine war against us and end our support of England. I guessed about six weeks, the time it would take for the Germans to regain the initiative in Russia and capture Moscow. We had an answer the next day—but it was not war with Germany. In the first few hours after the news about the Pearl Harbor disaster, Tom Shaw and I huddled by the radio. Impatient to do something—anything—I rode a streetcar to the White House. A crowd was assembling on the Pennsylvania Avenue sidewalk—silent, respectful, curious as black limousines with cabinet members and officials, whom I probably should have been able to identify but couldn't, drove through the northwest gate. Soldiers arrived. The police asked us in muted tones to cross over into Lafayette Park.

At noon on Monday, the eighth, I stood at the House wing of the Capitol. Security, primitive by later standards, allowed our small crowd to be close as Roosevelt slowly made his way into the building supported by his son James, elegant in his Marine Corps dress uniform. This was the first time I had seen the president. I knew, as did everyone, that he had suffered polio years earlier, but that he moved with such difficulty was startling. Newsreels never showed him in motion. I raced four blocks to the apartment to listen to the "Day of Infamy" speech to the Joint Session. "Hostilities exist . . . I ask that the Congress declare that a state of war exists between the United States and the Japanese Empire . . . We will gain the inevitable triumph." Returning to the Capitol after the speech, I watched as Roosevelt posed for still camera shots—no motion pictures were allowed of his awkward gait as he went to his car. He drove past, smiling and waving. I went home and wrote, "He was grey and very aged."

And then to the phone. What was my status? If I was not commissioned soon, the Oakmont Draft Board would lose patience and toss me into army boot camp. Mott, with the dogged persistence that I was to learn was one of his positive traits, found the answer. Because my application had been filed in Boston, notice of its acceptance had been sent there. It was bogged down in the chaos prevalent everywhere. Lost, too, was the telegram ordering me to active duty in the Office of Naval Intelligence. All this was straightened out in the next few days, and on Saturday, December 13, I was sworn in as an ensign and assigned to duty with Mott.

Hitler, however, had foolishly declared war on the United States on

Thursday, the eleventh, to the great relief of the British. Had he not done so, outraged public and congressional opinion would have forced Roosevelt to concentrate our effort against Japan, leaving aid to Britain vastly diminished. The president did not return to the Capitol to ask for a declaration against Germany. A written message sufficed. In those far-off days when anyone could walk into the building at any time, it was a simple matter for me to enter the visitors' gallery of the House of Representatives, hear the presidential message read by the clerk, and watch the House vote without debate. The vote would have been unanimous except for the "nay" of Jeannette Rankin of Montana, who voted just as she had on April 6, 1917, when she was the only naysayer on the occasion of that declaration of war as well!

I went to work in Mott's office still in a civilian suit. One could not order a uniform without documentary evidence of status as an officer. Military tailors were so rushed that two weeks went by before I was properly clad. I seemed to be always showing my ID to guards throughout the Navy Department. When the tailor handed over two uniforms at last, I headed for Tom Shaw's apartment. Proudly, I emerged, eager to exchange a proper military salute for the first time. A small boy on the front steps looked up at me and said, "My daddy's a policeman too!" An ensign, alas, commands little respect.

Mott's office, "A-3-c," was at the bottom level on the organizational chart of the Office of Naval Intelligence, but it was at the top in terms of the information it handled. It had custody of the most secret telegrams coming to ONI. In the benighted practice of the times, only *one* copy of a highly classified message was provided, no matter how important the message might be from the commander in chief of the Pacific or any other top official. Mott, or whoever was the senior officer in "A-3-c" in his absence, would decide who in the Office of Naval Intelligence should see the message. One of us youngsters would trudge about the building, usually going first to the director of ONI, a rear admiral. We would wait respectfully (and *silently*) until he had pondered it, initialed it, and handed it back. Then on to the next designated officer. This was a preposterously inefficient system of conveying information that fell of it own weight as the war heated up, but by then I had moved on. As the newest recruit in Mott's shop, I often was assigned the watch from midnight to 8:00 a.m. Incoming cable traffic was light during night hours. There was plenty of time to dig into office files. Here were the details of the December 7 losses at Pearl Harbor and the catastrophe at Clark Air Base in the Philippines where MacArthur had failed to heed the lessons of Pearl Harbor and his air force was destroyed. (We got army cables as well as navy messages.) I learned the most secret of all secrets—that the United States and England had broken many of the Japanese and German codes. Although the duties of Mott's watch officers could have been handled by any clerk, civilian or military, it was the highly classified character of the information to which we were privy that required us to be commissioned officers.

Because the hours were irregular and the street-car ride from Shaw's apartment on Capitol Hill was tedious, I left the apartment with warm thanks for Tom's hospitality and moved to a rooming house on Seventeenth Street within walking distance of the Navy Department. Weeks flowed by pleasantly. New friendships with fellow officers emerged, and there was always the thrill of knowing far more than the newspapers reported. Mott, usually gregarious and outspoken, in late February '42 grew silent and preoccupied. Early in March, he confided in me. The naval aide to the president, Captain John L. McCrea, had broached the possibility of his being assigned to a very confidential place in the White House known as the Map Room. Mott could not be transferred there until the officer who had set up the room moved on. This was a well-known movie actor and Naval Reserve officer, Robert Montgomery, a favorite of FDR's. Mott was ecstatic but intensely nervous lest Montgomery decide to stay or someone else nudged in. If he was picked, Mott said, at the first opening for a Map Room Watch Officer, he would ask for me. Now it was my turn to be ecstatic! I could not conceive of a more exciting post for a prospective teacher of American history than to be at the White House during the nation's greatest war.

Chapter Two

The Map Room

The first White House Map Room took shape in a cluttered temporary space in the West Wing of the White House. In the hectic days that followed the Pearl Harbor attack of December 7, 1941, the naval aide to the president, Captain John Beardall, took over what was known as the Fish Room. This windowless room directly across a corridor from the president's Oval Office owed its name to the trophies Herbert Hoover had caught on his fishing weekends at his camp on the Rapidan River in Virginia. Roosevelt's much larger deep-sea catches replaced Hoover's fish, and the room kept its name. (It is now known as the Roosevelt Room with portraits of Theodore and Franklin to maintain a bipartisan atmosphere.) Beardall placed maps of battle areas on easels positioned around the room; brought in safes where classified messages from military commands and cables from Churchill, Stalin, and other leaders could be filed; and added desks for the young army and navy officers who stood watch around the clock ready to brief the president on war events whenever he had a break in his schedule.

Prime Minister Winston Churchill arrived in mid-December, bringing with him his own portable map room, which he set up in a second-floor White House bedroom across the hall from the Queen's Bedroom, which he took over as though he owned the place. Roosevelt was a daily visitor to the prime minister's sophisticated presentation of military fronts and vivid displays of allied and enemy naval fleets. Enchanted, Roosevelt told Beardall after Churchill's departure, "Fix up a room for me like Churchill's."

Beardall plucked Lieutenant Robert Montgomery from the Office of Naval Intelligence. Montgomery, fresh from duty with the U.S. Naval Liaison Office in London, was familiar with Churchill's underground

War Room, far more impressive than the traveling map room he had brought to Washington. The War Room was the command center for the British war effort, Churchill being minister of defense as well as prime minister. Impressed by what he had seen in London, Montgomery responded to Beardall's instruction to "fix up a room like Churchill's" with a grandiose proposal for an American underground war room to be dug under what was then known as Ickes Park, the area between the Department of the Interior and Constitution Avenue where the War and Navy Departments were located. (The Pentagon was still in the early states of construction.) Montgomery proposed that top admirals and generals and civilian officials gather in this war room for a once-a-day presentation of the war situation. He envisioned himself as the ideal "presenter." His proposal went nowhere. The only digging that took place was a tunnel from the White House under East Executive Avenue to the "gold vaults" of the Treasury Department, where Roosevelt could be moved to safety in the event of a German attack on Washington. (This was as ridiculous as the panicky mounting of antiaircraft guns on the roofs of downtown buildings. The Germans had neither land planes capable of transatlantic flight nor any aircraft carriers.)

Thwarted in his grandiose scheme, Montgomery came down to earth. He would leave the Fish Room—it was too exposed to newsmen and the numerous West Wing visitors—and relocate to the White House itself. He found the perfect spot in the Trophy Room, so named for the gifts—official and unofficial—that were sent to the president and Mrs. Roosevelt. The room was on the ground floor, directly across the corridor from the elevator the president used in going between his living quarters on the second floor and his office in the West Wing. He could catch the overnight news first thing in the morning and stop in again at the end of the day. Security was ideal. This area was off-limits to all except the official family.

Montgomery had the paneled walls covered with soft wallboard for their protection and so that the maps could be readily changed. Desks and file cabinets were placed in an island in the center of the room so that the president, in his wheelchair, could study the maps at close range. The maps of battle areas were covered with clear plastic. Grease pencil markings showed the dispositions of enemy and allied troops. Charts of the oceans were studded with colored pins—blue for U.S. ships, orange for Japanese, red for British, black for German, gray for Italian. The pins were of different sizes and shapes to denote the category—battle-ship, cruiser, destroyer, submarine, or special troop ships such as the *Queen Mary* and the *Queen Elizabeth*. Pins of capital ships bore their names—as did a ship of whatever size on which a member of the Roosevelt family was embarked.

When I arrived in the Map Room on April 28, 1942, pursuant to a cryptic order from the director of Naval Intelligence to report to the naval aide to the president, I found there to be six watch officers, three army and three navy, maintaining the room twenty-four hours a day, seven days a week. One officer from each service was there until mid-evening, with a lone officer remaining during the night. Our "boss" was Captain John McCrea, who had succeeded Beardall as naval aide. Soon after I arrived, the last of the West Point and Annapolis graduates departed for troop or sea duty. Watch officers were to be reserves only, men whose future careers would not be tarnished with too much "state-side duty." My assignment was due to Bill Mott, now assistant to McCrea. He was carrying out the promise he had made a few weeks earlier.

Nominally in charge of the watch officers, Mott pretty much left us on our own after making sure we were properly instructed in our duties. As he led me into the Map Room for the first time and closed the door, he pointed to a cartoon of three monkeys posted on the inside of the door. Under the first monkey, whose eyes were wide open, was printed "sees everything." Below, in pencil, was written "something." Under the second monkey, holding a hand to an ear, was printed "hears every-thing." The penciled note: "a little." The third monkey, with hand over mouth, "tells nothing." Below, in pencil, "less." Mott said the penciled words were written by Secretary of War Henry Stimson as dictated to him by Roosevelt one evening when they were conferring in the room. Map Room watch officers, it was obvious, were expected to be discreet in word and action.

Several times a day officer couriers from the War and Navy Depart-ments brought locked leather pouches crammed with telegrams, re-ports, and documents. From these the watch officers updated the maps and selected the items they thought important enough for the naval aide to show the president. Mott explained that, however interesting the war news might be, the most important papers I would be handling were the cabled exchanges between the president and Prime Minister Winston Churchill, with those between Roosevelt and Stalin or Chiang Kai-shek not far behind.

"When you get a message that is to go to Churchill," he told me, "the first thing to do is type it in the proper form, give it the next number in the Roosevelt-Churchill file, and then phone the navy code room to send an officer to pick it up. All outgoing messages to Churchill [and Stalin and Chiang too] are coded and sent by the navy. The incoming ones are brought to us by officer courier from the War Department."

"Why is that?" I asked.

"Simple. The president doesn't want any place in Washington except the Map Room to have a complete file of these messages. This way, snoops in the navy might find out what he asks Churchill, but they won't know the answer. Army will get an answer to an unknown question. Sure, people can make good guesses, but they'll never know the whole story.

"Navy codes all the outgoing stuff; army decodes the incoming. The only time the Map Room might code and decode would be if the president were away on a long trip. If he's just at Hyde Park or some place close, stuff gets to him by White House pouch. We've been told that if he's going to be away for some time, cryptographic equipment will be brought here and we'll be taught how to code and decode stuff that is too hot to go by pouch. Then we'll be handling not only Churchill and such but back-and-forth things from the cabinet and Congress. We're likely to be damn busy then."

I learned that the Map Room was expected to follow up with the naval aide or Harry Hopkins if action was not taken in timely fashion on messages and papers that required action. Hopkins, the president's closest adviser, had lived since before the war on the second floor of the White House in what today is known as the Lincoln Bedroom, a few doors from the president's own quarters. Hopkins was the only presidential staff member with access to the Map Room and its files. Not even the president's longtime press secretary, Steve Early; his trusted speechwriter, Judge Samuel Rosenman; or the director of war mobilization, former Supreme Court Justice James Byrnes (dubbed by the press as "assistant president") was eligible to enter our sanctuary. Roosevelt was certain that the army and the navy would be reluctant to entrust the Map Room with their most secret information if "politicians" were allowed to nose around.

As a recently commissioned ensign, I had been thrilled not many weeks earlier to hand a cable to a rear admiral directing Naval Intelligence. Now, I was taking papers directly to the commander in chief if something important arrived during evening hours when I was the lone watch officer on duty. If the president wished a message sent that could not wait until the next day, I would be summoned to his second-floor study. I took upstairs one night a message that caused much grief. In the Solomon Islands campaign in the Southwest Pacific the Japanese had sunk a cruiser skippered by Captain Daniel Callaghan with heavy loss of life, including Callaghan's. Callaghan, the naval aide before Beardall, was much beloved at the White House. On those occasions when the evening watch officers had gone upstairs, we wrote notes for the naval aide to read the next morning so that he would know what "his boys" had been doing. With experiences such as these, my Map Room colleagues and I became a close-knit group, highly conscious of the importance of the information with which we were entrusted and the privilege of associating with the president and his intimate staff.

As I had in the Office of Naval Intelligence, I delved into the files to learn of events before I had arrived at the White House. One of the most revealing items was a letter Roosevelt had sent to Averell Harriman in London for personal delivery to Churchill. Harriman, the Lend-Lease coordinator in England, had been drawn into Churchill's inner circle. This was shrewd of the prime minister. It gave him a direct line to Roosevelt, and he knew that his opinions and wishes would not be warped by the American embassy or by the State Department. His distrust of both dated from before Pearl Harbor when Joseph Kennedy, then U.S. ambassador, was notoriously anti-British.

The Roosevelt letter of March 18, 1942, was remarkably revealing. "By the time you get this," Roosevelt had written, "you will have been advised of my talk with Litvinov [a Soviet envoy Stalin had sent to Washington to plead for more military assistance] and I expect a reply from Stalin shortly. I know you will not mind my being brutally frank when I tell you that I think I can personally handle Stalin better than either your Foreign Office or my State Department. Stalin hates the guts of all your top people. He thinks he likes me better, and I hope he will continue to do so."

This example of Roosevelt's egoism—that he could "handle" Stalin—was a foretaste of what I was to see for the next three years. Roosevelt was deaf to Churchill's warnings throughout the war as to the character of Stalin and his regime and probable Soviet behavior after the war. FDR was to side with Stalin against Churchill when the three met in

Teheran in late 1943 and at Yalta in early 1945 and, in the interval between those meetings, in various cabled exchanges. To what extent Roosevelt's stance abetted Stalin's expansion into central Europe, and strengthened the Soviets during the Cold War, will be endlessly debated. There is no question, however, that the written record lends some credence to the criticism that Roosevelt "sold out" to Stalin. In my judgment, this was not his intention in the slightest. It was unwitting, born of FDR's supreme self-confidence that he could "handle" any one, any time, in any situation.

As for Roosevelt's relations with Churchill, it's an open question as to who "handled" whom. Each thought he had the better of the other. Eager to see for ourselves how the two leaders related to each other, we in the Map Room awaited the prime minister's second wartime visit in June 1942 with keen anticipation.

Churchill had grown to mythic stature in the eyes of most Americans. His leadership of Britain during the Nazi blitz, his eloquent defiance of Hitler and Mussolini, and his inimitable rhetoric had made him well known and much admired, thanks to radio and newsreels. He was a demigod, except to a dwindling few who muttered that all he cared about was saving the British Empire. When he had flown to Washington two weeks after Pearl Harbor, I was so eager to catch a glimpse of the great man that I waited outside my Seventeenth Street rooming-house one Sunday morning. The presidential limousine sped by en route to church, too fast for any look. By June 1942, my situation was quite different. I was on duty in the Map Room, and Churchill was to be a White House guest. I was sure to see him close-up.

Map Room officers had frequent occasion to take papers to Harry Hopkins's second-floor office (which, incidentally, had been McKinley's map room). One fine June morning, with a report for Hopkins in hand, I came face-to-face with Churchill as he emerged from the Queen's Bedroom in a silk dressing robe with the ever-present cigar in hand. He came into Hopkins's office, calling for "Harry." Not wearing my naval hat, I did not salute but straightened sharply up and gave a "Good morning, Sir" greeting. The prime minister responded with something that sounded like "umph" and, as Hopkins was not around, turned and left. That was all there was to the encounter, but the thrill I felt cannot be understood a half century later by anyone who did not live through the emotions of World War II.

Back in the Map Room, I wrote: "Of course he looks like his pictures—but a bit heavier, shorter, more stooped and balder than my mental picture of him. He seemed in a foul mood." Indeed, he should have been. The British had just been disastrously defeated at Tobruk in North Africa by German forces under the seemingly invincible Field Marshal Erwin Rommel. It looked as though all North Africa—including Egypt—might soon be in Nazi hands. Churchill was later to say of this time that he was the saddest Englishman in America since Burgoyne.

My quick look at the P.M. (as he was usually called by all at the White House) was the only one I had. All of us in the Map Room were disappointed that the president never brought him in and that he had not brought his traveling map room as he had six months earlier. We were intensely curious as to how we might measure against it.

A few weeks after Churchill's return to England, the Map Room acquired a new "customer." Roosevelt had concluded that he needed help in resolving arguments between the navy and the army and its air force over strategy and the allocation of scarce resources. He needed an officer senior to George Marshall of the army, Ernest King of the navy, and "Hap" Arnold of the army air force. He recalled retired admiral William D. Leahy, who was serving as ambassador to what was known as Vichy France. Roosevelt had known Leahy since World War I, when FDR was assistant secretary of the navy. As president, he had appointed Leahy chief of naval operations, governor of Puerto Rico, and ambassador to the puppet government of France. Roosevelt gave Leahy the title of chief of staff to the commander in chief. Leahy was to preside over meetings of the Joint Chiefs (Marshall, King, and Arnold) and be the president's link to them. He was installed in a spacious suite of offices in the just-completed new East Wing of the White House so that he would be close at hand.

The hastily built East Wing, replacing the small one that had been not much more than a guest entrance, provided badly needed office space and covered a bomb shelter deep underground. There would be no need to use the long tunnel to Treasury in the event of trouble. (Shortly after the war, White House Chief Usher Howell Crim told me that Roosevelt was claustrophobic. He had been taken by the Secret Service to inspect the new shelter and then ordered Crim to see that he was never taken there again. "If bombs fall, just take me out to the South Lawn," Crim told me he'd said. Crim noted that $800,000 had been spent on the unused shelter—all taken from Civil Defense funds intended for Washington. No harm done—the city didn't need the funds anyway.)

Admiral Leahy seemed incredibly old to us youngsters, having graduated from the Naval Academy in 1897. Recalled to active duty in this new position and in the uniform of a four-star admiral, he was a formidable figure. But I took to him at once. He was quiet, friendly, and eager to learn all that we could provide. Not everyone, however, was pleased at his arrival. Harry Hopkins saw Leahy as a rival for the president's attention on war strategy. Hopkins had been to London and to Moscow. He felt he knew the score as an old sailor could not possibly know it. Hopkins had helped Roosevelt draft cables to Churchill and Stalin; indeed, he had written some. Sensing that Leahy was an intruder on his turf, Hopkins pulled a fast one by preparing a directive for the president to send to Leahy: "I am anxious to get the cables to me from the Prime Minster and other heads of government in various countries, and my replies to them, coordinated through Harry because so much of them refer to civil things." This rationale was pure nonsense. Hopkins was jealous!

There were also fundamental differences of opinion between the two men. Hopkins shared Roosevelt's disdain for the State Department. When I asked Hopkins once why we sent cables to Churchill through naval channels rather than through normal diplomatic ones, he answered, "Ever since the Tyler Kent case, the Boss doesn't trust State." This reference to the theft of classified messages by a code clerk in the American embassy was a brush-off. The fact was that Roosevelt preferred to handle foreign affairs that interested him and ignore the rest. Leahy, by contrast, always thought of the diplomatic and foreign policy implications when strategy was considered, wanting to know "What does State think?" and wanting to be sure that State was kept informed. As an example, at the American-British landings in Morocco in November 1942, Leahy scribbled a note he passed to me: "State through diplomatic missions to inform our friends and allies in Latin America that we have landed to prevent an invasion of Africa by Germs and Wops." (In language that in later years would be regarded as "politically incorrect," Leahy used the epithets of his youth—Limeys, Frogs, Wops, Chinks, Japs, Krauts or Huns, and Russkies.)

The Leahy-Hopkins situation festered for months. On the eve of

Churchill's third visit in May 1943, Leahy's aide unburdened himself on me. The admiral was not seeing all the Roosevelt-Churchill-Stalin traffic. He was not faulting the Map Room. He knew we could provide copies only by Roosevelt's specific directions—which he all too often would not give. This put Leahy in the embarrassing position of having to ask Sir John Dill, head of the British military mission in Washington, for information. Churchill regularly and routinely provided Dill with copies of his exchanges with the president. Even more distressing to Leahy was Hopkins's indifference to his need for accurate, current information. I witnessed it one afternoon when the two were in the Map Room. Leahy, showing rare irritation, spoke sharply to Hopkins. "Harry, give me the prime minister's dispatch you have in your pocket." Harry calmly reached in his jacket and did. The two left in silence.

Our day-to-day work left little time for speculation about such palace jealousies and intrigues. We were busy keeping our maps ("charts" in naval terminology) up to the minute on much besides fleet locations. The president was especially interested in the convoys sailing around the northern tip of Norway to the Soviet port of Murmansk. Losses by German U-boats were horrendous, but the convoys had to keep sailing with tanks and weaponry if the Soviets were to stay in the war. Roosevelt's interest in our charts was at its peak as the date for the invasion of North Africa in November 1942 neared and our blue pins inched across the Atlantic. The relatively quick campaign that followed was not matched in the southwest Pacific, where the struggle to wrest the Solomon Islands from the Japanese was protracted, bitter, and very costly in lives and ships lost.

Despite anxieties about the war, FDR, always interested in anything pertaining to the navy, busied himself with minutiae to an extent that astonished me. He demanded that the name of every new frigate be submitted to him for approval, and he was irked to the point of writing sharply to Admiral King that the navy had instituted a "commendation ribbon" without seeking his permission.

As 1942 turned into 1943, the president began dropping in on us less and less frequently. Admiral Leahy and the naval aide would wait impatiently in the Map Room for "three bells" to sound in the corridor—the Secret Service's signal that the president was on the move. They would take the messages that the watch officers thought the president should see, with their own papers, and greet him as he emerged from the elevator. Trotting alongside his chair, pushed by a valet, Leahy and the aide would begin their oral briefings. Any time from ten minutes to an hour later, Leahy would return to his East Wing office, stopping to leave with us the papers he had shown the president. Meticulously, he initialed each with a large "P" and "WDL." Our Map Room group was careful to preserve all items that Admiral Leahy had "Peed" on. Otherwise, routine dispatches usually went into a "burn bag" destined for the incinerator in the basement of the West Wing. (The use of shredders as a means of disposing of classified papers was far in the future.)

The president's lessening personal interest in visiting the Map Room gave rise to the phenomenon characteristic of bureaucracies large and small: makeup work to keep all hands busy. Lieutenant Mott wrote three pages of instructions of information he wanted the naval watch officers to obtain from the Navy Department. Word of our nosing around soon reached Admiral King. We found ourselves being told, "If the president wants to know this, Admiral King will be glad to tell him personally." Despite the rebuff, the job continued to be fascinating.

The year 1943 began with busy preparations for Roosevelt's January flight to Casablanca to discuss with Churchill the next steps following the successful landings in French North Africa two months earlier. FDR was as elated as a kid facing spring break. He would make history as the first president to fly while in office. He had not been in a plane since flying to Chicago in 1932 to accept the Democratic nomination. (Cousin Theodore Roosevelt had boasted that he was the first president to fly, but he had not flown until several years after leaving the White House. Nothing seemed to please Roosevelt more than doing something "Cousin Ted" had not.)

The Map Room had served in September 1942 as the communication link with the president when he made a two-week rail trip to inspect war production plants and military installations in the West. We had learned the hard way that our cryptographic system of one-time pads for sending classified messages was slow and difficult. It was so bad, in fact, that Charles Berry, the Map Room officer on the presidential train, had not been able to decipher many of the messages we sent. For this trip, Naval Communications came to our rescue by installing electronic coding machines (ECMs in navy jargon) temporarily in the Map Room and providing instructors to teach us how to use them.

Because I was the only bachelor on the Map Room staff and was presumed to have time on my hands, Captain McCrea asked me to prepare a paper on the natives of northern Africa, "the Berbers in particular."

"The president is curious about them," he said. "And find a book or two about Morocco he can read on the way over." This request would seem to have little to do with the war or the forthcoming conference, but we had heard of Roosevelt's chagrin that Churchill always seemed to know more than he about people, places, and customs. This time, he would be the better informed.

My friendship with Tom Shaw, my former "landlord" in the Capitol Hill apartment, came into play. I phoned Tom at the Library of Congress and made an appointment, saying I wanted to do a little research on some African questions. Tom was no dumbbell; he caught on instantly. At the library, neither Roosevelt's name nor any travel was ever mentioned. I returned to the White House with books containing everything Roosevelt might want to know about his destination and more than I needed to write a nine-page essay about the natives, "the Berbers in particular." When the presidential party returned, McCrea said they had read and enjoyed the paper and the books. I phoned Tom with warm thanks.

Tom and I played this game for all of Roosevelt's later overseas destinations—Cairo, Teheran, Yalta, and Malta. Since Tom checked out all books in his own name, there was no trace of the White House interest. Our security was airtight, and we had a little fun.

As those of us on the Map Room staff readied ourselves for the Casablanca trip, we daily heard Admiral Leahy's tart views on the French. In his tour as ambassador in Vichy, he had acquired an intense dislike for Charles de Gaulle. Whenever de Gaulle's name came up, Leahy would snort something like: "Well, for Christ's sake, if you could send him someplace in a plane with one wing, it would be the best thing in the world." Roosevelt had expected to learn heavily on Leahy for advice on French questions, but pneumonia forced the admiral to drop out at Trinidad on the first leg of the flight.

For weeks thereafter, Leahy fretted at his absence from the Casablanca Conference. He would mutter to us in the Map Room that the president had swallowed hook, line, and sinker Churchill's strategy for continued activity in the Mediterranean after North Africa was cleared of the Germans. Like General Marshall, Admiral Leahy favored the earliest possible assault across the English Channel against "the Huns." He was astonishingly candid in his remarks to us youngsters in the Map Room, trusting us and letting fly his feelings. He often expressed contempt for air power and snorted at aviation enthusiasts who claimed the war in Europe could be won by bombing German cities. Only a massive invasion would end the war—and it could not be through Churchill's "soft underbelly of Europe."

Leahy's analysis of the German defeat at Stalingrad was blunt. "It shows what happens when the civilian head of a country directs strategy." Although Hitler inspired this comment to me, it was clearly a swipe at Churchill and, equally, an expression of the conviction I had often heard from Leahy that Roosevelt should leave strategy to the Joint Chiefs of Staff.

Churchill was expected to return to Washington for his third wartime visit in May 1943. "I'm all involved in this British invasion of the U.S., which has me nearly crazy," Leahy confided one morning in the Map Room. Leaving as little to chance as possible, fearing both that Roosevelt would shoot from the hip without much thought and that Churchill's bombast would sweep all before him, Leahy prepped the president to seize the lead in strategic discussions. He gave Roosevelt a "talking paper" with which to open the meetings. It was a strong restatement of the position the U.S. Chiefs had been stressing since Pearl Harbor. Still smarting from Churchill's success at Casablanca in persuading the president to invade Sicily after the Germans were licked in Africa, Leahy was determined to keep FDR from being talked into further "Mediterranean adventures."

"All operations in Europe," Leahy's paper read, "should be judged primarily on the basis of the contribution . . . to defeating Germany at the earliest possible date." Invading other islands or the Balkans—as Churchill ardently wished—was just plain wrong, the Joint Chiefs were convinced. While we in the Map Room were well aware of the differing American and British views, they were far beyond our responsibilities. All we could do was watch the struggle with fascination.

We were intrigued on learning that this time the "P.M." would again bring his traveling Map Room. But when its director, Captain Richard Pim, of the Royal Naval Volunteer Reserve, arrived and was introduced to our shop, he at once proposed that he move in with us. His room would be superfluous. Such information as the Admiralty and the War Office might send him that we did not have could be posted on our walls each day. We had a happy collaboration for the next two weeks and enjoyed the opportunity we had missed the previous June of seeing much of Churchill, who popped in without warning, sometimes at very strange hours. Unlike the previous June, when Churchill had been depressed by the bleak news, things were going well. One morning, just before he walked in, I had pulled three round black pins from the Hydrographic Office chart of the mid-Atlantic. When I told him this, he fairly bounced for joy. Three fewer German submarines was indeed good news. "Three! Three! Three! We've really got him!" "Him," of course, was the enemy. While German subs continued to be a serious menace, May 1943 was, in fact, a real turning point in the Battle of the Atlantic. Convoys month by month reached Europe with steadily diminishing losses.

A second turning point was in Africa. I was standing the evening watch alone when the door was flung open. In zoomed Churchill. "Any news, Lieutenant?"

"Yes, sir, great news."

I handed him a copy of a dispatch from Allied Headquarters that I had just received announcing the surrender of the last German forces in North Africa.

"Wonderful, wonderful, I'm off to our Embassy. I must show them this."

And out he went with my precious dispatch, leaving me nothing to pass to the president.

My chagrin was pale compared to that of my army counterpart a few nights later. Forgetting Churchill's nocturnal habits, Captain Ogden Kniffin had stripped off his uniform to bed down when Churchill, with the always present cigar, blew in at about 2:00 a.m. "Kniff" guided Churchill around the room, briefing him on the day's events on all the fronts while garbed only in socks and undershorts. Henceforth, we were careful to keep our pants on when the prime minister was in town.

All Map Room staff members had vivid memories of experiences there. For me, one stands out above all others. It, too, dates from the May 1943 Churchill visit. I had the solitary night watch and was on the alert for a possible intrusion by the prime minister. Well past eleven, not only did he arrive, but so did the president and a clutch of admirals and generals. Roosevelt and Churchill needed to answer a forceful message from Stalin, who, now that North Africa was cleared of the enemy, demanded to know when he could expect Allied action on the continent. It was sorely needed to relieve Nazi pressure on Soviet armies. After a very convivial dinner upstairs, the group had come down to the Map

Room, where they could speak freely, about a reply to the prickly Soviet comrade.

Roosevelt and Churchill were in a quandary. They could not tell Stalin their future moves because they had not been able to reach agreement. The give-and-take that night across the Map Room's navy-gray steel desks was vigorous. General Marshall took the lead for the Americans in arguing the primacy of the cross-Channel strategy. The British favored an invasion of Italy. The night wore on. Finally, Field Marshal Sir John Dill picked up his pencil and wrote an evasive answer to Stalin that ducked the issue.

"We are fully aware," he wrote, "of the importance of exerting the maximum pressure upon the Axis at this particular time, but we would have you remember that all the Anglo-American forces with which to exert pressure have to be brought and maintained over many miles of sea." Dill handed the paper across the desk to Marshall, who changed "many miles of sea" to "long and exposed sea lanes." He and Leahy made a few editorial changes. Marshall read the text aloud. No one had any suggestions. All knew it would not satisfy "Uncle Joe," as Stalin was known to them, but they had nothing to say that would have satisfied him.

And so Admiral Leahy handed the message to me to type and send on its way to Moscow.

After all had left, I scribbled a note: "This message to Stalin written in lengthy Map Room midnight conference—P.M. and all his group, with President and Marshall . . . on our side being overwhelmed by British oratory."

(The conference ended a few days later in compromise. The Americans agreed to an invasion of Italy after Sicily was captured, but no more Allied forces would be sent to the Mediterranean area. All additional forces, essentially American, would go to England for a cross-Channel invasion of France set for May 1944.)

For a break from the talks, Roosevelt drove with Churchill to the rustic retreat in Maryland's Catoctin mountains then known as Shangri-La. In those days it was a tedious three-hour drive over country roads; later presidents, beginning with Eisenhower—who renamed the retreat Camp David—would travel by helicopter and reach it in minutes. The president and his guest fished in a brook well stocked with trout for the occasion. One of the few informal pictures of the two ever taken was snapped there. Churchill kept the pressure on. If—or when—there was a cross-Channel invasion, he wanted Marshall to be the commander. Roosevelt refused to make a decision and asked the Joint Chiefs to join them. The naval aide returned from the excursion in a sour mood. The prime minister had kept the president up until all hours and never stopped pressing his interests. And everyone, growled the aide, was annoyed at Harry Hopkins, who kept barging in and trying to take over whatever talk was under way. There was general relief when Churchill set an early date for return to London.

As the departure date approached, I overstepped the limits appropriate to my status. My father, as a hobby, was much interested in book design and fine printing. He especially admired the work of Bruce Rogers, the foremost typographer of the time. Dad called my attention to an item in the latest sales brochure of his favorite New York rare-book dealer. Rogers had designed and printed a broadside of the Atlantic Charter in a limited edition. (This was because of Dad's interest in Rogers's work, certainly not an interest in Roosevelt, of whom he could say nothing good.) I promptly ordered two copies. Emboldened by daily contact with the prime minister, I asked Captain Pim how I could get Churchill's signature on one. "Oh, that's easy," he replied. "Have Harry Hopkins ask him. The P.M. will do anything for Harry." And so I did.

The morning Churchill was leaving for London and there was no sign of my charter, I assumed the worst—that it had been tossed aside. In came Pim. With a smile, he handed me the tightly rolled paper tied with a bit of red tape. (Yes, literally, "red tape.") "Here it is, Elsey. The P.M. was eager to sign it when he saw it. His things were already packed. We had to hunt for his pen. He signed it, all dripping wet, just out of his bath."

Not many minutes later, Churchill came in for a last-minute look at the maps. I thanked him warmly, getting a cursory nod and this: "I've never signed it before. Now you must get the president to sign it and you will have something there."

Only much later in the day did his words sink in. Encountering Hopkins in the corridor, I thanked him for his role and asked what Churchill meant when he said he'd never signed the charter before.

Hopkins thought for a bit and answered: "That's probably right. Actually, there never was a formal piece of paper prepared for them to sign. They just radioed the text from their ships back to London and Washington for release."

This was beginning to be interesting. I took my charter to Roosevelt's private secretary, Grace Tully, and asked her to add it to the collection of books, photos, and other stuff piled on a table in her office awaiting the time Roosevelt would ask for "all the autograph things." I waited weeks, again assuming the worst. But one day a messenger tapped on the Map Room door and handed me my charter, rolled up this time with a simple American rubber band, enhanced with a second signature.

(A digression: American versions of the charter, whether in textbooks, reference works, or broadsides such as Bruce Rogers's, place "Franklin D. Roosevelt" and "Winston S. Churchill" below the text because that was how the document was released by the White House Press Office. However, all British versions omit the names. The explanation: Before turning over the text to a communications officer on the cruiser *Augusta,* for transmission to the White House, Roosevelt in his own hand wrote the two names at the bottom of the page. That copy is in the FDR Library at Hyde Park. By contrast, Churchill had the text radioed from his ship to London with no names subscribed. Hence the disparity persists to this day between American and British versions, the American giving the clear impression that the two men had signed the charter. More on this later in the narrative.)

A few days after "the Brits" had left town, the air force liaison with the Map Room invited me to join a group flying to the naval base in Key West to observe tests of a new submarine detecting device. A plane equipped with a Magnetic Airborne Detector (MAD) would try to locate one of our subs that would be constantly changing course in an effort to avoid being found. While my colleague boarded a plane with air force scientists, I boarded an S-15, one of our subs too old for use against the Japanese. We surfaced and dived repeatedly, day and night, while MAD sought us. The tests were regarded as a success, and the equipment was approved for production. As we had seen in our Map Room reports, the Allies were slowly winning the struggle with German U-boats, but anything that would help cleanse the Atlantic was very welcome.

As interested as I was in submarine activity in the Atlantic, I cared much more about U.S. subs in the Pacific. I read the action reports of those on which college classmates were serving. Thinking higher-ups might find such reports of interest, I began stripping out some of the administrative details and passing them to the naval aide. Successes were passed along as well as failures, to give a true picture. The *Guardfish,* for example, ran aground in a Japanese harbor, escaped, and completed her war patrol. The *Whale* experienced exasperating torpedo failures and returned to port with no sinkings to her credit. I was gratified to have a note from Harry Hopkins: "Both the President and I have read the submarine reports with the greatest of interest. They are fascinating reading."

Another break from the Washington routine came in mid-July. Captain McCrea had left as naval aide in February to assume command of the USS *Iowa,* the first of a new class of the largest battleships of our fleet. (*Iowa* was one of the battleships under construction that Jim Risk had pointed out to me in the Brooklyn Navy Yard in September 1941.) Probably not expecting to be taken seriously, McCrea, in saying farewell to the Map Room staff in a small ceremony attended by Roosevelt, quoted the notorious actress Mae West: "When you have nothing much to do and lots of time to do it in, why don't you come up and see me sometime?" My closest Map Room buddy, Bob Myers, and I decided to do just that when we read a report that the *Iowa* would be conducting speed tests, sailing from the Brooklyn Navy Yard. With the brashness of youthful naval reservists, Bob and I headed for New York and informed a startled duty officer at the yard that we were accepting an invitation from the commanding officer of the *Iowa.* After a check with the ship, we were told to be back for a 3:00 a.m. departure the next morning.

McCrea was a surprised but perfect host. After breakfast with him in his cabin, we were given a complete tour of the ship by Charley Berry, a former Map Room colleague who had left us to continue serving under McCrea. During most of a very long day, Bob and I were on the bridge with the captain while the *Iowa* tested her engines for maximum speed. It was especially exciting to plow directly through an outbound convoy of merchant ships headed for England. Maintaining perfect formation, each freighter saluted the massive floating fortress as we passed. Feeling a special affinity for the *Iowa,* Bob and I followed her every move for the rest of the war.

Key West and the *Iowa* were but momentary breaks from Map Room duty. A real change came when Mott left to attend the Naval War College. McCrea's successor as naval aide was Rear Admiral Wilson Brown, Naval Academy 1903, a dozen years older than McCrea but sufficiently junior to Leahy to treat him with the proper respect. Brown fitted in easily. He had known Roosevelt since the First World War. This was his fourth tour as naval aide, having served as such for Coolidge, Hoover, and FDR in the midthirties. Brown named me to succeed Mott as the naval executive officer of the Map Room. I was no longer to stand watches but would be on duty daily, supervising my fellow naval reservists and ensuring that we had an uninterrupted flow of information from the Navy Department. Brown wrote the necessary orders allowing me unrestricted access to "Magic" and "Ultra" information and to review each day's collection of super-secret files maintained in Admiral King's office of which no copies were permitted.

I also became heir to handling the numerous requests that flowed to the naval aide from Mrs. Roosevelt. She had established herself in the eyes of the public as being accessible to any one at any time on any subject. Appeals from the serious to the silly came her way and, if they related to the navy, to me to look into. Anguished parents appealed when an errant son was court-martialed. A girlfriend insisted that the boy in a news photo was her fiancé, although the navy had reported him "killed in action." Without exception, the department was able to support its actions and "Mrs. R" accepted the answers I provided. I took particular delight at her request to look into the food situation at Princeton University. I was assured by the secretary of the navy that "President Dodds had taken corrective action with regard to a contract with the Howard Johnson Company and that the food 'is entirely satisfactory now.'"

As for Eleanor Roosevelt herself, we in the Map Room rarely saw her. I had first met her when, soon after I reported in April 1942, she had come in to ask Captain McCrea a question regarding Franklin Jr.'s ship. Some weeks later I was heading for the Map Room from the West Wing when "two bells" sounded. She rounded a corner sharply and bore down on me. I saluted with a "Good morning." She returned the salute with "Good morning" and a warm smile. I wrote later that day: "She is not as unattractive in the flesh as photographs and cartoons have made her. Very tall, slender, tanned, wavy hair, and friendly eyes. She is so cheerful and quick to respond that I like her." (Such a remark would have put my father into a fit.)

Other new duties came my way with Mott's departure. With a law degree from George Washington University, he had enjoyed scrutinizing court-martial cases of naval officers who had been tried in the navy's legal system for various offenses and recommended for dismissal. Since all officers were commissioned personally by the president—in theory, if not in fact—only the president could revoke a commission. Massive trial records came to the White House for review and action. The procedure was as old as the navy itself. The system might have worked in peacetime, but it was preposterous to burden the president or his staff in time of war. I inherited from Mott the trial records of sixty-seven officers. Some had languished at the White House for months as not even the naval aide, let alone the president, had time to look at them.

The status of the officers was in limbo. Some were in naval prisons, while others were free but unassigned. One of my first actions was to recommend to Admiral Brown that the president authorize the secretary of the navy to act for him in these matters. It was soon done. Why so simple a solution had not been adopted years earlier baffled me. I was happy to be rid of the mess and to no longer have to know or care about the miscreants, even though reading salacious details about the sexual antics of some of them, highlighted in a few cases with photographs, had brightened dull hours of long night watches.

Almost immediately after Mott's departure, I was caught up in a tussle between our navy and the admiralty in London. Admiral King was furious (his usual state of emotion) over what he regarded as British sloppiness in protecting security in the antisubmarine campaign. The Brits were releasing, King felt, too much information, too soon, about Allied successes in sinking U-boats. The Nazis were sure to conclude that their messages were being read by the Allies—which, of course, they were. King feared the Germans would change their cryptographic systems, at great cost to us.

Roosevelt turned to Brown, who, in normal naval fashion, passed the buck to me. "Get over to the department and get all the facts, and tell them that from now on the White House will release information on the submarine campaign. We'll coordinate from here with the British and the Canadians."

I quickly found out—again—that Admiral King liked the White House no better than he liked the British. But he had no choice. From then on, information on the antisubmarine efforts of the Americans, British, and Canadians was released simultaneously in Washington, London, and Ottawa after personal clearance of the releases by Churchill and Roosevelt. To add to King's outrage, the release in Washington was made neither by the White House nor by the navy but by the civilian Office of War Information. I became a regular and welcome visitor to Elmer Davis, OWI's director, and an equally regular and unwelcome visitor to King's staff when it was time to draft the monthly release.

Aside from an occasional fracas with Admiral King's office, things moved smoothly in mid-1943 as we looked forward to another summit meeting. Roosevelt tried hard to persuade Stalin to meet him one-on-one and said he would go anywhere Stalin wished. But he couldn't "handle" the Soviet dictator on this: Stalin said he could not leave his post. While this dithering was under way, on July 25, 1943, Mussolini's Fascist government collapsed. We and the British were caught by surprise. The president was enjoying a weekend at Shangri-La. When he returned to the White House at 10:10 that night, I handed him transcripts of radio broadcasts from Rome that the navy had translated and I had brought up from the department. "Then it's really true!" he said in a tone of real surprise. For the next twenty minutes he stayed, reading all the scraps of information I had, including a flash message from Churchill.

Mussolini's fall was so unexpected that the State Department and the military were unprepared. Roosevelt, rarely at a loss for words, had nothing he felt he could say at his scheduled press conference on the twenty-seventh. When asked for his "first reaction to the fall of Mussolini," he quipped, "Why, you know, I don't have reactions, I'm too old for that." This brought hoots of laughter from the reporters crowded around his desk in the Oval Office. No other questions on Italy were asked. Standing behind the press gang, I reflected that he'd done it again. By a seemingly nonchalant remark, he had evaded discussion of matters for which we embarrassingly had no contingency plans. I was also amused by all the laughter. A mild witticism, if uttered by a big shot, is thought to be very funny. From someone else, it might bring a wan smile.

The new situation in the Mediterranean added to the urgency of another meeting with Churchill, despite Roosevelt's desire to have a private session with Stalin first. Wincing at the thought of Washington in August, Churchill suggested Quebec, to which Roosevelt agreed—provided Churchill would spend a day or two at Hyde Park. Constant cable traffic since the May meetings made it clear that Churchill was still red-hot for an aggressive Mediterranean strategy, now even more so with Mussolini's ouster. General Marshall was positive that if Churchill's wishes prevailed, there could be no cross-Channel invasion of France in

1944—if ever. Marshall was also vividly aware of the power of "British oratory." When Churchill proposed to FDR that the American Chiefs of Staff meet with him and their British counterparts for several days of discussion before the president joined them in Quebec, Marshall discreetly spoke to Admiral Leahy. Thus this simple alert from Leahy to his boss: "General Marshall and Admiral King consider it unwise for the U.S. staff to be exposed for several days to the Prime Minister in the President's absence."

I was charged with setting up a temporary Map Room in Quebec under Leahy's guidance and hence was privy to this insight that not even such formidable men as Marshall, King, and Arnold were confident of their ability to hold their own against Winston Churchill's brand of "British oratory." Roosevelt understood Leahy's warning. When all hands assembled in Quebec, the president backed Marshall to the hilt. The conference ended with the ironclad commitment to invade Normandy in May 1944, with a simultaneous landing in southern France. Stalin could at last be sent the assurances he had asked for three months earlier.

Before such a message was sent, however, my army colleague Ogden Kniffin and I had seen more of Churchill in our temporary Map Room than we had of him in May at the White House and more, too, of FDR than usual. The conference was held at the Citadel, a historic fortress overlooking Quebec and now the summer home of the governor-general of Canada. Our room was next to FDR's bedroom. His first act on arrival was to inspect us. Churchill brought his own map room with Captain Pim and a small crew who were installed a long corridor's walk from our map room. We vied with each other for speed and quantity of war news. Pim had it over us for Mideast and South Asian affairs. We easily outdid him on Pacific events. Kniff and I had more visitors than the White House Map Room itself ever had in so short a time. We became used to "pop-in's" by the president, Churchill, Secretary of the Navy Knox, Admiral King (his usual dour self, but favorably impressed with the completeness and accuracy of our naval information), Lord Louis Mountbatten, British Foreign Minister Anthony Eden, our ambassador to the Soviet Union, Averell Harriman, and on and on.

Churchill, with his usual weird hours, was fascinated by our maps and photographs of the Aleutians where our army was fighting to evict the Japanese who had invaded Attu, Kiska, and some smaller islands a year earlier. A fog-shrouded campaign among sharp ice-covered peaks was new to him. Heavy naval bombardment of Kiska was taking place on our arrival in Quebec. When the army landed, to its astonishment, there were no Japanese. They had evacuated under cover of mists and clouds. Only barking dogs greeted the invaders. Churchill, for the rest of our days in Quebec, could not resist jokes about barking dogs, to Roosevelt's discomfiture. Despite the Kiska fiasco—a happy one, as casualties would have been horrible had the Japanese remained— Admiral Leahy commented, after our return, that he felt Churchill had a better understanding of the grand scope of the war in the Pacific from his many visits to our Map Room than he had had before. Heretofore, Leahy said, the P.M. had thought too much about Burma and the Middle East. While it was pleasant to hear such a comment, I suspect Churchill's Pacific education came more from Ernest King and the other U.S. Joint Chiefs, with whom he met several times. This was in contrast to Roosevelt, who never deigned to meet the British Chiefs.

As one who had majored in history and enjoyed historical mementos of all kinds, I was happily surprised one afternoon just before we left Quebec when an aide to the governor-general came into the Map Room. The governor-general's wife was Princess Alice, the youngest granddaughter of Queen Victoria. In the years before World War I, she had traveled extensively, visiting her relatives on assorted thrones throughout Europe.

"Would you be so kind," I was asked, "as to inquire of the president if he would honor Her Grace by inscribing a leaf in her album?" "Of course" was the only possible answer.

I leafed through the album, rebound more than once to accommodate new pages. Here were signatures of Hohenzollerns, Hapsburgs, and Romanovs mixed with dozens of lesser kings, queens, princes, and minor nobles with indecipherable titles. The princess had resumed her travels after that war. The names of relatives and nobility were succeeded by the those of presidents and prime ministers.

When FDR was wheeled into the room that evening, I laid the album before him. He forgot all about the war. We exchanged pleasantries about some of the deposed but not forgotten personalities. "Oh, how my mother would have loved this!" he smiled as he found a blank page at the end. He signed with a flourish, using my Waterman fountain pen. Late that night, when the P.M. came in, my pen was useful again. (I still have it.) Churchill spent even more time than Roosevelt in leafing through. He had known many of the signers himself and had acerbic comments about more than a few.

The days following the Quebec Conference were almost as exciting as the conference itself. Events in Europe were happening fast. After a short stay in Hyde Park with FDR, Churchill decided to come to Washington despite the heat rather than return to London. He stayed nearly two weeks, wanting to be with the president when Allied troops landed in Italy on September 8 to begin a tortuous climb up the peninsula toward Rome. Captain Pim came with Churchill, not to set up his room, but to move in with us as he had in May. Once again, we were a "joint operation."

Captain McCrea had enjoined the Map Room staff—and Admiral Brown repeated the words—"Tell no one what you see or hear at the White House and remember the army and navy orders: 'No diaries during the war.'" I obeyed to the extent of "no diary" and so have no record or recollection sixty-plus years later of many events. I did, however, make an occasional note of a conversation or intriguing situation (as the reader will have discerned). I wrote such a note as Churchill was readying to leave in mid-September:

> Since returning from Quebec . . . we have had two masters instead of one. The Prime Minister has been here & those who stayed home . . . have had their wishes fulfilled by seeing him here many times over. He is in rare form these days—full of high spirits & colorful words. When I first saw him in June '42, he was in the dumps. The dark day when Tobruk fell made him, as he put it, the saddest Englishman in America since Burgoyne. Last May, he was in good humor because the North African campaign was drawing rapidly to a close. Now he is positively jubilant by the glowing success of Sicily, Mussolini's end, Italian capitulation, & our landing on the mainland. In the spring he was given to snarling "the bastard" when Hitler was mentioned; now he shrugs his shoulders (or wiggles his upper parts—a man of his girth hardly has shoulders) at the name. Emotion no longer called for. The game now is to beat Hitler as quickly, cheaply & thoroughly as we can. It is not to fight him, but to beat him. A very different matter.

Two evenings after the Italian landings, we arranged to have a speech of Hitler's piped into the Map Room with a running translation provided. Roosevelt, Churchill, General Marshall, and Harry Hopkins joined us. I wrote that "the P.M. sat quietly listening and chewing on the cigar, happily pleased at the dull, dead delivery, the sullen sodden words, and the wrath [of Hitler] in condemning Bagdolio's 'treachery.'"

While it had been fun to have Pim's good humor brighten our days, I noted, "We find the P.M. somewhat trying at times. He never sleeps—at eight in the morning until two the following morning he is apt to pop in for the latest news. When there is none, he demands some anyway & we give him a newspaper to chew on."

Relative quiet prevailed in the Map Room after Churchill's departure. The president began to slow down noticeably, leaving the second floor much later in the morning than before and rarely coming into the Map Room. His erratic schedule frustrated and irritated Leahy and Brown. They had no choice but to stand by in the Map Room awaiting his uncertain descent in the elevator and their dutiful walk with him to the West Wing. With plenty of time to shoot the breeze, shoot it they did. They spoke frankly, knowing that our ears were open but our mouths were shut.

Harry Hopkins was a frequent topic. Just before Quebec, a conservative newspaper had attacked Hopkins as "a dangerous liberal." Leahy let loose: "Sure, he's a pinkie. But he's frank about it. He's for the proletariat and the underdog. I didn't like him before I started to work with him, but I do now. By God, he delivers the goods. He puts his shoulder to the wheel and works. No matter what the problem is, he works and works hard because he sees the serious purposes in this war. When the war is over and he starts being pinkie again, we'll shoot him. It'll be all right to bump him off then. But he does a tremendous good in the war effort. He's got plenty on the ball. He can put his finger on the essential thing and work on it. He's always been associated with the down-and-outers. He doesn't care about money. He's always given away somebody else's to the down-and-out. If he had to work for it, it might be different. He always finds the essentials and follows them out. He's smarter than Hell."

Ironically, Leahy's belated awareness of Hopkins's value as Roosevelt's most trusted adviser came as Hopkins's influence was beginning to fade. His poor health put him out of action for long periods. He remarried. The new Mrs. Hopkins joined Hopkins in the Lincoln Bedroom, but the cramped quarters were not to her liking, and Mrs. Roosevelt resented the way she began instructing household staff to do things her way. Late in 1943, the Hopkinses left for a house in

Georgetown. The president saw much less of him. Leahy's old rival, more recently an admired colleague, was gone, and the admiral was indisputably top dog.

As Hopkins's influence waned and he was no longer a presence in the White House scheme of things and no longer a target of conversation, Leahy and Brown—to my considerable amazement—began to speak critically of Roosevelt. Both were concerned at his "globaloney," the derisive term applied to the views of idealists preaching a "One World" philosophy. They fretted aloud and often in the Map Room about Roosevelt's intent to give a future United Nations organization sovereignty over the islands in the Pacific that had been mandated to Japan after World War I. Leahy was adamant. Those islands had to be ours; they were essential to our security. But the president had told the Pacific War Council that he would "give" them to the United Nations. The Pacific War Council was an inflated name for the informal gathering of ambassadors of the nations fighting Japan in the Pacific whom Roosevelt brought together from time to time. It had no authority to do anything. It was—as Leahy saw it—a forum for FDR to talk freely, grandiosely, and unrealistically about the future.

Admiral Brown, usually quick to defend Roosevelt, joined Leahy on this issue: "There is no one with the president at these council meetings to check or control him. He might promise the moon, and the ambassadors all take him seriously. He tells them what we are planning to do. That's a great danger. There's no telling whom they pass these secrets on to."

The Map Room staff suddenly had a more immediate concern than the future of Japanese atolls. One morning, the army lieutenant colonel who served as executive officer under Admiral Brown for army matters failed to show up. Days went by. Admiral Brown gave us no explanation for his absence, nor did General Watson, the military aide to the president, his nominal commander. The mystery deepened when his tight-lipped brother, a colonel on duty in the War Department, came by to pick up personal possessions such as a pair of reading glasses and to drive away the missing officer's car, which had been left in a White House parking area. Leahy, ordinarily so talkative, had "no information." Only many weeks later did we learn that the lieutenant colonel had been arrested by military police for homosexual activity with an employee of the Mayflower Hotel where he had been living. We found that he was being held incommunicado in a psychiatric ward at Walter Reed Army Hospital and would be there until all future operations of which he had knowledge had taken place. This was the military's mindset at the time—homosexuals were automatically regarded as security risks. A court-martial, to throw him out of the army, was ruled out—too great a chance of publicity that would embarrass the White House.

My Map Room associates and I were dumbfounded when we heard the facts. We were naive about homosexuality. A West Point graduate! That it existed in all areas of society was not generally known in those days. We were saddened; I think all of us liked the man and had seen a bright future for him. He had been selected for promotion to full colonel and was a prospect for an important post in the forthcoming invasion of Normandy. The event sobered and matured us.

In the fall of 1943, I made a procedural change regarding presidential exchanges with Churchill, Stalin, and Chiang. I prepared an "action sheet," on which were recorded the time an incoming message was received, who got copies, and what action followed. The author, or authors, of outgoing messages, was noted and relevant cross references were included. Such a simple procedure should have been instituted in the Map Room's early days, but McCrea and Brown had stepped on my suggestions with the sharp rebuff: "This is none of our business." By October 1943, however, I had convinced Brown that details of authorship and handling had historical significance and would be scrutinized in the future. (My graduate school training in history was showing. Years later, Professor Warren Kimball of Rutgers University, when editing the wartime correspondence of Churchill and Roosevelt, described the action sheets as "invaluable historical tools" and regretted that the procedure had not been started earlier.)

By late October '43, we were anticipating another summit, although where was still unsettled. Stalin finally agreed to leave the Soviet Union but would go no farther than Teheran, where his troops were firmly in control. Roosevelt also wanted to meet Chiang, but Chiang could not join Churchill, Stalin, and Roosevelt in Teheran, as Stalin did not want to provoke the Japanese—with whom the Soviets were not yet at war—into attacking Soviet Far Eastern territories. Cairo was agreed to as the place for a U.S.-British-Chinese talk. As for Soviet-Japanese tensions, Ambassador Harriman cabled as the Cairo and Teheran sessions were shaping up, "There is no doubt in my mind that the victories of the Red

Army and the growing sense of strength and security had had an influence in setting aside their fears of offending Japan. There have been a number of indications. . . . I have the feeling that they want the Pacific war ended as quickly as possible after the termination of hostilities in Europe."

Reports like this whetted Roosevelt's appetite for the meetings, and ours too. But Admiral Brown said there could be no temporary Map Room as at Quebec; distances and space on planes made it impractical. However, we would "know everything," as the president had decided that all communications from anyone in Washington would flow through the Map Room. We were to use our judgment as to whether to send them by pouch or encrypt them on our machines and transmit them through the Army Signal Corps.

Roosevelt, in arranging the meetings, was less than candid with Churchill. When Stalin finally cabled the president agreeing to a date in Teheran, the latter did not promptly pass on the word to the prime minister. Map Room staff prodded Admiral Brown—and Admiral Leahy, too—that Churchill should be told. He got the word belatedly, not from the White House but from his ambassador in Moscow, whereupon he shot off a hot, somewhat spiteful cable to the president. FDR did not bother to acknowledge it until he was leaving Washington to begin the long journey.

I recorded my reactions when the party had left. "Roosevelt wanted the affair to be his own personal doing. . . . He made numerous arrangements which were not in accord with British wishes and he showed no inclination to change them after Churchill objected." When Churchill "screamed in protest" at Roosevelt's inviting Soviet Minister V. M. Molotov to be present at meetings of the U.S. and British military staffs, Roosevelt simply ignored the cable. He wanted, I was convinced, to show everybody who was "The Boss."

The presidential party left Washington on Armistice Day, crossing the Atlantic on McCrea's *Iowa* to Oran, Algeria, and then flying to Cairo, Teheran, back to Cairo, on to Tunis, Malta, and Dakar, before reboarding the ship there and arriving home on December 16. The Teheran and Cairo conferences have been amply described in histories of the period, and, as I have no firsthand knowledge, no further mention of them is called for. I shall, however, mention one event that occurred on the eve of the party's departure from Washington. Admiral

Brown handed me sealed envelopes with the order to deliver them in person to Dr. Vannevar Bush, director of the Office of Scientific Research and Development. I had no inkling of the contents until Bush, on examining the contents of one of the envelopes, said I should take them to Brigadier General Wilhelm D. Styer in General Marshall's office. I knew then that the documents related to the development of the atomic bomb, as General Styer was one of my father's contacts in the Manhattan Project, as the effort to build an atomic bomb was code-named. I stayed mute, giving no indication that I knew Styer to be a deputy to General Leslie Groves, who was in overall charge of the bomb effort.

(Digression: My father was spending four days a week for much of the war as a consultant to the company building a plant at Oak Ridge, Tennessee, that was to produce the special form of uranium needed for an atomic bomb—and did produce it for the Hiroshima bomb of August 1945. The other three days a week were "Westinghouse Days," where he was especially concerned with electrical equipment needed for high-altitude military planes. Although Dad was mute regarding his work, I guessed from his itineraries what he was up to.)

Similarly, I gave no indication to my Map Room associates that I understood the implications of various cables from Churchill that dealt cryptically with "Tube Alloys." (*Tube Alloys* was the code name for the joint British-American atomic research efforts. The Manhattan Project specifically related to U.S. activities to construct atomic bombs.) Only after the war did I learn from Admiral Brown that even he was unaware of what the Manhattan Project was all about and that "Tube Alloys" was a mystery to him (as it was to all the rest of the Map Room group). The paucity of information in the Roosevelt archives at Hyde Park on the development of the atomic bomb is partially explained by the fact that, a few days after Roosevelt's death in April 1945, Leahy and Brown ordered a search of White House files for everything relating to the Manhattan Project. Once again, I was a messenger carrying files to Dr. Bush, and, again, I gave no indication that I knew what I was delivering. The secrets held until after the bombs landed in August on Hiroshima and Nagasaki. (The secrets held, that is, from the American public. The extent to which Soviet espionage had succeeded came later as a dismaying surprise.)

The winter of 1943-1944 was one of nervous anticipation. British and American troops were slogging slowly up the Italian peninsula.

Progress in the Pacific was also slow and costly as Admiral Chester Nimitz's and General Douglas MacArthur's forces sought to evict the Japanese from the island chains north of Australia. Reports from all battle fronts came in as usual, but they sparked little interest from Roosevelt. His attention—to the extent that he evinced any—was focused on the buildup for the forthcoming invasion of France and on European political questions. With ever rarer presidential visits, the Map Room staff relied on Leahy, Brown, and Major-General Edwin ("Pa") Watson for excitement. Leahy continued his tirades against de Gaulle: "The only thing to do with that s.o.b. is to shoot him . . . we should have done it a long time ago. He only plays politics. We should take money, food, and arms away from him. Ike is too soft on him; the Brits have got to him." And on another pet peeve of the chief of staff, "The Brits want to sew up the Mediterranean. But we want to win the war!"

Not all Admiral Leahy's barbs were directed abroad. He had his disagreements with other members of the Joint Chiefs—King, most often. "Ernie is trying to get complete control of everything to do with the navy. He's put out a plan to reorganize the navy that's unworkable. This is no time to reorganize!" He sputtered as well to Roosevelt, who, not wanting to implicate Leahy, wrote to his naval aide: "I think that before all these changes are decided on that Admiral King might come in to speak to me about them. F.D.R."

The Map Room staff was fascinated and wondered how all this would turn out. We didn't have long to wait. Checked by the White House on his big plans, King vented his spleen where he could. Two days after the presidential memo, King wrote back to Brown. Map Room officers were no longer free to request whatever information they felt was needed, specifically, "certain dispatches that are not ordinarily routed there." I was convinced that this was a knee-jerk reaction to FDR's reining him in. He was retaliating in a petty way.

By February 1944, our action sheets were flagging a number of unanswered messages. We kept pointing this out to Admiral Brown. Brown, defensive of his boss, responded that the president had "good reasons for not answering which are unknown to us, that his sense of timing is marvelous and that he waits until the opportune moment to reply." I was not convinced. In another of my personal notes, I typed, "I cannot say that I agree. I think it is mostly forgetfulness and indifference." A few days after Brown's most recent defense of the president, on February 19,

1944, "Pa" Watson was in the room. Unanswered messages again were a topic. "Yes," said Watson. "He's always slow, late. He can never be hurried or moved by anyone now. Can't anyone, not even the Mrs., move him. No one, not even Jesus, can move him."

But all this was more than the "forgetfulness and indifference" I had noted. Harry Hopkins was no longer at the president's elbow to keep things moving, to draft a cabled response, to suggest an action, to mediate a dispute, large or small. Above all, Roosevelt was really slowing down, and his interest in almost everything was flagging. Hoping that a long rest in a more pleasant atmosphere than Washington would revive body and spirit, that spring Roosevelt spent a month at the luxurious plantation in South Carolina of financier Bernard Baruch. The Map Room staff was instructed to keep intrusions to a minimum, and this edict prevailed after his return. The admirals still awaited his uncertain morning descents from upstairs, but they no longer carried to the Oval Office a sheaf of army and navy dispatches. Watch officers typed brief summaries of war news on a single sheet. And often even that was ignored.

This I learned when I returned to Washington in late July, having been detached for temporary duty in March with the naval forces preparing for the Invasion of Normandy. That is the subject of the next chapter.

Chapter Three

Normandy

President Roosevelt's decision that the Map Room should be staffed with reserve officers and that they should remain on duty there for security reasons was challenged on occasion. Mott, eager for postwar transfer to the regular navy, knew he had to break away. FDR approved his request to attend the Naval War College in Newport, Rhode Island, to be followed by assignment to the Pacific Fleet. Mott's departure brought a change for me. I was now the NOIC, jargon for naval officer in charge. On duty each day, I supervised four naval reservists junior to me and took on miscellaneous tasks for the naval aide to the president and for Admiral Leahy.

Some months later came my chance to leave the confines of the White House. Samuel Eliot Morison, my Harvard professor and long an acquaintance of Roosevelt's, sought a Naval Reserve commission and FDR's blessing on his proposal to write the history of the U.S. Navy in World War II. The president approved, and Morison was soon in the Atlantic studying the battle against German submarines. After observing the invasion of French North Africa by U.S. and British forces in November 1942, Morison headed for the Pacific, where he spent most of 1943. Back in Washington that December, he correctly judged that the great naval actions in 1944 would again be in the Pacific and that he should be there. But he surmised—as did most Americans—that 1944 would also see the long-awaited opening of the Second Front on the European mainland. He fretted with me about his lack of information. Where and when might the invasion take place? Having been with Roosevelt in Quebec, I knew the answers, but security kept me from saying anything. On the assumption that an invasion would take place and that he would miss it because he intended to head back to the

Pacific, Morison proposed that I take leave from the Map Room and be his eyes and ears for whatever would take place in Europe. I responded that his standing with the president was such that any request he made would surely be granted.

Thus, in mid-March 1944, I was on the *Queen Mary,* one of the world's largest ocean liners, which, like its sister ship the *Queen Elizabeth,* had been converted by the British into a troopship. About 14,500 American soldiers and a few hundred sailors were headed for the invasion buildup in England. Only a dozen or so U.S. naval officers were aboard. Each of us was assigned duties to augment the ship's complement. My post was on the port (left) flying bridge, so-called because it extended about fifteen feet beyond the ship's side to provide visibility when the ship was docking. In wartime, it had a more important use—as a lookout post for German submarines. The "Queens" sailed at 26.5 knots, a speed too great for any antisubmarine escorts. Hence, we were alone—and vulnerable. Every pair of eyes was needed. When I was not on duty at my station, I was permitted to remain on the enclosed bridge with the navigator, the helmsman, and other British officers. I knew, from Map Room experience, that every few minutes the ship would change course slightly. The zigzag pattern was designed to make a submarine attack more difficult. I also knew that German submarines were now being deployed in "wolf packs." While helpful against a single sub, the zigzag course would be of little avail if several subs attacked simultaneously from different angles.

The most important information secreted in my head was that the British had cracked the German naval code and that Ultra, the name for information so learned, enabled the Royal Navy to know each day the location of most wolf packs. Thus it was no surprise to me when we veered in mid-Atlantic sharply from our planned route and headed north toward Iceland. From cryptic conversations among the ship's officers on the bridge, I learned that the Admiralty in London had ordered the change. I was certain that Ultra had learned of a wolf pack athwart our original route. So closely was the source of such information guarded that it's possible not even the ship's captain knew the exact reason for the change. Thanks to the timely warning, we arrived safely—but late—at Glasgow.

(Memories of the Atlantic crossing came flooding back in July 1998 when my wife, Sally, our son, Howard, and I visited our daughter,

Anne, and her family in California. We went to see the *Queen Mary,* long out of service, moored at Long Beach as a tourist attraction. The ship had memories for Sally also. She and her cousin "Tot" Ivison had sailed to England on her in 1948 after her transformation from troop-ship back to passenger service. I made my way to my 1944 duty station on the flying bridge. In the kind of coincidence that seems too improb-able to be true, a man of my vintage approached and asked if I had ever been on the ship before. When I replied that I had left New York on St. Patrick's Day 1944, he stood mute. Then he said softly, "I was on her too—the same trip. I was in the army, and I knew I was headed for the invasion." We shook hands silently, remembering that many of our shipmates never made it back.)

Arriving in London by train from Glasgow by way of Edinburgh (where I had time for some sightseeing), I found a ready welcome. Admiral Brown, my White House boss, had written to Admiral Harold Stark, the chief of naval operations at the time of Pearl Harbor and now the senior naval officer in England. I also had a letter of introduction to Gilbert Winant, the American ambassador, and various notes from Morison to Oxford University professors he thought I should meet. I never made it to Oxford but took full advantage of the other door-openers. From Winant, one afternoon at tea in his office, I learned that Roosevelt had been seriously under the weather and was resting at the baronial es-tate of financier Bernard Baruch in South Carolina. This cast an inter-esting light on a piece in a London tabloid about FDR, his Map Room, and his "holiday," which I copied and sent home to my fellow Map Roomers. The London story reported that Roosevelt was in "top form," an example of the skill of his press secretary, Steve Early, who fed the press information far removed from the truth. White House "spin" is not a new invention. Another gossipy London newspaper story, full of inaccuracies, included these bits about Roosevelt: "He now stops every-day in his new [*sic*] Map Room studying military developments on se-cret charts. I am told that he is very proud of this Map Room and has chucklingly boasted 'It is now better than Churchill's even though he has got a long start.'"

In two letters to Admiral Brown, I reported on the effect of his letter to Admiral Stark. There seemingly was nothing I wanted to see or do relating to the navy's preparation for the invasion that was denied. My letters are full of names, naval abbreviations, and details that will interest only a scholar, but they are in my files for anyone wishing to plod through them. Most interesting of all the places I visited was Prime Minister Churchill's Map Room, the godfather of ours at the White House. The London operation far surpassed ours. It was the center from which Churchill, serving as minister of defense as well as prime minister, dispatched orders to the British navy, army, and Royal Air Force. Ordinarily no foreigner and surely no one of my junior rank would have been admitted to this sanctum sanctorum containing the greatest secrets of the war, but the officer in charge, Captain Pim, knew me well from our cooperation in Washington and Quebec and was a gracious host.

In due course, I boarded the *Ancon* in Plymouth harbor. This was a converted cruise ship of the Panama line, serving as the headquarters for amphibious landings. She had seen active duty at the invasions of Sicily and southern Italy the year before. Now she was the command ship for "Force O," the naval transports and landing craft destined for Omaha Beach, the code name for a section of the coast of Normandy. Success at Omaha was essential to the success of the whole invasion, since it was the center point of the entire British-American effort. Once aboard, I was put to work as a badly needed member of the Force O Intelligence staff.

Omaha Beach is almost flat, sloping gently seaward. At low tide, almost fifteen hundred feet of sandy beach are exposed. This the Germans had studded with thousands of wooden, cement, and steel obstacles, many armed with mines set to demolish any landing craft trying to land at mid or high tide. The German defensive strategy was clear. If troops landed at low tide, they would be easy targets for machine guns firing from concrete pillboxes on the high bluffs behind the beach. If they tried to land as the tide was coming in, their craft wouldn't make it through the mine-studded barriers—so the Germans hoped. In the crowded quarters of Force O's Intelligence group, we daily updated our charts of the beach with data obtained from low-flying photo planes. The defenders had stopped work on some two hundred strong points above and behind the beach, believing them invulnerable to air or naval attack, and were concentrating on adding beach obstacles at a frightening speed. Commander Curtis Munson, the force intelligence officer, was a veteran of the Sicilian and Italian landings. Nothing like the Omaha defenses had been seen before. His yeoman agreed: on May 27, he shook his head and said, "This one won't run according to the book. This one *won't*. It'll be a new book." Three days later, at the last possible moment for the printers to do their work, we released beach obstacle information to be overprinted on charts to be given to all the ships and landing craft to be involved in the landings a few days hence.

We had a bit of diversion from our frantic preparations in the form of a royal visitor. I told the story twenty-five years later in an address at a symposium at the Eisenhower Library in Abilene, Kansas, and my remarks have been oft repeated:

> Only if one were designated a Bigot—the awkward code name for a person who had the proper security clearance and had a "need to know"—was he entitled to be told the date and the hour and the place. We were so security minded that when King George VI visited *Ancon* on May 25 at Portland, and asked what lay behind closely drawn curtains in our Intelligence Center, the junior officer standing with me answered "Very secret information, Sire," and remained motionless before the curtains. The King took the hint and moved on. An angry captain demanded of my companion some minutes later why he had been so rude to the King. He received the entirely correct answer: "Sir, nobody told me he was a Bigot!"

General Dwight Eisenhower, supreme commander of the Allied invasion forces, set June 5 as D-day. Troops began boarding transports on June 1, and tanks, trucks, and all the paraphernalia of the complex operation started the loading process. By Saturday, June 3, ninety thousand men were aboard. All ships were "sealed," that is, no one—for security reasons—could go ashore. The danger of a leak was too great. I was an exception, leaving the ship a couple of times on errands for Commander Munson. Last-minute newcomers to the *Ancon* were several well-known war correspondents, fretting for all they were worth at the "no liquor on a naval vessel" rule. Ernest Hemingway was the most conspicuous and about the noisiest. Bandages covered fifty-two stitches on his head. A taxi accident in London? A drunken brawl? His stories varied from day to day. The correspondents brought a welcome touch of color and frivolity to the formal atmosphere of the ship. Despite the imminence of the invasion, we officers were in well-pressed standard blue uniforms with well-starched white shirts and equally starched manners. (Even on D-day, we remained in "blues" unless going ashore. One of my fellow reservists was sharply chastised that day for incorrect dress. Such was the regular navy.)

Bad weather forced Eisenhower to postpone the attack until the sixth. With an unexpected twenty-four-hour calm on the *Ancon,* I sought out Rear Admiral John Hall, the Force O commander. "We are ready," he said, "and I do not expect to be repulsed on any beach." The weather was still atrocious when the slow-moving convoys got under way after dark on the fifth. *Ancon* weighed anchor at 2:00 a.m. on the sixth. Our crossing was uneventful, but troops in smaller ships and landing craft were miserable. Heavy seas and unexpectedly strong tidal currents played havoc with the precise and detailed plans for beach touchdown at H-hour, 6:30 a.m. An overcast of clouds at Omaha forced the heavy bombers to overfly the beach area in the half hour before the scheduled landing lest their bombs fall on our ships or craft. Thus the German defenses were unscathed—and ready and waiting.

The first reports to us on *Ancon* after H-hour about conditions on the several sectors of Omaha were alarming. Because of the tides, landing craft were missing their designated targets, few tanks and artillery were making it ashore, and those that did were easy targets for German fire. The navy had trained special teams to be among the first to land. Their job was to blast lanes through the beach obstacles so that small boats could bring in troops safely. Few of the teams made it ashore, even fewer succeeded in opening lanes, and none managed to mark its lanes with flags. The tide was rushing in faster than expected, concealing the mined obstacles at a frightening pace. The few troops that had managed to cross the beach unharmed were huddled behind rocks and dunes at the foot of the high bluffs. By 8:30, the navy beach masters had signaled for all landing attempts to stop. I asked Commander Munson for his estimate. "It's in the balance now. You can't tell which way it's going. The Germans will probably try to hold the beaches until nightfall and then come after us. It doesn't look good. The obstacles are bad, and there are lots of mines." This assessment from a veteran of amphibious landings was not what I had hoped to hear.

Nor was it what Admiral Hall had expected. He wanted Munson's personal assessment of the beach situation, and Munson was eager to see what was happening for himself. There would be future invasions— one was scheduled for southern France in August—and there was a war to be won in the Pacific. What was going wrong here? Was it just the weather or, more serious, were our intelligence and our planning at fault?

Munson commandeered an LCS(s), a small high-speed scout boat armed with two 50 mm guns. When I asked to go with him, he said I could not unless I had the admiral's permission. (Munson was one of the few who knew I was on loan from the White House, and he did not want to be responsible if something went amiss.) Admiral Hall was much too busy to be asked, so I approached his chief of staff, Captain E. H. von Heimburg, whom I'd known in Washington. "If you want to be a damned fool and get your head blown off, you can go" was his response. Before anyone could object, I was in the scout boat with Munson.

Our skipper was Lieutenant Phil Bucklew, who had gained fame for his bravery in the landings in Sicily and Italy the year before. "Buck" had come out to the *Ancon* to report, but Munson said, "You can report to me. Let's go!" Buck's job had been to lead in the first wave at H-hour of DD tanks, DD standing for dual-drive, that is, tanks able to swim as well as move on the ground. They were equipped with large inflatable canvas bags to keep them afloat. The plan called for them to be launched three miles offshore, navigate in, and provide protection to the navy teams that were to clear paths through the obstacles. But the seas had been too rough. Most of the tanks sank within minutes, carrying their crews to the bottom. Few made it ashore, and they were too late to help the demolition teams. Buck was bitter at the loss of "his" tanks. He burst out to Munson in words I wrote down: "All the High Command does is carry out the plan. They sit far out and can't see what's happening. There is no pliability. The plans are too rigid." Buck was convinced that if senior officers had been close enough to the beach to judge the sea conditions, the DD tanks would have been brought much nearer, would have made it safely, and would have provided cover for the demolition teams, making the landings better in all respects.

It was true that the command was far offshore—eleven miles to be exact—but the situation now had passed out of the hands of admirals and generals. If Omaha's several sections of beach were to be taken and held, it would be by the courage of navy coxswains manning small landing craft and the sheer guts of the combat troops that made it ashore. Skippers of destroyers, abandoning their designated positions, moved in so close that some scraped bottom. They provided the fire against German strong points that the missing and delayed army tanks and artillery had been counted on to furnish.

On our way in, we plowed through the flotillas of landing craft loaded with tanks, artillery, and troops that were staying out of range of German guns. All scheduled landings were at a standstill; craft were called in whenever a section of beach was thought to be reasonably safe. Munson wanted to go ashore and find Lieutenant Commander Joe Gibbons, commander of the navy demolition teams. The closer we got, the less possible this seemed. Thick gray columns of smoke rose from wrecked, burning landing craft. Beach areas were jammed with burning trucks and wreckage of all kinds. Exploding gas drums spit fire and oily smoke into the air. A few undamaged trucks in our vision were jammed against sand dunes. Would bulldozers be able to clear paths before the rising tide swamped them? We passed the slender antenna of a sunken tank and grazed another unseen menace, possibly one of our sunken tanks if not a German beach obstacle. Torn canvas from one of the drowned DD tanks made Buck swear again, so angry was he at the blunders—as he saw them—that had lost so many lives.

I was surprised, as was Munson, at how much closer together the beach obstacles seemed, as the tide closed in on them, than they had appeared in aerial photographs. Munson realized it would be impossible to find Gibbons—if he was still alive—and told Bucklew to cruise along the coast, seaward of what we hoped was the outermost line of obstacles. Everywhere was the same: wrecked, swamped, broached, burning boats; tanks, guns, and trucks in a flotsam of fuel cans, cartridge cases, life belts, soldiers' packs—and bodies of men killed by enemy fire or drowned in the onrushing tide. We passed an LCT (tank landing craft) upside down, a seemingly impossible position for a broad-beamed, flat-bottomed boat, but there it was, with its bridge half buried in the sand. The next LCT we approached was no luckier. German mortar fire hit her ramp as she was unloading a truck. With a great flash, the truck exploded. Flaming fragments hit the sea around us.

At no time could we see clearly the top of the bluffs that rose behind the beach. Smoke was too dense. But here and there we could make out that some of our men were there and appeared to have cleared out the Germans in their area. With steadily increasing, more accurate fire from destroyers, with more army tanks and artillery being landed, and with a degree of order seeming to be emerging from the confusion, there was nothing more to be seen or learned. Munson ordered a return to the *Ancon.* His yeoman's prediction of May 27 had been amply borne out. This was a military operation that had not gone "by the book."

As Bucklew turned seaward, his luck ran out. We hit something with considerable force—one of the beach obstacles? We began taking on water. In trying desperately to avoid mines, Buck lost control and we broached on some rocks. A helpful landing craft pulled us clear. It was obvious that we could not make it to the *Ancon.* Buck tied up alongside an LST (tank landing ship). Munson hailed another fast boat, and we moved on, leaving an exhausted Bucklew to watch his LCS(s) go to the bottom within an hour.

As Munson and I climbed a cargo net to reboard *Ancon,* with his usual aplomb he merely said: "That wasn't so bad. Suppose Buck had hit an obstacle that was mined. We wouldn't be here."

Just before midnight on D-day, the ship sounded its first air raid warning. The first German planes we had seen all day—a pitiful three—flew over, all that remained of the powerful Luftwaffe that had once controlled the skies over France. *Ancon*'s gunners shot down one; it fell into the sea a hundred yards to starboard. The weakness of German air defenses surprised not only the Allied top command. Commodore C. D. Edgar, commanding a follow-up convoy on D-day afternoon, told me a couple of days later that a German prisoner brought to his ship refused that night to go belowdecks. He was confident that the Luftwaffe would be arriving to annihilate the invaders, so completely had he been taken in by Nazi propaganda.

I went ashore midday on D+1, the seventh. The difference was scarcely believable. The last of the German pillboxes, gun emplacements, and trenches were empty. Prisoners were corralled behind barbed wire. Paths had been blasted through the beach obstacles, and bulldozers were carving roads out of the gullies that led from the high ground down to the beach. Convoys with fresh troops were arriving on schedule from England. Work was beginning on a landing strip for small planes at the edge of the bluff.

With no further work to do in Force O's Intelligence Center, I was free to begin interviews for Morison's history. One of the first was with Brigadier General W. M. Hoge, commander of the army's Special Engineer Brigade charged with opening up roads and building the airstrip.

Three miles inland, it was not as peaceful as at Omaha. "The Germans still have some punch," Hoge said. "We damned near lost Vierville early this morning," referring to the closest French village. By the next day, the problem was one of logistics. Ships were too slow in unloading to meet the army's needs. Admiral Hall came ashore to discuss unloading with Hoge. Hall commented to me while we were on "Easy Red," a key segment of Omaha, "This is the most strongly defended beach I've ever seen. In another month, we might not have made it. The DD tanks were a complete failure." Everywhere I went in the next few days, I found the same opinion. German beach defenses, especially the obstacles, were being strengthened at such a pace that, instead of "writing a new book," we came close to having "no book at all" at Omaha.

Those landing at our sister American beach on the Cherbourg Peninsula, named Utah, happily had an easier time of it. The terrain was not formidable, German defenses were slim, and paratroopers had landed behind the beach during the night before H-hour, discombobulating the defenders. However, the Germans fiercely defended the land between Omaha and Utah for a couple days, and it was not until the ninth that I made it to Utah to track down friends who could fill me in on the navy's role in the landings there.

On one beach or the other daily, when I was not aboard a destroyer, the *Ancon,* or the *Bayfield* (the Utah headquarters ship), I also made contact with Forrest Pogue, an army historian who was attached to the army's field headquarters—a tent city put up on June 10 several miles inland. On the afternoon of the twelfth, on returning to Omaha from a discussion with Pogue, I was surprised at the commotion. General Omar Bradley and a cluster of lesser brass were there awaiting some distinguished visitors: General Eisenhower and Chief of Staff George C. Marshall and their aides. Marshall had come to see for himself the hard-won initial success of the invasion that he had so long advocated over British obfuscations and delays. While Bradley and his associates briefed Marshall on the D-day struggle for Omaha, I ventured over to greet Colonel Frank McCarthy, Marshall's top aide. We knew each other well from Map Room contacts. McCarthy was more surprised to see me than I him, as he had not realized I had left the White House temporarily. After hurried greetings and a few words from me on the D-day situation, he left with Marshall and the others for Bradley's tent city. I thought no more about the encounter until I learned, weeks later, that McCarthy had thoughtfully phoned the Map Room on his return to Washington and written my father that he had seen me and that I was okay. These were gracious acts, typical of the way General Marshall had trained his associates to remember always the human side of military life.

Except for four days in the third week of June, when a fierce storm stopped all landings and the troops pushing slowly inland were almost out of ammunition and supplies and I was trapped on the ship, I spent the time interviewing army and navy men who had good stories to tell about the assault. Some nights I bunked with Pogue in his large tent-covered foxhole at army headquarters. After the storm abated, I returned to England on the *Ancon*. The Germans still held Cherbourg, the only port in the invasion area capable of taking big ships. Capturing it was a priority. Pounded by our battleships and heavy cruisers, and penned in by our army, the Germans threw in the towel on June 25. The next week, I crossed the Channel on a PT boat in heavy seas. (If you want to shake up your liver and all the rest of your insides, try that.) I especially wanted to interview the men of the underwater demolition teams who were scouring the Cherbourg harbor for German mines. Until they were finished, no ship could safely enter the port. A couple of days later I flew back to England on a hospital plane filled with wounded men.

By now I had the kind of eyewitness stories Morison wanted for the account he would write of the navy's role in the Normandy landings. Statistics and dry-as-dust formal reports would be found in the documents that would be written in the coming months and sent "through channels" to the Navy Department. I packed four large Naval Intelligence locked pouches with maps, photographs, operation plans, army and navy orders, and voluminous notes and dispatched them to Morison's Washington office. Back in London, I made farewell and thank-you calls. I chanced to be in Churchill's Map Room on July 20 when Deputy Prime Minister Clement Attlee walked in. (England had a coalition government during the war; thus Attlee, leader of the opposition Labour Party, was deputy to Churchill.) Attlee knew all about the British and Canadian landings on their three beaches, but he had not yet met anyone to interrogate on the American assaults. He gave me a real third-degree going over. At the hotel that night, I wrote about him: "Short, dark, bristly shopkeeper—rather wild hair. No polish. No

suavity and no concern about it." All this, of course, was in reaction to
my admiration for the charismatic Churchill. Polish or not, just a year
later Attlee's party trounced Churchill's, and he became the prime minister. As such I was to see him at the conference in Potsdam when I was
there with President Truman in July 1945.

Churchill's flamboyant minister of information, Brenden Bracken,
whom I'd come to know a year earlier in Quebec, joined us. He
breezily told me that I wouldn't find Roosevelt in Washington and
then launched into talk about the "buzz bombs." They were Germany's latest secret weapon, rocket-propelled missiles for which the
Allies had no defense. Landing indiscriminately throughout the
London area, they were unnerving to the populace, who had hoped
the invasion had ended such troubles. Pim spoke of Churchill's reaction the day before when he was urged to head for the bomb shelter as
radar was warning of approaching missiles. "Tell them," said Churchill, "to go and bugger themselves!" "Shocking language from a
prime minister," grinned Pim.

As I was leaving the Map Room, Pim handed me photographs of the
maps of the invasion area taken on the morning of the landings. "This
is how a *real* Map Room looked"—a teasing reminder of an April news
story quoting FDR's remark that his Map Room was better than
Churchill's. Pim also handed over a parcel wrapped in well-used brown
paper and tied in oft-knotted string. "Something to read on the flight
home," was all he said. Hours later, I opened the package to find a
copy of Winston Churchill's *Thoughts and Adventures* inscribed, "To
Lieutenant Elsey from Winston S. Churchill 1944 July." This is a cherished possession, well protected in a slipcase later ordered for it by my
father. I hope it will be equally cherished by future members of the
family.

It was back to the States by air—an army plane to Northern Ireland
and a navy seaplane to the maritime terminal of LaGuardia in New
York, with a refueling stop in Labrador. Eighteen hours in the air—
splendid time for those days. From New York, I phoned the Map
Room. FDR's absence, as Bracken had said, was confirmed in carefully
guarded language, as we never spoke openly about the president's
whereabouts. With no reason to scurry back, I boarded a flight to Pittsburgh. The monthly newsletter of the Westinghouse Research Laboratory reported what happened there:

BELIEVE IT OR NOT. Dr. H. M. Elsey returning from the Sharon works goes to a Pittsburgh garage for his car to drive home to Oakmont, and finds that his son Lt. George Elsey had unexpectedly returned from England and was waiting at the garage for the attendant to bring the car to him. All the more miraculous are these facts: A postponed test at Sharon caused the Doctor to shorten his stay there, he then got a bus to Pittsburgh only because the driver made an extra trip around the block. In the meantime, over in England, Lt. Elsey had his planned trip home cancelled by a higher priority rating and boarded the plane a day later. To the minute, both father and son arrived at the garage for the car.

Mother, Dad, and I had a splendid weekend reunion. Then it was back to Washington to await Roosevelt's return from a conference at Pearl Harbor with Admiral Nimitz and General MacArthur and a resumption of Map Room duties.

(In 1949, as I shall describe later, I returned to active duty for some months to assemble and organize materials for volume 11 of Morison's fifteen-volume history of the U.S. naval operations in World War II. And much later still, in 1969, on the twenty-fifth anniversary of the invasion of Normandy, I spoke at a commemorative seminar at the Eisenhower Library in Abilene, Kansas. My paper was printed with those of the other participants in *D-Day,* a volume published by the University Press of Kansas. Generous portions of my remarks were also included in *Assault on Normandy,* a publication of the U.S. Naval Institute Press issued in 1994 on the fiftieth anniversary of the invasion.)

Chapter Four

Back to the White House

When I returned to the White House late in July, Roosevelt was still in the Pacific. He had left Hawaii for a vacation cruise to Alaska. With the White House unusually silent and the "final campaign" in Europe appearing to be going well, the press began to speculate on the "final campaign" against Japan. A popular weekly of the day, *Collier's,* went overboard. Asserting that there were six "roads to Japan," its imaginative correspondent wrote: "These routes are contemplated by our Pacific strategists every hour of every day on the master charts that wall the secret Map Room in the White House. These charts show Allied and enemy naval, air and army bases. The global battle lines are drawn in infinite detail. . . . At least once and frequently several times daily, President Roosevelt, his War and Navy secretaries and the Joint Chiefs of Staff sit in the air-conditioned room somewhere in the lower regions of the White House and ponder these maps." No such meetings ever took place, but we bought extra copies of the magazine and enjoyed sending them to parents and friends with a wry comment or two.

Roosevelt returned to the White House on August 17 and was wheeled into the Map Room at once. Having been told of his uncertain health, I was pleasantly surprised at his high spirits. He stayed with us a half hour, reading up on the top news of the moment and the Allied landings in southern France of two days earlier. We already had photographs of those landings, which he tried to match with a rubber terrain model of the beaches placed on the floor in front of his chair. A wire from the front, hand delivered from the War Department just as he was arriving, reported that the initial assault had cost fewer than one hundred lives—a very happy contrast from the Normandy landings of ten weeks earlier.

News from northern France was equally cheering. Eisenhower reported that armored units under General George Patton were within twenty-five miles of Paris and that he had canceled an airborne operation as unnecessary.

FDR looked at us and grinned: "The next thing we'll see is a picture of old George on a horse, with his spurs, riding under the Arc de Triomphe!" (Patton's ability to publicize himself was second only to MacArthur's.)

Harry Hopkins had hurried in from his house in Georgetown to welcome Roosevelt and came in just as the president was reading the last of the dispatches. He was greeted with a warm "Hello, Harry. How are you doing? Are you going to come up with me and have some coffee?" Hopkins's response was equally warm, but it was not a first-name salutation. Despite their intimacy of many years, Roosevelt was always "Mr. President" to Hopkins, just as he was to almost everyone. The only people I ever heard use the baptismal name were Mrs. Roosevelt and Churchill, to whom the president was "Franklin," and Supreme Court Justice Felix Frankfurter, to whom he was "Frank."

I had assumed I would resume routine duty in the Map Room, but Admiral Brown had other ideas. I was to work on studies and projects of his choosing. He was tired of the cubbyhole off the corridor leading to the West Wing and, to the intense irritation of the White House ushers, he chose the Library as his office. This was a handsome, paneled room on the ground floor a few steps from the Map Room. Standard navy-issue desks and file cabinets were installed for him and for me. They clashed with the dignity of the Library's furnishings, adding to the ushers' woes.

My first assignment related to the forthcoming Second Quebec Conference with Churchill. A squabble was under way as to how Germany was to be administered by the Allies after her defeat. How would the country be parceled out to the Soviets, the British, and us? Roosevelt insisted that the American zone of occupation should front on the North Sea so that our troops could be supplied directly from its ports. The British, he said, should be south of us. Churchill countered that, if that were the case, his supply lines would cross over ours, with confusion for everyone. He wanted to be on the north. Hopkins mused one morning, on a now rare visit to the Map Room, "The president feels very strongly on this. I'm trying to find out why." "Simple," said Leahy.

"The president doesn't want our supply lines to have to go through France. God damn it, nobody wants to go into France!"

At Brown's direction, I worked up a paper on the evolution of the fracas—the roots of which went much deeper than the Churchill-Roosevelt cables indicated. Maps were included. Leahy took the paper for the president to read en route to Quebec. There Churchill won the argument: logic was on his side.

While other Map Room officers ran the second Quebec Map Room, I eavesdropped from Washington. At a distance from the action and without the personalities of the prime minister and the president to overwhelm me, I was appalled at Roosevelt's continuing haphazard and irresponsible treatment of the State Department. At Dumbarton Oaks, a great estate in the Georgetown section of Washington, an international conference was under way planning the organization that was to become the United Nations. Two days before the Quebec Conference began, Stalin had cabled Roosevelt insisting that each of the sixteen "independent" members of the Union of Socialist Soviet Republics be members of the new organization. FDR pocketed the cable and left for Canada. The head of the U.S. delegation at Dumbarton Oaks was Undersecretary of State Edward Stettinius. Not informed of Stalin's position until the Soviet delegation told him, Stettinius appealed to Hopkins, who knew nothing of the matter either. Hopkins phoned Admiral Brown in Quebec, relaying State's request for information on the only matter, according to Stettinius, left unresolved at the conference. Presumably, Brown checked with the president. We were told to take a copy of Stalin's cable pronto to Stettinius at Dumbarton Oaks.

As he had a year earlier, Churchill accepted Roosevelt's invitation to spend a few days at Hyde Park before returning to England. While they were there with Hopkins and Leahy, but with no one from State, a sweeping statement on new U.S.-British policies toward Italy was drafted. I suspected a heavy British hand. Secretary of State Cordell Hull, having learned in due course from the British embassy that a "manifesto" was to be issued "this evening," sent an urgent message to Roosevelt—still at Hyde Park—through the Map Room asking for a delay. Latin American nations had been promised that the United States would take no action with respect to an Axis nation without consulting them. FDR, we were told, spoke with Hull by phone. Hull's appeal was to no avail; the statement was released on September 26. Similarly, when

I rather cautiously suggested to Admiral Leahy that Stalin be informed in advance, Leahy's reaction was sharp. "It's political, isn't it? Why tell him?"

Such an off-the-cuff way of doing business, without involving interested and knowledgeable parties, all too often left the diplomats and the military floundering. The British general, who was supreme allied commander in the Mediterranean, cabled the Combined Chiefs of Staff in Washington on October 4 asking what the September 26 statement meant. He did not know, he said, what he was expected to do!

Still another fiasco erupted after the Second Quebec Conference. While there, Roosevelt had approved a paper prepared in the Treasury Department, proposing that Germany, after the war, be stripped of her industries and reduced to agricultural status. Neither the State Department nor any military officials had been consulted. When word leaked of this proposal, dubbed the Morgenthau Plan since it had been slipped to the president by Secretary of the Treasury Henry Morgenthau Jr., all hell broke loose. Although Hopkins had been with Roosevelt and Churchill at Hyde Park, he had not earlier been with them in Quebec. He asked me for the documents about this "Plan," assuming there would be a copious file in the Map Room. I replied: "Nothing."

Reasons for concern were obvious. A postwar pastoral Germany would present an open door for future Soviet westward advance. Suspicious minds at State, War, and Navy surmised that communist sympathizers in Treasury had put one over on Morgenthau and Roosevelt. (They were later proved correct.) Hull's outrage at the audacity of a fellow cabinet member, as well as well-founded concerns about the danger of the proposal in which Hull was supported by the Chiefs of Staff, led Roosevelt to disavow the Morgenthau Plan. Just one more example, as I saw it, of how not to do business.

Italian manifestos and Morgenthau Plans were matters Admiral Brown and I could do nothing about. There was one we could do something about. That was planning the disposition of the Map Room papers and other highly classified White House records. While it did not seem likely that Roosevelt would lose the November 1944 election to Governor Dewey of New York, it was at least a possibility. Whether he would leave the White House the coming January or later, his files would go to the library on the Roosevelt estate in Hyde Park. How "secure" was the library? The admiral took the matter up with the president, who suggested I go with him to Hyde Park on October 5, look over the library, and suggest necessary alterations to meet security requirements for top-secret papers. Accordingly, on the appointed evening, I checked in at the presidential train parked underground for security reasons at the Bureau of Printing and Engraving on Fourteenth Street in southwest Washington. Expecting to go to one of the cars designated for staff and Secret Service, I was surprised to be told, "Lieutenant, you are with the president in the *Ferdinand Magellan*." This was the president's heavily armored sleeping car, with bulletproof windows, built for him by the Pullman Company at the outbreak of the war. I found I was to be the president's only guest in that car.

Arriving minutes after I did, Roosevelt sent for genial Bill Hassett, his correspondence secretary; Louise Hackmeister, the head White House telephone operator, who would run a small switchboard at Hyde Park; Mary Eben, his personal librarian; and Dorothy Brady, a personal secretary. All were invited for a nightcap. The president had just made the second of his admitted "political" speeches of the campaign and was eager for compliments. They were profuse, as was to be expected from this group. "I never mentioned his [Dewey's] name and I won't ever," he grinned. He urged highballs on us but drank only orange juice himself while he had his Scottie, Fala, entertain us with tricks. Despite a heavy cough, out came the ever-present cigarette holder and a pack.

"Hackie," Dotty, and Mary, knowing what was expected of them, began entertaining FDR with stories. Hackie had one about the misadventures of some sailors on shore leave that brought forth the familiar "I love it, I love it!" Mary Eben, turning to business briefly, got his approval of Christmas gifts for cabinet, staff, family, and friends. "I can't wait any longer, Mr. President, I have to place orders now." Coughing heavily, Roosevelt complained about Washington weather. "I'll be voiceless and miserable by Saturday." Pointing to Dotty Brady, "You have to be born here to survive Washington weather."

At 11:15, Roosevelt dismissed us, saying, "Children, it's late. Time to turn in." But before the others left for their sleeping car, he said. "Wait. I've got a new chair. It's very light. It all folds up." And he demonstrated. This was the only time in the three years with Roosevelt that I ever heard him refer, even indirectly, to his disability. I had not known until I reported to the White House that he could not walk at all—nor did anyone except his closest associates. The public was used to seeing him standing tall and erect on the arm of a son or an aide, or moving slowly with support. As for his new chair, as with earlier ones, he never moved it himself. He was always pushed by a valet or an aide or, when in the Map Room, by one of us.

It was an all-night trip to Highland, New York, a small village on the west side of the Hudson River, opposite Poughkeepsie. Roosevelt always insisted on traveling at a low speed. That this greatly inconvenienced the railroads, by delaying the trains behind his, was of no concern to him. When we disembarked, he told me to climb into his White House limousine, which was awaiting us. As escorts, we had one New York State Police car and a single Secret Service car—nothing like today's parade of cars that encompass every presidential move. And we obeyed the local stoplights, unthinkable today. Knowing that I was a stranger to the area, FDR pointed out landmarks and told anecdotes about historic personalities as we headed north to Hyde Park. It was raining hard when we arrived at his house. He was quickly carried inside without the delay of being pushed in a chair up a ramp.

Bill Hassett and "the girls," following in other cars, were invited to join us for breakfast. "Have your eggs any way you want them," the host declared. But when he said, "Scrambled for me," everyone meekly concurred. He had milk. "I used to drink coffee so strong the spoon would stand up, but I haven't had any since rationing started." That was not enough to deter the rest of us.

I made copious notes of events of the next couple of days, but there is no need to record the trivialities. Roosevelt was at home to relax, and a lot of that relaxation took the form of gathering us around while he told stories. Hassett told me later that he felt like throwing up at hearing the old chestnuts again, but at the time he was a perfect listener and chuckled heartily at the appropriate times. We heard all about Mrs. Vanderbilt, whose mansion was a few miles up the road, wearing pearls with her black silk nightgowns and decorating the chamber pots with elaborate bows before the place had modern plumbing. We were assured that the Roosevelt bees were the oldest honey producers in Dutchess County. And there were the legends about "Elmer Poughkeepsie." (I never did find out whether "Elmer" was real or only a myth.)

When I was alone with the president in the small fieldstone library, some yards from the house, we talked about current war matters. He queried me sharply as to who actually drafted the monthly submarine press releases that always seemed to raise Admiral King's blood pressure. He asked about Bill Mott, "Where is he now?" I explained his recent transfer to the staff of Admiral Richmond Kelly Turner, commander of a major Pacific Fleet Task Force. Once again, Roosevelt showed his knowledge of senior naval personnel. "Kelly," he said, "is a 'no' man. Whatever he's told to do, he says it can't be done. But he's a good officer. He comes around and does it damn well. He's very different from me. I'm a 'Happy Thought' man. I'm always 'Can do!'"

Roosevelt mused about Pacific amphibious operations and the islands that were our targets. "My spies tell me," he said, "that the navy wants them all. The United Nations should have them." (This phrase was already in common use to denote the future organization.) "My spies say the navy is drafting a bill for Congress to give the navy responsibility for running all those islands after the war. I asked the navy who gave them authority to draft such a bill. I didn't get any answer. You know how hard it is for me to get information from the navy. Giving those islands to the navy is the worst option. Out of every hundred captains, there are always two or three who are no good. They're the ones that Ernie King would say, 'Send them out to run Guam!'" (FDR's remarks on these Pacific islands confirmed the fears Leahy and Brown had expressed so pungently in the Map Room months earlier, that he was "going to give them away.")

Our talk switched to Europe. For some reason, prisoners of war were on Roosevelt's mind. He asked my opinion of the German POWs I'd seen in Normandy. I explained they were a very mixed bag. Except for the crack 352nd regiment at Omaha Beach on D-day, very few of whom surrendered or were captured, most prisoners seemed to be from Eastern Europe, not German at all. He commented that the Germans were tough and "hopeless to retrain." We could do nothing with them. The "Wops" were different; we now had 140,000 of them working. He told the oft-repeated joke about Italian soldiers captured in North Africa. A GI guard asked an Italian captive why his group was so happy. "Because we're going to New York and you're going to Rome!" FDR roared at his story.

From the Germans and Italians, Roosevelt moved on to the French. "Pétain was a traitor. He should spend the rest of his life on Reunion Island." I ventured that Pétain had redeemed himself by siding with us and the British when we invaded North Africa. "Maybe," he said, but he was not convinced.

Then we were back to World War I, when he was assistant secretary of the navy. As he had said many times, his boss, Josephus Daniels, "didn't know a damn thing about the navy. He was as dumb as that secretary back about 1830 who was amazed when he went on a ship the first time and looked down a hatch and said, 'Why, it's hollow!'" (This was a really tired old chestnut, and false, but as a mere lieutenant I didn't challenge the commander in chief.)

When we came into the present again, we talked about the zones of occupation in Germany. Forgetting—or ignoring—that the U.S.-British-Soviet European Advisory Commission had already agreed on the precise boundaries of the areas to be administered after the German surrender, he remarked that he hoped "Russia would get lots of Germany. Stalin already has a million German prisoners. He makes Napoleon look like a piker."

As I was expected to do, I expressed admiration for the library, which, by the end of the second day, I knew pretty well. Did I have any suggestions? "Yes. I hope a Map Room can be added as a postwar exhibit." "Good idea," was the response. (Years later, a fanciful exhibit purporting to be "The Map Room" was developed with scant regard for accuracy.)

"Anything else?"

Hesitantly I proposed, "Perhaps your study could be altered to resemble the Oval Office."

This was not well received. He had designed his study and liked it exactly as it was. I was regaled with an account of everything in the room, the most recent addition being the carpet given him at Teheran by the shah of Iran. No one was going to make any changes.

When left on my own and not exploring the mansion or the library, I walked around the spacious grounds. I was startled when a soldier, whom I had not seen, stepped out from a well-camouflaged guard post, saluted, and said, "Lieutenant Elsey, you have a phone call." Until then, I had been oblivious to the security curtain surrounding the estate.

The call? The president wanted me to join him for more rambling conversation. Although a presidential election was less than a month ahead, we might as well have been on the moon as far as politics was concerned. The only political note was the sudden death of Wendell

Willkie, Roosevelt's opponent four years earlier. Roosevelt was shaken. Willkie had become a staunch internationalist, and FDR was counting on him as a partner in postwar international affairs. I felt the loss on a personal basis, as Willkie's only son was a college and graduate school friend. Aside from that shadow, I had a very happy interlude away from Washington and a very heady experience for a twenty-six-year-old.

I reported on the trip to Admiral Brown. We agreed on what should be done if—and a very unlikely "if"—Roosevelt should lose the election to Dewey. What we did not foresee was FDR's sudden death the following April. Our contingency plans then went into effect. The great mass of papers accumulated in the White House over twelve years went to the National Archives for temporary storage until the Hyde Park Library was prepared to receive them. Some extremely sensitive documents were returned to the War and Navy Departments or, as I have noted earlier, to Dr. Vannevar Bush if they related to the Manhattan Project. President Truman directed that a small group of papers relating to relations with the British and Soviet governments be held at the White House for ease of reference. These were placed in a special file safe in my office to which I alone had the combination.

Back to 1944. My next assignment from the naval aide was to work up a report on China. The war against the Japanese invaders was going poorly. Chiang and American officers were at loggerheads. How, asked Brown, did we get into such a mess? When I told Admiral Leahy of my assignment and asked for his help, he spoke freely. "I used to think China was important and potentially powerful. I hoped that, after we'd sunk the Jap fleet and knocked their planes out of the sky, the Chinese would finish off Japan. But now China is weak and divided. The communists run a lot of the country and ignore Chiang." Leahy went on: "I'm for helping Russia. She has big interests in Manchuria—all over the Far East. Let her carry the ball and to hell with China."

Over the next month, with copious interruptions, I wrote a sixty-five-page report summarizing U.S.-Chinese wartime relations. Brown passed it to Roosevelt, who somewhat later returned it with the not-very-exact characterization: "I have read this Lend-Lease report in regard to Chiang Kai-shek by Elsey and it is excellent. Please thank him for me. F.D.R." Since my paper was far more about the politics of the struggle between Chinese leaders and American military and civilian advisers than it was about Lend-Lease, I wasn't sure that Roosevelt really had read it. The note was appreciated, anyway.

Some thirty years later, I had a long-distance call from a retired army historian who asked my permission to publish the "China Report." I didn't know what he was talking about until he refreshed my memory. I answered that the paper was included in the public files of the Roosevelt Library and my permission wasn't needed. The historian, Riley Sunderland by name, wrote a long interpretive foreword. In due course, it was published, Sunderland later writing that it was very useful to scholars. That was pleasant to hear, but, despite his too-effusive praise, I doubt that it contributed much to historical knowledge.

Another scholar, Eric Larrabee, concluded in *Commander in Chief* (1987) that my report was written at Roosevelt's instigation: "Roosevelt's political radar told him that if Chiang's regime went down, he himself would be subject to partisan attack for having 'lost China' (as his successor subsequently was). To prepare against this eventuality, it would be prudent to have at hand an analysis of the historical record showing how hard the President had labored to sustain Chiang Kai-shek despite the latter's failings." This was an understandable, but incorrect, assumption.

Many of the copious interruptions I faced while compiling the China paper were due to the presidential election. As a naval officer, it was improper for me to participate in a political event, but because my involvement was so indirect and was at my superior officer's direction the impropriety was ignored. Roosevelt's campaign speechwriting team consisted of Judge Sam Rosenman, a longtime political adviser; Broadway playwright Robert Sherwood; and Harry Hopkins. Admiral Brown told the triumvirate that they should turn to me for any facts relating to the war needed for speech purposes. I became the "legs" for the three, but not all aspects of my research had to do with war issues. Bob Sherwood asked for dope on Christopher Columbus for a radio address aimed at Italian voters. This was easy. I walked to my apartment and returned with Morison's biography, *Admiral of the Ocean Sea*. Sitting at the big table in the Cabinet Room—the site of the campaign speech factory—Sherwood and I developed what we hoped was the right political pitch.

One war-related episode involved our nemesis—Admiral King. Harry Hopkins wanted a rousing statement about the victory our navy had just won in the Battle of the Philippine Sea where the majority of the surviving Japanese fleet had been sent to the bottom. Hopkins would have Roosevelt boast about his farsightedness in building up our navy over the opposition of isolationist Republicans. I knew whom to ask in the Navy Department for the facts, and a splendid statement was quickly written. Admiral King was so sensitive on anything going to the White House, as I have mentioned more than once, that the draft had to be submitted to him for his personal OK. It was due at the White House at 11:00 a.m. on October 27, the date traditionally celebrated as Navy Day.

With no sign of any response from King as the hour approached, I went to his office. A nervous aide took me in, saying, "Lieutenant Elsey is here, Sir, for the Philippine statement." King gave us his usual icy glare, plucked a paper from the pile on his desk, tossed it into the in-box for looking at whenever he damned pleased, and pointed to the door. When the statement finally reached the speechwriters, the clock had run out. Another Ernest J. King episode to remember.

The next assignment of substance, after the China paper, related to U.S. wartime relations with France. Dr. William Langer, distinguished Harvard professor and international relations scholar, now in Washington on war work, sought access to White House files relating to France. Admiral Brown and I saw the president on the afternoon of November 27 in the doctor's office while he was having the daily rubdown and sinus treatment. After clarifying some confusion about "William Langer," with the president at first thinking we were talking about the isolationist senator from North Dakota of the same name and us assuring him that this was a very different Langer, he turned to me and said, "You're the curator in chief." I was to comb the White House files and work up a synopsis on our troubled relations with the French. He would review and "censor" it. Maybe it could be given to the professor, but no outsider—absolutely no one—could have access to his raw files.

As with the China project, I went early to Leahy. As our former ambassador to the Vichy government, he was a fount of information. He spoke pungently, as always. Newspapers were full of stories about "Nazi collaborators" being tracked down as France was being liberated. De Gaulle was getting rid of his political opponents—in Leahy's view, many of them "the better elements in France." Talk with the admiral was fascinating, but it did not contribute to my progress. Plowing through file cabinets, particularly the "PPFs"—the president's personal files—was necessary.

I had barely started when Leahy "borrowed" me. His assistant in his White House office had taken emergency sick leave. I was asked to fill in. I sat in on his daily briefing by the secretary of the Joint Staff and his sessions with Charles "Chip" Bohlen, one of State's top experts on the Soviet Union. Fluent in Russian, Chip had been Roosevelt's interpreter in the Teheran meeting with Stalin (and would be again at Yalta two months hence). Roosevelt fortunately had taken a liking to Bohlen. Leahy capitalized on this. He had struggled against Roosevelt's habit of leaving State in the dark and had finally won the president's consent to his meeting with Bohlen each day for frank exchanges of views and information. Bohlen would carry word back to State of FDR's exchanges with Churchill and Stalin and in turn would convey State's views to Leahy. This was better than nothing, but still a hell of a way to do business. I came to know and admire Bohlen and worked well with him in the Truman years. Thanks to the Leahy-Bohlen linkage, State's opinions and judgments were now taken into account and were reflected in the top-level messages that Leahy now controlled with Hopkins being on the sidelines. Thus, with Roosevelt scarcely being aware—or possibly not being aware at all—a degree of coordination of diplomatic and military views was at last being achieved in the Roosevelt-Churchill-Stalin discourse.

When Admiral Leahy was tied up in meetings, I had to entertain his visitors. One was Admiral Richard E. Byrd, an internationally famous aviator almost as well known as Charles Lindbergh for his flights over the North and South Poles and an early transatlantic flight. He came to report on a mission so confidential that we were keeping it secret from our closest ally, Britain. The United States was preparing for postwar commercial flights in Pacific regions. Byrd, in a navy cruiser, had been surveying obscure Pacific islands as possible refueling bases. (Jets were in the future; propeller planes were limited in their range.) Unfortunately for Byrd, his ship suffered an explosion and a fire, serious enough to cause Byrd to break radio silence and report he was heading for the nearest port. The British picked up the broadcast. Irked at the unexplained presence of an American cruiser in "their" area of the Pacific, they asked for an explanation. They, too, were thinking ahead to postwar civilian aviation and had their eyes on strategically placed islands. One was Clipperton.

Clipperton is about 660 miles southwest of Acapulco, Mexico. It fitted perfectly into a Britain–Bermuda–British Honduras (now Belize)–Clipperton–Marquesas–New Zealand–Australia route. The British, our navy learned, were planning to land an exploratory team on Clipperton. Admiral King objected—vociferously. If anyone was going to put an "observation post," it would be the United States Navy. The French government, getting established in Paris, spoke up. Uninhabited and ignored until now, Clipperton had belonged to France since the 1790s, or so the French claimed. Roosevelt was alerted. The State Department told the British embassy to "lay off." King ordered the immediate establishment of a "weather observation" base on the island.

The French were more incensed than ever and announced that a "shark-fishing expedition" would be sent to Clipperton. By now, four nations were involved as the United States enlisted the Mexican government in the scrap. The Mexicans refused to allow the French "shark-fishers" to leave any Mexican port, the "fishers" being French military personnel.

Leahy and Brown had me watch the Clipperton affair closely and bring every army, navy, and State cable or paper on the subject to their attention. In due course, Roosevelt instructed State to sooth French nerves by assuring them we respected French sovereignty, but Leahy felt so strongly that we should "take" Clipperton that he had me write a full account for the new administration when Truman became president. Truman, however, had much bigger things to worry about. Clipperton, still French and still with no permanent residents, was forgotten as jet aviation made frequent fueling stops unnecessary. Forgotten also were the island specks that Admiral Byrd had sought to identify as Pacific stopovers.

While I was pinch-hitting as Admiral Leahy's White House aide, the Atlantic Charter made the news again. In December 1944, the British government was under heavy fire for its efforts to restore the king of Greece to the throne of his country newly liberated from Nazi control. Under attack in Parliament, Churchill vigorously denied he was violating the charter's third provision, which expresses "the right of all peoples to choose the form of government under which they will live." In an emotional moment, Churchill burst out to the House of Commons that he had never signed the Atlantic Charter. His words provoked astonishment on both sides of the ocean. Roosevelt, at his next press conference, was asked if Churchill's statement was true. The president answered, "Nobody ever signed the Atlantic Charter." He explained that as soon as the text had been agreed, it was turned over to radio operators on his and the British ship and sent to London and Washington for release to the press. "There is no formal document—complete document—signed by us both," he flatly declared. Both had obviously forgotten their response to my request.

Skeptical reporters began snooping. Calls to the Roosevelt Library at Hyde Park were answered, "Yes, we have a typewritten copy with both names, but they are in President Roosevelt's handwriting." The State Department knew nothing more than what was stated in the original White House press release. Finally, the *Chicago Sun's* Washington reporter wrote: "Found: A Signed Atlantic Charter. There is, after all, a copy of the Atlantic Charter signed by Winston Churchill and Franklin D. Roosevelt. It is engraved on the very finest paper, but it is not at the Roosevelt Library, in the White House, or in the Library of Congress. A young aide to Fleet Admiral William D. Leahy, chief of staff to the commander-in-chief, is the proud owner of the document. He had a copy of the charter made, on the basis of the press release issued at the time of the Atlantic meeting, and on one of Mr. Churchill's visits to Washington, got his signature. He also asked the President to sign it. Some day it may become one of the most valuable historical documents of the war."

Where the reporter got his story, inaccurate in many details, I never knew. I kept quiet. Soon the curiosity died down, except for scholars who refused to accept that so important a policy statement, incorporated into the United Nations Declaration of January 1942, signed by twenty-six nations in a White House ceremony, had never been validated by formal signatures. Questions continued to arise until finally put to rest by the chief of the diplomatic branch at the National Archives. In a *Washington Post* interview in 1979, Dr. Milton Gustafson said: "There is no official signed copy at all, though there is one souvenir. . . . Roosevelt and Churchill never got around to putting a copy on paper and signing it. Later a young naval aide who had access to both Roosevelt and Churchill got a printed copy and had both sign it. His name is George Elsey; he is now president of the American Red Cross, and he owns the only signed copy of the Atlantic Charter." That ended the questions, except for the final one: what should I do with it?

My relationship with Admiral Leahy, already close, grew even warmer during the weeks I was in his White House office. "Unification" was much on his mind. Postwar reorganization of the armed forces was being widely discussed in Congress and in the press. If they were "unified," Leahy feared the navy would be dominated by the army. I heard his dire predictions of what would happen if this were to come about. One bill sailing through Congress, however, merely amused him. It would create a new five-star rank for him and seven other officers. It was said to be necessary so that our most senior men would not be outranked by British field marshals and admirals of the fleet. "Poppycock," was Leahy's retort when I told him the bill had cleared both houses. "We're winning the war now. More stars don't mean a damned thing." Nevertheless, he seemed pleased when, the morning Roosevelt signed the bill into law, his secretary and I placed a vase with five red roses on his desk.

Despite his status as the ranking American officer in the American armed forces during World War II, Leahy's diffidence, his aversion to personal publicity, and his unwillingness to court the press meant that he was largely unknown to the public. Mrs. Kermit Roosevelt, a Theodore Roosevelt daughter-in-law but an ardent Democrat, told me of an episode at Hyde Park just before the '44 election. She came downstairs one morning and found an elderly gentleman in civilian clothes who looked vaguely familiar. When polite prebreakfast conversation lagged, she asked in what she admitted might have been patronizing tones, "Do you live here?" "No, Mrs. Roosevelt, I am the chief of staff to the President."

Released by Leahy when his regular aide returned from sick leave, I joined the Map Room staff in preparing reference materials for Roosevelt's forthcoming meetings with Stalin and Churchill at Yalta in the Crimea. Bob Bogue, a navy lieutenant, and Hal Putnam, an army captain, were to be in the party to handle communications and maintain a temporary Map Room. I would once again help hold the fort at home. All was not sweetness and light in the cables flowing back and forth with the prime minister. As he tried to do before Quebec in 1943, Churchill proposed that the American Chiefs of Staff meet with him and the British Chiefs at Malta for some days prior to everyone's flying on to Yalta. Roosevelt made his displeasure known. As before Quebec, he did not want Marshall, King, and Arnold exposed to Churchill's bombast. Churchill then promised, "I shall only arrive [in Malta] in time

to welcome you on February 2." Despite that promise, he was in Malta
two days earlier for sessions of the American and British Chiefs of Staff.

Roosevelt had left Washington on January 22, crossing the Atlantic
on the cruiser USS *Quincy,* two days after he had taken the oath of office in a simple ceremony on the south portico of the White House. It
was later gossiped that he had been too ill for a traditional ceremony at
the Capitol. Nonsense. Wartime conditions ruled out the customary pa-
rades of tanks and soldiers, flyovers and festivities. Some two thousand
invited guests stood in melting snow on the south lawn and then dirtied
up the mansion with their muddy shoes for a reception that left almost
everyone thirsty and hungry.

After the ceremony, the president secluded himself in the Red Room
with family and a very few longtime intimates for a buffet lunch. It was
my assigned task to admit no one to the Red Room who was not on a
very short list. This was not a Map Room assignment but was the task
of a White House aide.

White House aides were young army and navy bachelors who, in addition to their regular duties, were summoned to the White House from
time to time to assist in greeting guests, managing receiving lines, and
generally being hospitable at luncheons, teas, dinners, and other social
events. A year earlier, Admiral Brown had designated me as such an
aide. I was, he said, the first Naval Reserve officer to be named an aide.
"There just aren't any Annapolis men around," he said. My first assignment had come a week or two later when I had laid the president's
wreath at the mast of the battleship *Maine* at Arlington Cemetery in a
ceremony commemorating the Spanish-American War. Later assignments were few as the war curtailed practically all social events at the
White House. All aides, however, were mustered for the inauguration.
My post at the Red Room door was not an easy one. There were many
who thought their position or rank entitled them to push past a lowly
junior officer, but I had FDR's personal list and stuck to it, even deny-
ing admission to a godson of his who swore all kinds of revenge.

Ten days later, January 30, was Roosevelt's sixty-third birthday. Since
early New Deal days, birthday balls had been held to raise money to
fight infantile paralysis, the disease that had cost Roosevelt the use of his
legs. Roosevelt had never attended one, so his absence this year was not
remarked. Eleanor Roosevelt, however, had made it a practice to drop
in briefly at every birthday ball held in Washington and did so this year.

I was the aide to greet her when she arrived at the Hotel Washington and escorted her around the ballroom as she greeted as many as she possibly could before moving on to another hotel for more of the same, always cheerful and apparently tireless.

What Roosevelt was thinking that day, on learning from a Map Room dispatch that Churchill was already in Malta with the Combined Chiefs, despite his promise to arrive only in time to meet the president, I could only imagine.

From Malta, Americans and British alike flew on to the Crimea for the Yalta Conference, a meeting that has been so extensively discussed—and "cussed"—that I'll make no mention of it other than a few references to our Map Room messages. In an incoming one from Yalta, I was ordered to track down Harold Stassen, former governor of Minnesota and now a Naval Reserve captain, and tell him that the president wanted to meet him before he left for the organizing meeting of the United Nations to be convened in San Francisco in a few weeks. (Stassen was a Republican member of the U.S. delegation. Roosevelt was looking for a good Republican "internationalist" with whom he could work after the war as he had hoped to do with Wendell Willkie.) I also had to fly down to Norfolk to discuss with naval authorities plans for the president's return.

With Yalta behind us, I was free to return to the long-delayed paper on U.S.-French relations that William Langer had sought and that the president had told me to prepare for his review. Files searched, the paper was quickly written and handed to Admiral Brown to give FDR late in March. He took it to Hyde Park. From there it went with him to Warm Springs, Georgia, where on April 6, in a very feeble hand, the president wrote "O.K.F.D.R." When the paper and the memo came up by the daily pouch from Georgia, we in the Map Room were shocked at the handwriting, so different from the bold initials we had been used to seeing.

While distressed, we were not really surprised. Even us "kids" in the Map Room knew Roosevelt had begun to talk loosely and inaccurately about very significant issues. His constant talk about "unconditional surrender" bothered many. Chip Bohlen told me in mid-March that, in the State Department's view, "Unconditional Surrender stinks . . . it has strengthened German resistance." Leahy thought Roosevelt was off base in saying Grant had exacted unconditional surrender from Lee at

Appomattox and asked me for the facts. I produced the texts of the Grant-Lee correspondence of April 1865, and Leahy, fearing a "bad public relations bust" if FDR kept on erroneously talking of that surrender, told him the facts. That didn't stop him, however.

I last saw Roosevelt on March 29. Preparing for Warm Springs, he had himself wheeled into the library to look for books he might want to read. I rose from my desk as he entered and greeted him. There was no response. He appeared dazed, looked for a few moments at the bookshelves without seeming to focus on them, and motioned for the door. He was wheeled out through the Diplomatic Reception Room to his car and was gone.

Late on the afternoon of April 12, I walked across the corridor from the library to the Map Room for something or other, instantly put out of my mind by what I was told. Someone—I do not remember who—said, "The president is dead."

There flashed into my mind these never forgotten words. "So that is why they took him to Warm Springs." This unspoken thought conveys my sense of Roosevelt's last days—that he was no longer in control of himself or his situation; that an unidentified "they" had taken over; that he was a feeble shadow of a once powerful leader now in the hands of others.

Within the hour, the stunned silence in the Map Room was replaced with bustle and commotion. Messages flew in and out—from Mrs. Roosevelt to her sons abroad and at sea; from Churchill and embassies worldwide. Every phone rang. "Is it true?"

Admiral Brown arrived from a golf game at Chevy Chase Club. His first question was, "Do we know how to reach the president?" His question was met with uncomprehending stares until we realized he was asking about Harry S. Truman.

My aide's aiguillettes and white gloves were much in evidence the next couple of days. Other aides and I saluted on the North Portico as the casket was carried into the White House on April 13. All aides assisted in the funeral services in the East Room, crowded with American and foreign dignitaries. Much remarked by historians in later years but seemingly appropriate in the emotions of the moment, everyone stood when Mrs. Roosevelt entered the room, but no one stood when the Trumans entered. Harry Truman was not yet felt, by those present, to be The President, so great was the hold in their minds of Franklin Delano Roosevelt.

After the funeral, Admiral Brown suggested that, as a White House aide, I should go on the funeral train to Hyde Park for the burial at the library. "You might be needed." I begged off. Mother and Dad had arrived in Washington that morning for a long-planned visit. I could not desert them. I had taken my mother on a tour of the White House before the funeral, including the East Room where a military honor guard stood by the casket, and then had taxied her back to the Mayflower Hotel. My father was in one of his outrageous moods, able to talk of nothing but his dislike of Roosevelt and how fortunate the country was that he was gone. It was a painful weekend for many reasons.

Chapter Five

A New President

Roosevelt's death on April 12, 1945, was a shock to the whole world, coming with no warning. So it seemed, to all except the few who had seen at close range his rapid deterioration. The Nazis and Japanese were elated, believing they could hold their own in peace negotiations with a new, untested president. Allies were worried, the British especially. Could this scarcely known Truman stand up to Stalin?

No one could have been more curious than we in the Map Room. I had seen Truman for the first time at Roosevelt's January 20 inaugural ceremony when I stood only a few feet away on the White House south portico, on duty as a social aide. I next saw him, Mrs. Truman, and their teenage daughter, Margaret, when they joined the White House staff in a simple greeting party in the Diplomatic Reception Room on February 28 to welcome Roosevelt back from Yalta. Truman impressed us with his smile, cheerful handshakes, and vigor. So different was he in appearance and manner from FDR that it was hard to believe he was only two years younger than the gaunt man in the wheelchair whose hands trembled as he raised them to greet us.

Truman's schedule was crowded in the first few days after April 12. He had no time to come to the Map Room, limiting himself to Leahy's and Brown's briefings and initialing his approval on outgoing cables to Churchill, Stalin, and others that Leahy prepared. A break came on April 18. I quote the note I typed that evening (Colonel Park was the assistant military aide, Commander Tyree the assistant naval aide, Major Price an army Map Room watch officer):

President Truman paid his first visit to the Map Room today. He was scheduled to come in at 2:00, after his lunch with Mrs. Roosevelt.

Remembering that FDR was *never* on time, we were a little sceptical about how long we might have to wait for Mr. Truman. However, at 1:48, while we were still spitting and polishing, three loud raps on the door, and, a moment later, the usher threw it open and in came the President. He greeted Colonel Park cheerfully with a "Hello, Colonel, glad to see you." Park then gave him a brief story about the function of the room, and then said, "These, Mr. President, are the duty officers."

"Oh," replied the President, a little shyly to Park, "I'd like to meet them."

This diffidence made an instant appeal to us, and we all straightened and smiled, while he came around the room, shaking hands. It never occurred to any of us that we should have moved in a line past him. He was just a guy from Missouri, and we were not quite as sharp as we should have been, and so we let him come by us! That is, I think, about as good a contrast as we can ever find between FDR and Truman.

Commander Tyree gave the President a bird's eye view of the war in the Pacific, with a glimpse of things to come. The President said quietly, "Can you tell me where one ship is I'm particularly interested in, the *Missouri,* I've got some friends on her." She was pointed out to him, and he was told she been damaged a few days before. "Oh, that's too bad. Very badly?"

Major Price gave a ten minute story about the Asiatic war. Truman made non-committal remarks, a few uh-huhs and oh-yeses, and "where's Rangoon? If I know where that is, I know what Burma's all about."

Admiral Leahy came in, some time after 2:00, as did Admiral Brown. Both were surprised and amazed that the President had been on time.

The next day I wrote a note to my mother about the new First Lady. "Monday morning, bright and early, Mrs. Roosevelt and Mrs. Truman made a tour of the White House. Once again my office (the library) was invaded and inspected thoroughly . . . I was introduced to Mrs. Truman, of course, and as she cast an appraising eye over the room, she remarked on its attractive appearance. I may be thrown out!" (The premonition was correct. The naval aide and I were soon evicted.) My note also included an impertinent remark for which I should have been spanked. "Mrs. Truman," I wrote, "will make a good PEO First Lady; her slip showed." (PEO was a women's sisterhood that my mother greatly enjoyed and about which Dad and I teased her. I later learned from Mrs. Truman herself that she was indeed a PEO member.)

Truman thereafter came into the Map Room almost every day. In contrast to Roosevelt, he took a close interest in events on every front. His army experience showed. Admiral Leahy was indispensable in explaining planned future operations and ensuring that Churchill got immediate responses. Winant reported from our embassy in London how this surprised and gladdened Churchill. Leahy tutored Truman on Yalta, as well as earlier summits to the extent they were relevant, and on how cavalierly Stalin was violating his Yalta pledges. Leahy kept me hopping, pulling papers from our files.

On April 25, Truman, with Leahy at his side, drove to the Pentagon to use the "scrambler" telephone in General Marshall's office to discuss with Churchill an alleged surrender offer by Himmler, a high-ranking Nazi. Nothing came of this. I mention it only to disprove the oft-repeated statement that such a telephone was present in the Map Room or elsewhere in the White House and that Roosevelt had used it for frequent conversations with Churchill. Had such a system existed, Truman obviously would not have gone to the Pentagon. I still get queries and am met with disbelief when I deny that the White House had such equipment.

Three weeks after Truman took over, I wrote, "The wheel has turned full circle. Originally, the 'P.M.'s' were personal & private messages by F.D.R., too sacred for copies to be made. In his last months, F.D.R., however, left them in the hands of Leahy who took more and more authority. Still no message in Roosevelt's name was sent without his approval. Today [May 5] we have reached the opposite extreme. A Churchill message was taken to Blair House for Pres. Truman. An usher returned it with this instruction: 'Have Admiral Leahy handle without further reference to me.' Thus, Presidential messages are becoming 'staff papers.'" And, as far as Leahy was concerned, he made his wishes known to us in the Map Room a week later. When a "hot" cable arrived after-hours, he wanted us to call him only if the answer to this question was in the affirmative: "Will the war end any sooner if I act on it tonight?"

Of the many contrasts between the former and the current presidents, none was sharper than in their relations with the State Department. Truman was emphatic that there would be no secrets. Leahy was free, as he had long wished, to involve State in all matters and to make decisions on his own that he would not have dared to make in FDR's day. A prime example: As the British and Americans during the night hours of May 7-8 were preparing to announce the German surrender on the eighth, the Soviets protested that they were still fighting the Germans in the East and there must not be any proclamation of victory until all fighting had stopped. Eisenhower relayed a protest from his Soviet counterpart. A little after midnight, the Soviet embassy summoned the Map Room watch officer to come and pick up a message from Stalin to the president. It was a sharp demand to delay any announcement. Leahy had made it clear the evening before that if such messages came in they should be "buried" and not shown to Truman. Nothing should interfere with the president's planned May 8 radio address to the nation proclaiming "Victory in Europe." The president went on the air, not knowing of Stalin's objection.

I wrote about that broadcast, which was made from the Diplomatic Reception Room, next door to the Map Room:

> Trailed by most of the Big Shots in Washington, he went into the room and sat at the battered old desk which F.D.R. had used for years and sat behind a battery of 12 microphones. He stared at the speech which his secretary, Matt Connelly, laid under a tired goose-necked lamp and waited until nine o'clock.
>
> The guests murmured quietly and watched the President who sat alone. A little cluster of junior officers had followed the stars into the room, and we remained inconspicuously in the rear, watching the satisfied expressions of the victors: Admiral Leahy, General Marshall, Admiral King (actually smiling!), Justice Byrnes, Judge Vinson, Secretary Stimson (brisk despite his 77 years), Secretary Forrestal (grim as usual), Henry Wallace and the rest of the Cabinet . . . and many more. Field Marshal Jumbo Wilson and Sir James Somerville gave an Allied flavor to the group—but there weren't any Russians about.
>
> The murmuring died at nine and we listened to the seven-minute speech. . . . We got up for the Star Spangled Banner, piped into the room by radio, and then everybody turned to leave. But a radio announcer at the President's side spoke quickly to him and he called out, "Let's all sit down; we may get a chance to hear the Prime Minister."

We dropped back into our chairs and listened to the familiar tones
. . . as the speech was broadcast . . . we popped up for "God Save the
King" . . . and a few amused questions "Do we get Stalin too?"

Those who asked were not aware of Stalin's angry messages in the
Map Room protesting the timing of Truman's and Churchill's broadcasts.

Leahy, increasingly confident of Truman's confidence in him, acted
as he pleased. When, late in May, Churchill appealed to Truman for
American aid to bolster the British position in Syria, Leahy decided "to
sit on the message for a while," commenting to me, "It's a damned
British plot to get us involved. I'll have no part of it." When he did get
around to discussing it with Truman, he got the OK he sought—no
U.S. action with the British in Syria.

As Truman relied increasingly on Leahy, my role changed. Truman's
new naval aide replacing Admiral Brown was a political friend from
Missouri, Captain James Vardaman, USNR. Vardaman had no interest
in the kinds of papers Brown had had me write, whereas Leahy found
them useful. I was soon working almost exclusively for him preparing
such memorandums as "The Polish Problem since Yalta." In mid-May,
the admiral told me that Truman would appoint former justice Byrnes
as secretary of state to succeed Stettinius as soon as the conference in San
Francisco setting up the United Nations was over. This was to be a deep
secret until then, as Truman did not want "to pull the rug out from
under Secretary Stettinius." I was to help Byrnes in every way possible.
"You can be extremely valuable to him," said Leahy. "You know better
than anyone else where all the things are and how to find them. He will
want you to show him all the correspondence . . . prepare briefs . . . do
all sorts of things."

Most of my time for the next few weeks was consumed in writing
briefing papers for the prospective secretary of state, "Jimmy" Byrnes.
One Sunday morning, Leahy asked me to come to his office for a face-
to-face talk with Byrnes. In addition to the summaries of all agreements
Roosevelt and the Chiefs of Staff had made at the various summit meetings that he asked me to write, Byrnes also wanted to see the full texts
of all messages exchanged by Roosevelt and Truman with Churchill and
Stalin since Yalta.

"How long will it take to get those?" Byrnes asked.

"Ten minutes" was the answer that surprised him.

"How long will it take me to read it all?" was the next question.
"This afternoon, with hard work."

"I'm used to hard work!"

"Yes, Sir. I know that. I'll be right back."

I assembled the necessary files, saying to the Map Room duty officer,
"These are for Admiral Leahy." I kept Byrnes's name secret and returned to the admiral's office. Leahy waved Byrnes and me to a table
and said, "Make yourselves comfortable. A State Department man is
coming over, but you needn't leave! I have no secrets from you."

But Byrnes was alarmed. "State Department? I think we'll leave!" he
responded, so concerned was he with keeping his future role a secret.
Thus, he and I went to the Library, my former office from which the
naval aide and I had been summarily ejected two weeks earlier. Byrnes
read quickly, taking notes in his court-reporter shorthand. Asking for
more files, with a short break for lunch, Brynes worked until five
o'clock. He asked me to write a summary of "the Polish question," and
after a few minutes of pleasant chatter he was off.

For a month or more, Truman and Leahy provided whatever Byrnes
requested, usually through me to maintain security. I was as eager as
they were to see that the prospective secretary was well prepared and
that there would be no repetition of Roosevelt's cavalier treatment of the
department and its boss. I was, therefore, personally aggrieved—indeed, angered—when Byrnes in his 1947 memoir, *Speaking Frankly,*
wrote that secret information on the Yalta agreements had been kept
from him. I drafted a blunt letter reminding him of all that had been
done to fill him in before he became secretary. By 1947, he had had a
very public falling out with Truman. I went over my draft letter with
Clark Clifford (then my boss and Truman's special counsel). On Clifford's advice, the letter remained unsent. Had it leaked, it would only
have added to the bitterness of the Truman-Byrnes feud, to no one's advantage.

Although Admiral Leahy was now very obviously taking Harry
Hopkins's place as the president's top adviser, Hopkins—when not in a
hospital—still counted. Averell Harriman, home from the U.S. embassy
in Moscow, concocted the idea of Hopkins flying to meet Stalin in an effort to lessen tensions over Polish issues. They sold the idea to Truman,
who signed a telegram to Stalin that Hopkins would be arriving to discuss "outstanding problems."

Harriman and Hopkins, behaving as though it was still "the old days," forgot to consult or even inform Leahy, who learned about the trip when he reviewed the Map Room's log of VIP messages. The admiral blew off steam to me and then arranged for Hopkins to have a session with the Chiefs of Staff.

I was less concerned than Leahy that Hopkins would "give away the store." The day the telegram had been sent to Stalin, I had spent much of the afternoon with Hopkins in his small East Wing office. I did not feel his heart was in the trip. This was the first time I was with him that he was not ablaze with interest in current and future events. He talked about the past—and the Roosevelts. "Mrs. R. is OK," he said, but he didn't trust the children. He didn't think the Roosevelt Library staff was up to the job. "They don't understand. They can't comprehend what kind of a man he was. So complex. So complicated. Of course, there's some bad there, I know the pettiness and meanness. But so great!" Hopkins probed. Would I want to be the librarian? He could "put that over."

Hopkins didn't say a word about Stalin or Moscow or Poland. The trip would be his valedictory, and he was ignoring it before it took place. He was through, and he knew it. He offered a final word on Roosevelt: "It was lucky he died when he did." I protested, "One more month and he would have seen victory in Europe." "Yes, that was tragic, but still he was lucky."

I had scarcely finished assignments of interest to Byrnes when it was time to prepare for Truman's first (and only) summit conference with the British and the Soviets, to be held at Potsdam, a suburb of devastated Berlin. The San Francisco conference concluded, Stettinius resigned, and Brynes was secretary of state. On June 14, Admiral Leahy handed me a longhand list of papers Truman wanted on ten subjects. This was followed the next day with a note from his aide adding two more topics followed by the wry comment, "Delete all your social engagements for the duration!"

As well prepared for Potsdam as we knew how to be, army captain Frank Graham and I boarded the president's train on the evening of July 6. At Newport News the next morning, we carried our reference files to quarters assigned to us for a temporary Map Room on the cruiser *Augusta.* An electronic coding machine (ECM) had been installed so that we could have secure contact with the White House while at sea. Thus, we were able to give Truman, Byrnes, and Leahy twice-daily briefings on Nimitz's and MacArthur's actions. We left the ship in Amsterdam and flew to Berlin, whence we went by motorcade through unbelievable devastation to Babelsberg, a relatively undamaged residential area close to Potsdam.

As with the Yalta Conference, so much has been written about the meetings of Truman with Stalin, Churchill, and Attlee that I'll limit my account to personal experiences. The Berlin area was in that portion of Germany captured by the Soviets. We were conscious of Soviet troops everywhere. Soviet guards were even present in the small zone set aside for the presidential party, but with the conference identification cards Frank and I had, we were able to move freely.

Soviet troops were present in force around the Little White House when Stalin paid a courtesy call on Truman. Knowing when he was expected, I was on the alert by the front steps. With a roar of motorcycles, the entourage pulled up. As Stalin stepped out of his limousine, Truman's military aide, Harry Vaughan, bounded down the steps and rushed forward, right hand held out as if to shake the hand of a fellow Rotarian. Startled, Stalin froze in his tracks. His escorts bristled, not used to such an approach to their leader. Tension eased when Stalin accepted the outstretched hand briefly and then moved forward. He and Vaughan mounted the steps and disappeared into the house. I was not to see Stalin again, so tightly guarded were all the conference sessions of the "Big Three."

Frank and I had little time to leave our ECM, which was set up in a ground-floor room of the Little White House, since coded messages from Washington—and replies from the president—were exceptionally numerous. The president had instructed that all sensitive messages from Washington flow through the Map Room, and there was plenty to report on the Pacific war as well. I did break away one day to see the center of Berlin. Although the ruins of the Reichschancellery were verboten to almost everybody, my conference ID brought a salute from a Red Army captain and a bilingual escort. We made our way through the wreckage to Hitler's suite of offices, where I stood on the ruins of his marble-topped desk. Finding it hard to believe where I was, I picked up from a nearby room some of der Führer's stationery and a number of his bookplates, water-stained from the rain that had poured through the bombed roof. From another room came a pocketful of Nazi medals.

On another day, when there were few messages to decode, I hitched a ride in Truman's cavalcade to Cecilienhof, a palace of the last kaiser's family, where the Big Three sessions were taking place. The conference was nearing its end. Soviet army trucks were carrying off all the elegant furnishings except for those in the suite being used for the meetings. It was obvious that, after the final session, the rest of the furnishings would be hauled off to the Soviet Union. Accordingly, I felt no guilt in searching the library for a single volume that I could "liberate." I chose Sir Julian Corbett's *Principles of Maritime Strategy* bearing Kaiser Wilhelm's bookplate. To me, the book was highly symbolic. The last kaiser had engaged in a naval building race before World War I with his cousin, King George V, and was known to be a student of British naval thinking. I could think of no book among the thousands in the library that better epitomized the German-British rivalry that led to the Great War of 1914. (The kaiser's volume remains a cherished possession, but the Nazi trophies, aside from a Hitler bookplate or two, have long been disposed of.)

The conference recessed on July 25 so that Churchill could return to London for the counting of ballots from the parliamentary elections that had taken place weeks earlier. The count had been delayed until ballots from overseas sailors and troops arrived in England. We Americans naively assumed that Churchill's party would win hands down and that the victory celebrations would rival those of V-E Day, May 8. Admiral Leahy said he had friends in London he'd like to see, would I care to fly over with him? Of course! I phoned Captain Pim in the prime minister's Map Room and was invited to come again to the place that had been so familiar to me a year earlier. But how different the atmosphere was when I entered!

Innocently, I asked how the electoral count was going. Pim's answer, "Not good."

"You mean a smaller majority?"

"No, a minority."

The Labour Party was winning. Churchill was out; Attlee would be prime minister. Pim was maintaining his stiff upper lip and was cordial, but this was no place for an outsider. I left hastily. With Leahy as surprised as I was, we flew back to Germany the next day. Truman and Stalin waited impatiently until the twenty-eighth, when Attlee arrived. After courtesy calls all around, the conference resumed.

Neither the Map Room in Germany nor the one at the White House had any substantive role in policy matters, but—as on earlier occasions—our familiarity with subjects under discussion and the fact that we were not under the pressures our superiors faced gave us the opportunity to put a useful oar in the water from time to time. When a proposed statement by the president and the prime minister calling on the Japanese to surrender or face destruction (later known as the Potsdam Declaration) was sent by Frank Graham and me to our colleagues at home to be provided to the State, War, and Navy Departments for information, alert Captain Kniffin flashed back, "Shouldn't China be involved?" I took the query to President Truman. Embarrassed by the oversight, he marked up his copy to include China and told Frank and me to have the Map Room at home tell State to cable the text to Chiang Kai-shek asking for his concurrence. When that came in, the proclamation was issued simultaneously in Britain, China, and the United States. Japanese militarists in control in Tokyo overruled wiser civilian counselors, and the Potsdam Declaration, with its implicit offer to allow the emperor to remain on the throne if Japan surrendered, was rejected. That decision was tragic for Japan.

The Potsdam Conference is most remembered by the public—if remembered at all—as the place "where Truman decided to drop the bomb." Until a test at Alamogordo, New Mexico, on July 16, neither the military nor the scientists of the Manhattan Project had assurance that an atomic bomb would explode satisfactorily. A flash from home the day of our arrival in Germany told of the test's success, and Secretary of War Stimson flew over to report details that were too classified to be entrusted to cables.

President Truman made no specific decision at Potsdam to "drop the Bomb." He, Byrnes, Stimson, Marshall, and the few others he consulted in the weeks after he had first been briefed on the Manhattan Project by Stimson on the evening of April 12 were unanimous that bombs would be used *if they worked* to bring about the earliest possible surrender of Japan. All were concerned at the prospective loss of life that would be incurred if the United States had to invade the Japanese home islands. Hence the joy with which the news of the successful test at Alamogordo was received. The Potsdam Declaration was written with all this in mind. The declaration called on Japan to surrender its armed forces or face utter and total destruction. The statement was deftly worded to imply that the emperor's status would not be affected. Japanese rejection of it meant that atomic weapons would be employed. Thus, the "final decision" that resulted in Hiroshima and Nagasaki was actually made in Tokyo, by the militarists who controlled Japan when they rejected the Potsdam Declaration.

I was buoyed by the news of the successful July 16 test, gratified that the project that had absorbed so much of my father's energy for two years was on the verge of paying off. I queried the White House Map Room for Manhattan Project news and got a puzzled response that the subject was unknown. I had forgotten that my colleagues had not been clued in, as I had been, on atomic bomb developments.

On July 30, Stimson, now back in Washington, reported through army channels that a lengthy explanatory statement on the Manhattan Project was ready for release from the White House when weather conditions over Japan permitted a bomb to be dropped. Could he have Truman's permission to release the statement as soon as word of the drop was received in Washington?

I took Stimson's message to the president. He pondered it for a few moments, flipped it over, and wrote: "O.K. to release but not before August 2."

August 2 was the date set for our early-morning departure from Potsdam.

"I want to be out of here before this news is out," he told me. "I don't want to have to answer any questions from Stalin."

(Digression: So tight had security been that this is surely one of the few documents bearing Truman's signature or initials relating to the atomic bomb before its use at Hiroshima on August 6. Recognizing its historic significance, I made sure it survived when the Potsdam temporary Map Room files were stripped as we prepared to leave. I gave it to the Truman Library in 1979.)

Truman's desire to avoid questions from Stalin was born of the American and British agreement to keep secret from the Soviets their atomic energy research and weapons development. He had told Stalin at a break in the conference talks a few days earlier only that the United States had a "powerful new weapon." Stalin had replied that he hoped it would be put to good use, saying this so offhandedly that our group doubted he had taken anything in. Only much later did we and the British learn that Soviet espionage and communist-friendly American and British scientists had kept the Soviets fully apprised of our progress. Stalin would not have asked Truman any questions. He had no need to.

Another cat-and-mouse game of highest level secrecy also kept Frank Graham and me fascinated. Some senior Japanese civilian officials, aware that the war was lost and acting behind the backs of the military clique in power, were trying to persuade the Soviet government to act as an intermediary and ascertain the basis on which the United States would negotiate an end to the war in the Pacific. Not a surrender, but a "negotiated settlement" was the aim. This we knew courtesy of "Magic." Each day we read the deciphered exchanges between Tokyo and the Japanese embassy in Moscow. Stalin and his foreign minister, Molotov, gave Truman and Byrnes rather misleading accounts of this Japanese maneuver, not knowing that we knew much more than they were telling us.

Eagerly awaiting news from Stimson on "the bomb," which we hoped would bring an early end to the war—perhaps early enough that the Soviets would not jump in and claim fruits of victory for themselves—we flew to Plymouth, England, on August 2 and boarded the *Augusta* for the homeward journey. It was as uneventful as the eastbound crossing, made pleasant by Truman's confidence that the conference had been a success, that he had got along well with Stalin and Attlee, and that an early Japanese surrender was almost certain. Map Room traffic was light, but Frank or I was always on duty, expecting a flash at any hour from the secretary of war. Judge Sam Rosenman was a pleasant shipboard companion whom Truman had asked to come with us to prepare his speech reporting on the conference. As he had so many times before, Rosenman "borrowed" me to give him a hand on the speech.

On August 6 a flash message came from the navy. I passed it to Graham to carry to the president, who was lunching with the ship's crew while I decoded another "top secret." From Secretary of War Stimson to the president the flash message read simply: "Big Bomb dropped on Hiroshima 5 August at 7:15 p.m. Washington time. First reports indicated complete success which was even more conspicuous than earlier test."

Truman's exuberant reaction as he first announced the news to the *Augusta*'s crew and then to the newsmen traveling with us has been endlessly described. An invasion of the Japanese home islands at frightful cost in both American and Japanese lives would almost certainly not be necessary.

Stimson had dispatched a courier to Potsdam with the text of the "explanatory statement" referred to in his July 30 cable to Truman. The courier had arrived just thirty minutes before the presidential party left for the Berlin airport. Thus, when the flash on Hiroshima came, the president was ready with a solid explanation of the Manhattan Project to hand to the reporters on our ship.

When, later the same day, the excitement on the ship had lessened, I told the president of my father's consulting work on the Oak Ridge, Tennessee, plant where the uranium for the Hiroshima bomb had been produced. Truman reached for a copy of the statement—no longer top secret despite those warning words on the sheets—and endorsed it: "Best wishes to Dr. Howard M. Elsey and a Thank You for his contribution. Harry S. Truman."

(This and related documents, including the actual flashes from Washington with Admiral Leahy's initials and the significant "P," I preserved when the files from the temporary Map Rooms in Potsdam and on the ship were destroyed. I had a container made for them and gave the case and its contents to my Father. Dad, despite his lack of reverence for any Democrat, cherished them, and they remained in his study in Oakmont until his death in 1982.)

In a happy mood we docked in Newport News the next evening and entrained for Washington. Frank and I checked into the White House Map Room with our special cryptographic equipment at 11:00 p.m. on August 7, another mission accomplished.

The next afternoon, August 8, a message was flashed to the Map Room that Soviet Foreign Minister Molotov had summoned the Japanese ambassador to his office to inform him that the Soviet Union was at war with the Empire of Japan. So much for the hopes of the peace-seeking Japanese diplomats that the USSR might mediate a peace settlement with Britain, China, and the United States! I walked with Admiral Leahy to the Oval Office, where he broke the news to the president.

"They're jumping the gun, aren't they, admiral?"

"Yes, damn it. It was supposed to be the fifteenth. The bomb did it. They want to get in before it's all over."

Truman called Byrnes to join him, and at 3:00 he announced the news to a hastily summoned press conference in the Oval Office. I joined Truman, Byrnes, and Leahy in laughing as reporters stumbled into one another in their dash for phones in the Press Room.

With no word of any kind from Tokyo softening the blunt rejection of the Potsdam Declaration, Truman, Stimson, and Marshall saw no reason to interfere with the army's plan to release a second bomb when weather conditions were right. At 11:00 a.m. Tokyo time on the ninth, Nagasaki was devastated. The two bombs and the Soviet declaration of war seemed to do it. On the tenth, broadcasts from Tokyo gave reason to believe that the government had—belatedly—accepted the Potsdam Declaration. Had it done so one week earlier, there would have been no Hiroshima, no Nagasaki. But it turned out that "acceptance" did not mean "surrender," and it was not until further exchanges that Japan formally surrendered and Truman was able to announce late on August 14 that the war was over.

As the excitement of the war's end wore off, I had time to pick up loose threads left over from Roosevelt days. I worked with Judge Rosenman and executors of FDR's estate on the disposition of his most secret papers, which had been withheld and not sent to the National Archives. The Yalta documents and similar items would remain indefinitely at the White House for Truman's reference. (These are the papers that went to the file safe in my office for which I was the only person who knew the combination. Truman's Potsdam papers soon joined them.)

I also had time to return to a pleasant chore—the redesign of the presidential flag and seal. The flag in use since 1916 carried four white stars, one in each corner of a blue field with an eagle in white in the center. With the top army and navy officers now having personal flags with five stars, Roosevelt had felt his flag needed upgrading. Admiral Brown had given me the assignment, which fell into abeyance with the confusion of the transition and Potsdam.

I turned for advice to the Cambridge friend who had so encouraged me in my application for a commission back in 1941, James Risk. Jim, now a lieutenant commander, as a hobby studied flags, medals, and heraldic decorations. He advised me to call on Arthur Dubois, chief of heraldry for the U.S. Army. Dubois and I quickly came to an understanding. The new presidential flag should have a circle of forty-eight stars (Hawaii and Alaska were not yet states; stars would be added for them when statehood came). The circle of stars would surround the presidential seal, which should be in full color, as it was not in the old flag. Dubois seized the opportunity to correct an error that, purist that he was, had long bothered him. That the eagle's head faced to its left, or "sinister" in heraldic terminology, was all wrong. A "bar sinister," in a coat of arms, was an indication of illegitimacy. The eagle's head must face right, or "dexter," the direction of honor. While this formality of heraldry was interesting to a scholar, it would mean nothing to the public. What would catch public attention was that, in this new position, the eagle would be turned to the olive branches clutched in its right talon, away from the arrows in its left talon. And so I wrote the press release announcing that President Truman had modernized the presidential flag and had directed that the eagle in the presidential seal and flag turn away from "the arrows of war and face the olive branches of peace." In the autumn of 1945, with World War II just weeks behind us, this caught the attention of the public, and Truman was praised for capturing the mood of the country whereas, in fact, the change was due to Arthur Dubois's devotion to heraldic principles.

It was a thrill to stand on the flight deck of the navy's newest aircraft carrier, the USS *Franklin D. Roosevelt,* with President Truman in New York on Navy Day, October 27, 1945, and see "my" flag displayed for the first time. Later the same day, I served as aide to Mrs. Woodrow Wilson at the great naval review in the Hudson River. She was in tears from time to time as she recalled the similar great review she had witnessed with her husband at the end of World War I.

Social life at the White House began to pick up, and my aiguillettes and white gloves came out of the bureau drawer. Their first use in the Truman administration had been in May when Mrs. Truman, with the official thirty-day mourning for Roosevelt behind us, was invited to christen two medical evacuation planes in a ceremony at National Airport. I was her naval aide for the occasion.

The affair was a fiasco. Mrs. Truman slugged the nose of the army plane with the champagne bottle. Nothing happened. She tried again—the bottle did not shatter. She swung again—and again—and again—eleven times in all. The crowd in the bleachers, giggling at first, was hooting with laughter as Mrs. Truman, red-faced and irritated, handed the unscathed bottle to the army aide and crossed the ceremonial platform to the navy plane, nosed in on the opposite side. An alert navy crew member, having sensed the problem, had grabbed a hatchet from the plane's tool chest and was ready. I handed the navy bottle to Mrs. Truman. As she swung, the crewman, unseen by the crowd, hit the bottle from below. It shattered. The crowd roared and applauded heartily.

Mrs. Truman was not amused. On the way back to the White House, she was emphatic. "Never will I let myself be put in such a situation again. Never! Never! Never!" And she never did. She was even more distressed when she learned that cameramen had recorded the scene and the week's newsreels were showing it in theaters all over the country to the great amusement of all who watched.

The cause of her embarrassment? The champagne bottles had not been "scored," that is, deep scratches had not been made so that the bottles would break easily when hitting the soft aluminum nose of a plane.

I have scant recollections of social events in the first few postwar months, and had a wisecracking Map Room watch officer not made this entry in the daily log, which I stumbled across in 1999, this occasion would have remained happily unremembered:

30 November 1945. Hen party upstairs for Shirley Temple and 199 others. Comdr. Elsey aided.

The "Comdr." needs an explanation, as do my other changes in rank. The navy had abandoned its practice of promotion by "selection boards" as unworkable in wartime. Instead, promotions were generally given for officers according to the length of time they had held a specific rank. Thus on October 1, 1942, I and all other ensigns commissioned before January 1 of that year were promoted to lieutenant, junior grade. One year later, our group moved up to lieutenant. On October 1, 1945, even though the war was over, we became lieutenant commanders. The navy hoped that the goodly number of promotions that day would entice many Reserve officers to remain on duty awhile longer and not rush for the exits. There simply weren't enough regular officers to man the vastly enlarged fleets. I'll comment later on my final promotion to full commander.

I also "aided" at another event not long after. The president and Mrs. Truman were guests of honor at a reception at the Congressional Club, an association of wives of present and former members of Congress. It was a bit unusual to be invited to manage a receiving line away from the White House. All went smoothly, although I felt like gagging as I called the names of a few ladies whose husbands had been especially vicious in their criticisms of Roosevelt. (It was too early for such criticisms of Truman—they came later.)

When the reception ended, Mrs. Truman asked if I had a ride back to the White House. When I said I did not, she said: "Well, come with us." Despite the party, Truman was in an irritable mood. Congress was rebuffing his plans to enlarge the West Wing in order to provide more office space for the staff. "I'll just get a bulldozer, knock down the back wall, and they'll have to give me what I want."

"Harry," said Mrs. Truman in a stentorian tone, "you will do NO SUCH THING!" And she brought her fist down so sharply on a knee that I wondered if the poor man would be able to walk when we reached the White House.

Mrs. Truman was a lady to be reckoned with.

With Byrnes firmly established as secretary of state and that department now fully in the act, as it had not been in Roosevelt's war years, Admiral Leahy's role began to diminish. He no longer needed to speak for State as well as for the military. He was by no means a has-been, however. Truman valued him for the depth of this knowledge and turned to him for advice on many matters. Leahy, in turn, had me search the files. In early October, for example, the subject was Palestine. My five-page brief seemed to answer his questions.

In November, the future of "the bomb" was the hot topic that occupied Truman's and Leahy's minds. Prime Minister Attlee flew from London, and Prime Minister MacKenzie King came down from Ottawa. My only role was to lend a sympathetic ear to Leahy, who, day after day, would mutter that he was not at all in sympathy with the "do-gooders" who wanted to entrust the new United Nations organization with responsibility for atomic weapons research and control.

On Armistice Day, November 11, Truman took his guests down the Potomac on the *Sequoia,* then the secretary of the navy's yacht, as the new presidential yacht, *Williamsburg,* was still being fitted out. I was included in the party. Military Aide General Harry Vaughan, the new assistant naval aide, Lieutenant Commander Clark Clifford, and I sat in the dining salon behind the conferees but obviously did not participate in the discussion. The talk rambled for some hours. What resources do the Soviets have? Where are they located? Can the United Nations be made strong enough to control—or even keep an eye on—atomic matters? How can we trust the Soviets—they never gave us any secrets during the war but wanted everything from us. Such was the talk. At the tea break at 5:15, Philippine stewards were elbowed aside by Attlee's bodyguard, a Scotland Yard inspector who had made the tea. His face flushed when Byrnes went to the pantry door exclaiming, "This tea doesn't taste so good. Get me some bourbon!" With tea and bourbon consumed, talk resumed. "Well, let's talk about Korea," someone said. The casualness of it all astonished me.

Another break came before dinner. The group adjourned to the rear deck when a radio was tuned to the evening broadcast of a well-known gossip commentator of the day, Drew Pearson. Attlee leaned close to the microphone to hear better just as Pearson said, "Attlee leans toward world cooperation." The group howled with laughter.

In later years, I attended a number of meetings Truman held with visiting heads of government and wrote minutes for his files, but no occasion ever matched this Armistice Day on the river for its candor, intimacy, and high spirits. Hence, I mention it and will not bore a reader with notes of those later sessions.

Late in November, Leahy called me to his office. Truman had asked him, he said, to prepare a statement of our policy toward China. This was a surprise. Were we going back to FDR's day, excluding State again? Leahy explained that Truman was about to send General Marshall to China and wanted a crisp policy paper. He rambled on: "If the president lets State do it, they will produce some long thing of six or eight pages that won't mean anything and will get the president in trouble . . . the president is all right, he's behind Chiang. But those 'pinkies' in the State Department can't be trusted."

I was hearing an early expression of what was to become a torrent of mistaken criticism—that because some career diplomats were critical of Chiang's corrupt government—as they should have been—and were—correctly—describing the growing strength of Chinese communists, they were "pinkies," that is, communist sympathizers. Some splendid men whose skills and knowledge were sorely needed were forced out of the government in the "Red Scare" that blemished Truman's second term.

Searching White House files for information relating to Leahy's China policy statement was, I believe, my last such assignment growing out of my familiarity with Map Room records and other official files. With the war over, the Map Room was obsolescent, indeed, obsolete. High-level communications now flowed through normal departmental channels. Many tense military situations still existed, precursors of what was to become the Cold War, but they did not require twenty-four-hour coverage on up-to-the-minute maps. My Map Room colleagues were discharged one by one, being replaced by Army Signal Corps staff until the chief usher persuaded the president to throw all military out of the mansion. I had months earlier left my desk in the elegant Library for a small office in the East Wing, adjacent to Admiral Leahy's.

The Map Room's "last hurrah" was on December 22, 1945. Former stalwarts were invited back for a ceremony in the Oval Office in which the president presented each of us with the Legion of Merit, accompanied by a flowery citation that, to use a favorite expression of Leahy's, "would sound good if set to music." In my case, there was a follow-up honor. For reasons known only to the British, I was the only Map Room officer honored by them. On February 12, 1946, I was presented a medal as an honorary member of the Order of the British Empire by the British ambassador, the earl of Halifax. The accompanying citation, signed by King George VI, reads: "For services on the occasions of the visits to the United States of America of Mr. Winston Churchill when Prime Minister."

As the Map Room was being converted to its use as an Army Signal Corps office, files from the Roosevelt era were transferred to the National Archives for temporary storage until their legal status was determined and the library at Hyde Park was readied to receive them. Maps came down from the walls, and the map storage case was emptied. "Throw everything out," was the crisp order of Truman's naval aide. Captain—soon to be Commodore—Vardaman's sense of history was no better than any other of his senses. Knowing that certain maps that seemed useless now would be valued in the future, quietly and against orders I saved some.

A map of the Indo-China area had pencil markings showing Japanese naval forces approaching the Malay Peninsula on December 6, 1941. This had been shown to Roosevelt the night before Pearl Harbor, confirming his belief—a belief shared by all our senior military officers—that the Japanese were preparing to strike in that area. So focused was the High Command on that region that the next day's attacks in the mid-Pacific came as a stunning shock. This map, I felt, was one that must be saved. (I held it until June 2000, when I sent it to the Roosevelt Library.)

If that map symbolized the beginning of the war for Roosevelt, a map of April 1, 1945, symbolized the end for him. A map prepared that day and sent down to the president in Warm Springs, Georgia, laid out the army's estimate of what the situation would be one month later in Germany. It showed Nazi forces splintered into segments but still holding out. This was the last war map that he saw before his death on April 12. It deserved to survive, I felt, as I pulled it from the "to be burned" pile. It is now back in the Map Room at the White House, hanging above the fireplace mantel, with a note explaining how the room got its name and the significance of this particular map. I gave it to the White House early in the Clinton administration after Mrs. Clinton asked me if there were any relics that would signify the room's World War II role.

With the war in Europe ending three weeks after he took office, Truman's interest centered on the war in the Pacific. He studied with care plans for the invasion of Japan sketched on a large map of the western Pacific. This also was too good to be lost. Much larger than the ones mentioned above, it suffered some damage as it came down from the wall, but I folded the torn sheets with care. This map went to the Truman Library in 1998 and is on exhibit there.

I gave a final group of maps to the George C. Marshall Library in Lexington, Virginia, in 1999. They related to various issues that had much occupied Marshall as army chief of staff, such as the zones of Germany to be occupied by the victorious Allies.

Many of the maps we had found so useful in the Map Room were produced by the National Geographic Society. Later, as a trustee of the society, I talked the editor of *National Geographic* magazine into publishing a short article at the fiftieth anniversary of the end of the war on how the society's maps had been of use to the White House and government departments. I was delighted at the warm response from readers to the map story, published in the May 1995 issue. It is my only tie to the maps that I hated to part with but that now are in libraries that will preserve them and make them available for future students of the war years—which is, after all, why I saved them.

Well before Leahy's assignments died out and the Map Room was closed, I had plenty to do with tasks given by Vardaman and Clifford, his assistant. One onerous chore related to Truman's interest in Universal Military Training (UMT). Given his lifelong interest in the army, Truman was convinced that every able-bodied young man should have a year or two of military service. Vardaman dumped on my desk several volumes of congressional hearings on the subject, telling me to analyze them and prepare a concise statement of the pros and cons. A few days later, I was handed a draft of a proposed message to Congress and an outline of a speech on the subject. I was to bolster each on why UMT was necessary. My heart wasn't in it, but my exertions were useful. Congress ignored Truman's recommendation (which he futilely made year after year), but my literary efforts—that's an abuse of the word *literary*—seemed to please Vardaman and Clifford.

Clifford, who was buttering up fellow lawyer Sam Rosenman, asked to see the draft of a message being prepared for Truman to send to the Hill on the day Congress was to reconvene, September 6, 1945. Rosenman was pulling out all the stops, putting Truman squarely on record as an ardent liberal in the Roosevelt tradition. Clifford, still a political novice and far from the liberal stance he was later to assume, ostensibly wanted to assure that nothing conflicted with the UMT message. Actually, he was nervous about Roseman's wrapping so liberal a flag around Truman, but the die was cast. The message went as Roseman wrote it, and the liberal wing of the Democratic Party cheered.

Far more to my taste than promoting UMT was watching the struggle over the postwar organization of the armed forces. The army was pressing for "unification," which to the navy meant domination by its sister service. Leahy, Vardaman, and Clifford each asked me to stay alert for any "sneak" moves by the army. The new president, they feared, might be a pushover. When he was in the Senate he had signed a strongly pro-army magazine article on the postwar military structure that was ghostwritten for him by the army. I began a file that grew massively. Truman moved slowly and indecisively toward what became the National Security Act of 1947. I was to be much involved.

A snapshot of Mother, Father, and me taken in our yard in Oakmont in the summer of 1939 after my graduation from college.

Posted on the inside of the Map Room door when I reported for duty in April 1942 was this cartoon with penciled notations that I was told had been inscribed by Secretary of War Henry Stimson at FDR's direction one evening when both were in the room. Although the phrasing wasn't exactly grammatical, the point was clear: don't talk about anything you see or hear!

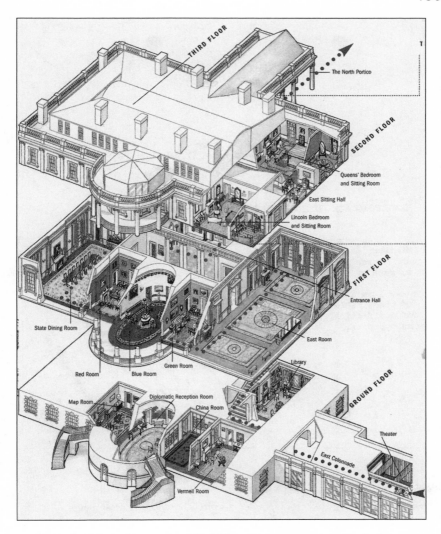

A sketch of the public rooms of the White House open to visitors before strict security measures were imposed, with a few other rooms that I mention in this memoir. These include the Map Room on the ground floor, next to the Diplomatic Reception Room; the Library, also on the ground floor, where the naval aide and I had our office in the last year of the Roosevelt administration; the Queen's Bedroom and Sitting Room on the second floor, where Winston Churchill stayed during his wartime visits; and the Lincoln Bedroom and Sitting Room, where Harry Hopkins lived for most of the war.

THE WHITE HOUSE
WASHINGTON

September 17, 1942

MEMORANDUM FOR ADMIRAL LEAHY:

I am anxious to get the cables to me from the Prime
Minister and other heads of government in various countries,
and my replies to them, coordinated through Harry because
so much of them refer to civil things.

I am asking him to see that all of the military aspects
of these cables are referred to you and the Combined Chiefs
of Staff and he will coordinate them and give them to me for
my approval.

This put-down of Admiral Leahy—inspired, if not actually written, by Harry Hopkins—was the result of Hopkins's resentment at the presence of a rival. The rationale that so much of the correspondence with Churchill, Stalin, and other leaders referred "to civil things" was nonsense. All related directly to the war.

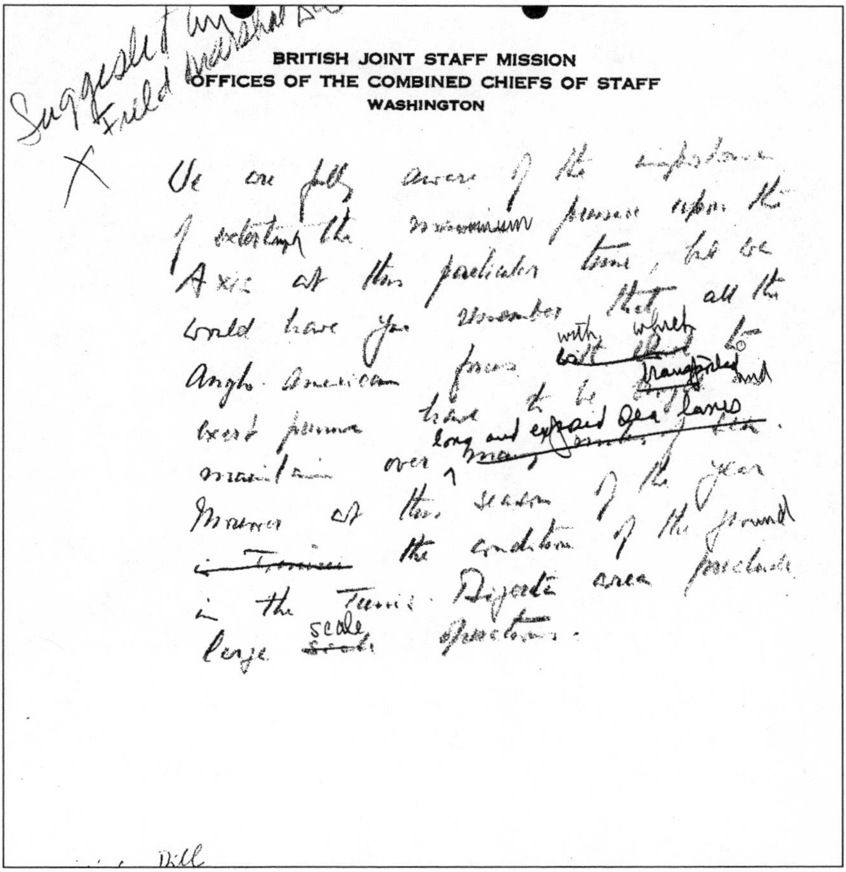

BRITISH JOINT STAFF MISSION
OFFICES OF THE COMBINED CHIEFS OF STAFF
WASHINGTON

[Handwritten draft message, largely illegible, with handwritten annotations including "Suggested" and "Field Marshal" in the top left margin and an X mark, signed "Dill" at the bottom]

The May 1943 draft by Field Marshal Sir John Dill of a reply to a petulant cable from Stalin demanding information on what action he could expect from Britain and the United States against Germany and Italy that would ease the situation on the Eastern Front. The answer was evasive because Churchill and his staff, meeting with Roosevelt and the U.S. Chiefs of Staff, could not agree on the next steps. Inked additions by General George Marshall and penciled notes by Admiral William Leahy.

Of this I wrote after Roosevelt, Churchill, and their associates had left: "This message to Stalin written in lengthy Map Room midnight conference—P.M. and all his group, with President and Marshall . . . on our side being overwhelmed by British oratory." I then typed the message in the proper form and sent it on its way to Stalin.

A gaunt lieutenant, junior grade, USNR, with Admiral Ernest J. King, commander in chief, U.S. Navy, and General George C. Marshall, chief of staff, U.S. Army. One of Marshall's aides is to his left. A British officer follows. Quebec, August 1943.

THE WHITE HOUSE
WASHINGTON

THE WHITE HOUSE
WASHINGTON

A16/France

SEC.

March 26, 1945.

MEMORANDUM FOR:

August 31, 1942

DOROTHY BRADY.

SECRET

You will recall that Dr. W. L. Langer
has written at the request of Secretary Hull
a history of our relations with France from
1940 through 1942. His work is "Secret"
and will not be published at present. Dr.
Langer requested permission to use White
House files to supplement the material he
found in the State Department. When this
request was brought to the President's
attention he directed me to have all available
information suitable for Dr. Langer put into
a summary, which he would "censor". The
President said he might add some comments
to the summary, and we could then send it
along.

MEMORANDUM FOR ADMIRAL LEAHY:

Attached is a copy of the message I sent to the
Prime Minister last night.

Will you show it to Admiral King and General
Marshall and tell Marshall to use his discretion about
acquainting Eisenhower with the contents of it.

The summary has been prepared by George
Elsey and Grace Tully thinks the President
might like to go over it while he is at
Hyde Park.

WILSON BROWN.

Roosevelt's bold signature on a 1942 memorandum contrasts painfully with his initials on April 6, 1945, six days before his death. We in the Map Room watched his health fade away.

As the senior in rank of the White House naval aides, I stood nearest the steps on the left side as President Roosevelt's coffin entered the White House.

With Army Captain Franklin H. Graham, I briefed President Truman on the previous day's attacks on Japan in late July 1945 in the president's quarters at Babelsburg, Germany, while Truman was participating in the Potsdam Conference with the British and the Soviets. No comparable photographs were taken at any of President Roosevelt's conferences, nor were any taken of the Map Room in the White House.

DRAFT PROCLAMATION BY THE HEADS OF GOVERNMENTS

UNITED STATES...UNITED KINGDOM...~~U.S.S.R...CHINA~~

Should china be asked?

(1) We, --The President of the United States, and the
Prime Minister of Great Britain, representing the hundreds of
millions of our countrymen, have conferred and agree that Japan
shall be given an opportunity to end this war.

(2) The prodigious land, sea and air forces of the United
States, the British Empire and of China, many times reinforced
by their armies and air fleets from the west are poised to strike
the final blows upon Japan. This military power is sustained
and inspired by the determination of all the Allied nations to
prosecute the war against Japan until she ceases to resist.

(3) The result of the futile and senseless German
resistance to the might of the aroused free peoples of the world
stands forth in awful clarity as an example to the people of
Japan. The might that now converges on Japan is immeasurably

Truman penciled a note to himself, repeating a question asked by the Map Room staff in Washington. After he had checked with Secretary of State Byrnes and the British, the "Little Map Room" instructed the Map Room at home to have the State Department, as a matter of extreme urgency, obtain Chiang Kai-shek's concurrence to having China be a co-issuer of what became known as the Potsdam Declaration.

WHITE HOUSE

MAP ROOM

TOP-SECRET   <u>6</u> August 1945

FROM: THE SECRETARY OF WAR
TO : THE PRESIDENT

NR : 335

    Big bomb dropped on Hiroshima 5 August at 7:15 P.M. Washington time. First reports indicate complete success which was even more conspicuous than earlier test.

                                  STIMSON

This is the flash from the secretary of war to President Truman reporting the Hiroshima bomb that I decoded and took to the president. He passed it to Admiral Leahy, who dutifully recorded his initials and the meaningful "P," before returning it to me. I paraphrased for security reasons this and a similar message from the navy so that the president could hand copies to reporters traveling home with us on the *Augusta*. Simultaneously, as previously authorized by Truman, the announcement of the bomb was being made in Washington.

Mrs. Truman's first public ceremony as First Lady, on Memorial Day 1945, was a painful event for her. "Never will I let myself be put in such a situation again," was her firm decision. She stuck with it!

I was on duty as a White House aide at an October 1946 reception in the Waldorf-Astoria Hotel, New York, given by President and Mrs. Truman for delegates to the General Assembly of the United Nations. My task was to ask the name of each person coming through the receiving line and repeat it clearly to the senior army aide, who would announce the guest to the president. (Some of the names were real horrors to catch and to repeat, especially those of the Middle East and the Orient.) None of the other aides had roles. In the jargon of the times, they were just "potted palms."

In this picture, Mrs. Franklin D. Roosevelt, wearing a large fur neckpiece and whose name I certainly had not needed to ask, had just passed by me. Ahead of her, bowing to Mrs. Truman, is Vyacheslav Molotov, the Soviet foreign minister.

I talked about Map Room and White House history with First Lady Hillary Rodham Clinton on June 23, 1994. We are in front of the last map prepared for President Franklin Roosevelt, a few days before his death in April 1945. I had saved it from destruction when the Map Room was closed and had presented it to the White House when Mrs. Clinton asked me if I had preserved any World War II mementos that could be returned to the Map Room to illustrate its role in that war.

24 September 1946

THE WHITE HOUSE

WASHINGTON

Suggest for consideration
that copies of
"American Relations with The
Soviet Union"
should be given to Secretaries Byrnes,
Patterson, Forrestall and Snyder,
and at a later date to members
of the Senate and House,
whose assistance you may
need in solving the Russian
problem, and who can be
depended upon to preserve
the secrecy of the report —
It would not be helpful
in the present situation
to permit the contents of
this report to have
any publicity

W,D,L.

Admiral Leahy's suggestions for distribution of the "Soviet Report," handed to me to present to President Truman. Before I was able to do so, Truman—nervous over the Henry Wallace fiasco—decided to sequester all copies.

In the first summer after World War II, 1946, Truman kept the White House aides busy with garden parties and other events for convalescing soldiers, sailors, and marines. In my summer "whites," I am on duty here as his aide at a South Lawn reception arranged by the Red Cross for soldiers from Walter Reed Hospital.

Standing beside the presidential car, the *Ferdinand Magellan,* while Truman was making one of his informal "whistle-stop" talks, Danville, Illinois, October 1948.

THE WHITE HOUSE

WASHINGTON

U. S. Naval Base,
Key West, Florida,
November 13, 1948.

My dear George:

In the midst of the myriad of congratulations that are being passed about over the President's victory, I wanted you to know that I think your contribution was second to none.

The part that you have played in formulating policy these past two years and in projecting that policy in an effective manner has been of tremendous value to the President. I have told him of the excellent work you did on the platform stops and I think he recognizes also how significant this contribution was to his winning.

Matt tells me you will be down here next week and I look forward with pleasure to you getting a rest here.

With best personal wishes, I am

Very sincerely yours,

CLARK M. CLIFFORD.

Mr. George M. Elsey
The White House
Washington, D. C.

A letter from my boss, Clark Clifford, about my work in the 1948 campaign, was much appreciated, as was the presidential invitation, relayed by Appointment Secretary Matthew Connelly, to join the president at Key West for "sun, fun, and relaxation."

THE WHITE HOUSE
WASHINGTON

THE WASHINGTON POST
Wednesday, August 17, 1949

Named Assistant To President

Associated Press Photo
GEORGE McKEE ELSEY
was appointed yesterday to a
$10,000-a-year job as administra-
tive assistant to President Truman. From Oakmont, Pa., he
formerly was assistant to Clark
M. Clifford, the President's special counsel. Elsey is 31

My appointment as an administrative assistant was duly noted—but with errors! The
Washington Post printed a photo of a Republican congressman from New York over my
name. The *New York Herald Tribune* wrote
that administrative assistants were men "with a
passion for authority." The president and the
White House staff had much fun teasing me.

At the Little White House on the U.S. Naval Base in Key West, Florida, December 19, 1949, on my first vacation with President Truman after having been appointed administrative assistant to the president.

This photo was taken March 9, 1951, at "Truman Beach" in Key West. From left to right, General Henry Vaughan (Truman's military aide) rubbing his chin, General Wallace Graham (Truman's physician), Truman (with the white cap and towel over his shoulders), Special Assistant to the President W. Averell Harriman, myself (looking in the wrong direction!), and Admiral Robert Dennison (Truman's naval aide).

The "old fort" whose wall Wally Graham and I climbed is in the background. Climbing was not difficult. The base was rough with good footholds, and the brick wall had plenty of crevices and openings for fingers and feet. It was fun!

Truman's White House staff was so small that we could gather around his desk for the morning conference. I am on the far left on a couch with a couple of other administrative assistants. Each of the other staff members had his regular chair—woe to anyone who sat in the wrong chair!

THE WHITE HOUSE /5 Feb 1950
WASHINGTON

Geo: The lies are beginning
to solidified and made into
historical "facts." Let's head
them off now while we can.
The truth is all I want for
history. If I appear in a bad
light when we have the truth
that's just too bad. We must
take it. But I don't want a
pack of lying, so called historians
to do to me (Roosevelt and to) what the New Englanders did to Jefferson + Jackson.

HST

An early 1950 chit from the president to me, showing his growing interest in his "legacy." They became more numerous as the second term was coming to a close.

This is the Oval Office as it is reproduced at the Truman Library in Independence, Missouri. I had felt the lack of anything at the Roosevelt Library in Hyde Park, New York, that resembled the White House, and I felt the same when I saw the first plans for the Truman Library. I recommended that a replica of the Oval Office be the centerpiece in a revision of those plans, and Truman agreed. The furniture, photographs, books—even the early TV set—are either the originals or exact copies of the ones that were in the room at the end of Truman's second term.

With Truman at the Pali (the great cliff above Honolulu). Truman, with binoculars, is standing next to Admiral Arthur Radford, commander in chief of the Pacific, on a rainy afternoon of sightseeing before taking off for the Wake Island conference with MacArthur. I am next to Radford with some newsmen. (This is where I lost one dollar in my bet with Truman, winning it back later in the day on another bet.)

Undated photo, on a Key West vacation with Truman, walking to "Truman Beach" for the morning swim. Truman is with the base commander, while I am with Averell Harriman and Irving Perlmeter, assistant press secretary.

Dear Mr. Sulzberger:— I am calling
your attention to your lead
editorial of May 9th 1951.

You say, "in domestic affairs
he (the President) has accepted
mediocrity and tolerated unworthiness and has never given
consistency or clarity to his
policies."

Now that is a very broad
and very untrue state-
ment—to put it mildly.
On Sept 6th 1945 a twenty
one point program was outlined in a message to the
Congress (copy enclosed in case
your editorial writer hasn't

THE WHITE HOUSE
WASHINGTON

usually accurate
ease take a look
where the paper
If and make the

: think I'm a fair
tise of a straddle-
th a couple of faro
' you're another ti
9. Either you shou
-against what I
t be on both side
anyway when the folks kne
the facts you can't fool them
When I get through they'll know

The first of the twenty-two pages of Truman's reaction to an editorial in the *New York Herald Tribune,* which he mistakenly thought had appeared in the *New York Times.* The letter, not sent when I pointed out his error, ended with two typical sentences: "When the folks know the facts you can't fool them. When I get through they'll know the facts."

The splendid Romanesque National Presbyterian Church at Eighteenth and N Streets facing Connecticut Avenue, Sally's family church, is long gone. It was the site of our wedding on December 15, 1951.

Sally and I leaving the National Presbyterian Church after our wedding ceremony.

COMMANDERS DIGEST

DEPARTMENT OF DEFENSE • WASHINGTON, D.C.

Vol. 4, No. 34   May 25, 1968

SWEARING IN—Secretary of Defense Clark M. Clifford looks on as Mr. George McKee Elsey is sworn in as Special Assistant to the Secretary of Defense and Deputy Secretary of Defense by Deputy Secretary Paul H. Nitze. Mr. Elsey succeeds John M. Steadman, who has become Air Force General Counsel. Mr. Elsey previously served with Secretary Clifford from 1945 to 1949, while Mr. Clifford was Naval Aide and subsequently Special Counsel to President Truman.

LBJ Asks Congress For Supplemental Funds for SE Asia

President Johnson has requested that Congress approve a $3.9 billion supplemental appropriation for fiscal year 1968 to support U.S. military operations in Southeast Asia.

In a letter to the Speaker of the House, the President urged Congress to give the request prompt and favorable consideration "so that we can meet our present military commitments effectively and without delay."

"Our hope is—and all our energies are directed toward—achieving a just peace as quickly as possible. However, until peace comes, we must provide our fighting men with all the support that they need to carry out their missions and to protect their lives," the President said.

Deputy Secretary of Defense Paul H. Nitze said the new supplemental appropriation replaces the $1.7 billion request made of Congress in mid-February, and raises the total Defense Department appropriation for fiscal 1968 to $76.8 billion.

The additional money, Mr. Nitze said, is necessary to cover the increased costs brought about by the seizure of the USS Pueblo by North Korea in late January, increased provocations against South Korea, and the Communists' Tet offensive in South Vietnam.

A majority of the requested supplemental appropriation is needed to "strengthen our own and allied forces in South Vietnam, including very substantial amounts for the procurement of helicopters, ground forces equipment, munitions and other combat consumables," Mr. Nitze said.

(Continued on Page 3)

U.S. Urges European NATO Members To Plan for Increased Commitment

United States officials have urged European members of the North Atlantic Treaty Organization to make plans to assume a larger share of the cost and troop commitments needed for the direct and immediate defense of Europe.

A greater share in the burden of maintaining a strong NATO force is necessary if the U.S. is to substantially reduce its grave balance of payments problems, U.S. officials told European defense ministers during a two-day meeting of NATO representatives in Brussels, Belgium, May 9-10.

U.S. officials said there is no immediate plan to send home the 260,000 U.S. dependents currently living in Europe, but because of the severity of the balance of payments problem, studies are being conducted to determine in what manner some of the pressure created by this problem can be relieved.

U.S. officials pointed out that the U.S. cannot indefinitely maintain its present force level in Europe, and would welcome any effort by its European allies to combine their individual defense efforts and develop future arrangements which would make these defenses as efficient and effective as possible within the considerable resources which could be made available to NATO.

An increased British commitment to NATO, announced during the conference by British Defense Minister Denis Healey, was described by U.S. officials as the type of move necessary to assist the U.S. in its balance of payments problem while maintaining

(Continued on Page 7)

A Pentagon bulletin regarding my swearing-in as special assistant to the secretary of defense and the deputy secretary (Clark Clifford and Paul Nitze, the latter administering the oath).

At the Red Cross convention in Washington, D.C., May 1971:
President Nixon: I am chairman and you are president. Is that right?
Roland Harriman: No, I am chairman. George, here, is president.
Nixon: Well, then, what am I?
Harriman: You are just the honorary chairman.

With entertainer Bob Hope, viewing some of the damage of Hurricane Agnes in Wilkes-Barre, Pennsylvania, as Hope was preparing for his telethon to raise funds for Red Cross disaster relief, July 1972.

Emperor Hirohito of Japan signing the Red Cross guest book on my desk while the empress and Red Cross staff watch.

Chapter Six

Into Everything

Having mentioned Clark Clifford's name a time or two, and since he will loom large in the coming pages, I should identify him. He was a successful St. Louis attorney before the war who numbered James Vardaman among his clients. Although both were above draft age, they had volunteered for Naval Reserve duty. Vardaman was assigned to the South Pacific and Clifford to a staff post in San Francisco. Truman thought it was a good idea to have reservists as his military and naval aides and brought Vardaman home to replace the elderly Wilson Brown as naval aide. While in the Pacific, Vardaman had acquired a dislike that bordered on hatred for career naval officers. At the White House, he set out to even the score with those he thought had treated him unfairly. Relations with the Navy Department rapidly soured. When Truman told Vardaman he would be going to Potsdam, Vardaman arranged for his former lawyer to be ordered for temporary duty at the White House. Clifford was to ensure that no Annapolis man would be snooping through Vardaman's files in his absence. Clifford, tall, handsome, and friendly, was immediately popular. Furthermore, he was energetic and highly capable, which could not be said of several of Truman's early appointees. Soon after Truman returned from Europe, Clifford's temporary assignment was made permanent. He would not return to San Francisco but would be assistant naval aide.

While Vardaman was absent for weeks at a time getting the yacht USS *Williamsburg* ready for presidential use, Clifford attended Truman's morning staff meetings in his place. He and I had established such a warm relationship that we were totally frank with each other. I was alarmed at the prospect of Sam Rosenman's departure at the end of the year. He had resisted Truman's appeal to remain, opting to return to

New York to a lucrative law practice. Truman said he would not replace Rosenman as special counsel, that it was a wartime job and no longer necessary. I told Clifford that I feared "a real vacuum." The Truman staff was already "too thin" and would be dangerously thinner without a special counsel. Clifford, in turn, told me almost every day how appalled he was at the haphazard manner in which decisions of the utmost importance were made at the staff meetings. "There is no policy-making body. It's just a collection of not-too-well-informed men, each one intent on his own job." "The president," Clifford said early in January 1946, "is floundering for assistance and support."

Privately, I wrote after the budget message, "after this good message, Rosenman leaves. Comes the deluge, Lord knows who will have brains then. There is no one of ability near the President with a positive program or even with any *ideas* on economic matters." And problems abounded, with strikes in major industries tearing the country apart.

I enjoyed working with Clifford. We got along well. My Map Room background was helping him in unexpected ways. For example, he phoned me one morning saying, "The president is going to see former ambassador Bill Bullitt this afternoon. Bullitt is going to Europe and says he will be glad to do anything the president would like while he is there. The Boss doesn't know what he should ask Bullitt to do: do you have any ideas?"

My response was quick and to the point. "He shouldn't ask him to do a damn thing. Bullitt is trouble. He'll just go parading around Europe saying he is a special emissary of the president. That was the problem with Roosevelt. He'd send cronies all around, and it just played hell with our embassies and the State Department. Truman certainly doesn't want to mess things up the way FDR did. Tell him to be polite to Bullitt but not say a word that Bullitt can use to promote himself."

A day or so later, Clifford said Truman was grateful for the alert; he'd caught the point at once. I should speak up like this any time I smelled trouble.

And speak up I did—constantly.

I was eligible, under the navy's complicated "point system," for discharge in February 1946. Naval procedures permitted a "spot promotion" to the next higher rank if a reservist, eligible for discharge, agreed to stay on active duty for at least six months if his commanding officer certified his services were needed. So "certified," I became a commander on my twenty-eighth birthday, after a scant four months as a lieu-tenant commander. This was possible in the chaotic days of demobiliza-tion when the navy was desperate to hang on to personnel to man ships, planes, and bases. I obviously did not fit that category, but the procedure for promotion was there. Clifford wanted me to stay. I was glad to. I foresaw exciting and challenging times ahead.

Much of the excitement of Truman's first winter in office related to foreign affairs. Secretary of State Byrnes was carrying on in his new post much as he had in his former one as Roosevelt's director of war mobi-lization. FDR had bucked problems to Byrnes on the understanding that "Jimmy will handle it and won't bother me." But Truman was not Roosevelt. Truman expected to be kept informed and to have the last word on foreign policy decisions. At long, contentious conferences of Soviet, British, and American foreign ministers that lasted through most of the fall of 1945 in London and Moscow, Byrnes made no effort to keep Truman informed.

Truman's boiling point was reached late in December when Byrnes cabled from Europe instructing State to arrange time on the radio net-works for a report on his London and Moscow meetings. When Byrnes arrived in Washington, Truman was on the newly renovated USS *Williamsburg,* on a holiday cruise down the Potomac River. It was intol-erable for Byrnes to report to the public before reporting to him. The Map Room watch officer wrote in the log on December 29, "Things got hot about 3 o'clock." Coded messages flashed back and forth between the yacht and the White House. Twenty minutes after a Truman mes-sage was carried across the street to Byrnes's office (in what is now the Eisenhower Executive Office Building), the Map Room reported that the secretary was flying to the Marine airfield at Quantico "within the hour." A launch carried Byrnes to the yacht, anchored in midriver, at 5:00. What Truman said to Byrnes is a matter of dispute that can never be resolved. Truman wrote that he gave his secretary of state a "dress-ing down," something Byrnes forever denied. Whatever the fact, Byrnes was not invited to join the presidential holiday party and left the ship at 9:20 p.m. (as duly recorded in the Map Room log) for a lonely winter's night drive back to Washington. Being so peremptorily summoned and then quickly dismissed could only have been embittering and humiliat-ing for Byrnes, who less than a year earlier had been hoping to be Roosevelt's running mate, with the speech nominating him to be given by the man who was now his boss and who, in Byrnes's judgment, was far less qualified for the presidency than he was.

Whatever had taken place, both men soon made efforts to improve their relationship. I was drawn in. At Truman's direction, Admiral Leahy told me to begin assembling copies of various papers from the Teheran and Yalta conferences for Byrnes. The admiral asked me about the legality of removing "FDR papers." His question arose because, at that date, all presidential papers were regarded as the personal property of a president or his estate. I told him, "We'll never get anything done if we go into that; we'd better go ahead and do what President Truman tells us to do." Leahy grinned and agreed.

On February 5, 1946, my twenty-eighth birthday and the date of my new rank, I carried copies of the papers Byrnes wanted to the secretary of state's ornate office. He thanked me for the information I had provided over the months and fired off surprising questions. Would I like to work for him at State? And didn't I agree that all the White House files of the Roosevelt administration that dealt with foreign affairs should be turned over to State? Withdrawing as gracefully as I knew how without answering either question, I reported the conversation to my official boss, Vardaman, and to my de facto boss, Leahy. Vardaman cared not a fig as to the disposition of Roosevelt papers, but Leahy cared very much. He would warn Truman at once, he said. "Irreparable harm would be done to our relations with Russia and France should some of the Roosevelt-Churchill remarks about those countries become public at this time." There were, in his opinion, "a number of people there [at State] who pass on highly classified information to the Soviet embassy."

Leahy went on to tell me of his recent luncheon with Prime Minister Mackenzie King in Ottawa. King had shocked him with details of Canadian complicity in Soviet espionage—even to the extent of sharing information on the Manhattan Project. That casual remark was the beginning of my knowledge of the depth and success of Soviet spying in Canada, England, and the United States that was to stun the country in the ensuing months.

Although the Map Room had evolved into an Army Signal Corps office, classified army and navy intelligence reports continued to be delivered there each day. The task of digesting the flow fell to me. Almost daily, I reported to Truman disturbing behavior by the Soviets in the Eastern European countries they occupied. When a lengthy telegram

from our embassy in Moscow analyzed Soviet conduct more percep-
tively than any paper I had ever seen, I made sure that Truman saw it.
(This has since become famous as the "Long Telegram" from George
Kennan.) When I talked with Leahy about it, he commented, "My
friends in the Department—if I have any left—tell me he's the best.
He's the best they've got, and that's not saying a hell of a lot."

(Digression: Some scholars have questioned whether Truman ever
saw Kennan's "Long Telegram" of February 1946. A copy of that telegram is in my papers at the Truman Library in Independence. In
October 2003, in a visit there, I verified that my copy had been initialed
by Admiral Leahy and bore his distinctive letter "P" as evidence that he
had reviewed it with the president.)

As the Soviets were keeping the European pot boiling, Churchill arrived in the United States for a Florida vacation and to accept Truman's
invitation to speak at Westminster College in Fulton, Missouri. Although he was now just a private citizen, Churchill's reputation was as
high as ever in our country. Seething at Soviet conduct, he felt the world
should recognize the dangers inherent in that country's ambitions. Riding with Truman on the presidential train to Missouri, Churchill spelled
out the views he uttered publicly on March 5 in what became known as
the "Iron Curtain speech." The speech, with its sharp denunciation of
the Soviet Union, aroused enormous controversy. Friendly feelings for
our wartime ally were still widespread, and Soviet activities, portrayed
so harshly by Churchill, were largely unknown to the American public.
Feeling the heat, the White House kept quiet, implying that Churchill
was speaking only for himself and that Truman had not known his
views in advance. This background guidance from the press office was
not accurate. Truman had been given a copy of the text on the train ride
west. But there was a more substantive reason for the White House to
distance itself from Churchill's blast. That was Truman's own ambivalence.

The president had grown so fond of his new "toy," the *Williamsburg,*
that he skipped off nearly every weekend for a Potomac River cruise.
Vardaman and Clifford were bored stiff to be cooped up with nothing
to do. It fell to me to be on the ship to receive any classified traffic and
to send such messages as the president might wish. One such cruise
came the weekend after the Churchill speech. When we were alone at
breakfast on March 10, I tried to engage the president in conversation

about Russia, but he wouldn't be drawn out. When I referred to some of the alarming reports from our military attachés on Soviet activities and our relations with the USSR, he simply commented: "Before we were trying to keep her in the war, now we're trying to keep her in the peace—and it's an entirely different thing." The Russian question "would be settled pretty soon."

I was so concerned at his seeming lack of alarm that I went to my cabin and wrote, "I, for one, am afraid that Mr. Truman is not yet fully conscious of the aggressions the Soviet Union has in mind. He keeps brushing aside reports on events in Eastern Europe & the Near East & Asia with a phrase like 'That's not so good, is it?' and then he's on to the next matter."

Truman's lighthearted, casual attitude continued through the spring of 1946 despite the briefs I provided, more open communications with State, and a steady flow of alarming information from the Joint Chiefs provided by Leahy. In time, it all sank in. Truman realized that the Soviet Union was ignoring promises made to Roosevelt at Yalta and to him at Potsdam. The "liberated countries" of Eastern Europe were anything but liberated. Suddenly exasperated, Truman told Clifford in early July to give him a list of agreements the Soviets had violated.

Before Truman had "had enough" of Soviet violation of agreements, he had been faced with a number of domestic crises. His initial reaction to them was similar to the attitude he expressed to me on "the Russian question." He took a light view of growing labor problems. When Clifford told him on March 9 that a Western Electric strike had been settled, he brushed the news aside with, "They'll all be settled pretty soon." He was, unfortunately, out of touch with reality and ill served by a trusted adviser, John Snyder.

Truman had named Snyder, a Missouri friend, to head the Office of Mobilization and Reconversion. Neither Clifford nor I was favorably impressed, but Clifford warned me to be careful in my comments, noting, "John is one of the Boss's closest friends." When Snyder was invited to address the prestigious Economic Club in Detroit in early February 1946, he asked Clifford to write a speech for him. Clifford gave me the job.

Why had Snyder turned to the assistant naval aide? "Because," Clifford explained, "he has no faith in his own staff. The speeches they write are full of 'New Dealisms.' John is desperately afraid someone will slip a New Deal idea over on him."

As labor problems grew worse, I had to agree with Snyder's self-depreciating description of himself to his White House intimates—"I'm just a small-town banker." In mid-May, I noted in another "eyes only" for myself, "He is far to the right but he is afraid to act that way. The vacillation, paralysis and 'sleeping sickness' on domestic matters is so apparent that Robert Hannegan, Chairman of the Democratic Party . . . is in a state of nervous hysteria. 'We are losing 2 million votes a day' he wailed during the coal strike."

During a turbulent spring, Clifford's star was rising. Vardaman had made himself so obnoxious to Secretary of the Navy James Forrestal, by telling the secretary how to run the Navy Department, that Truman had kicked him upstairs to a seat on the Federal Reserve Board.

(Another digression: Many years later—in 1984 or '85—Vardaman's transfer to the Federal Reserve Board came up in a surprising fashion. I was having a quiet talk with the Fed's former chairman, William McChesney Martin, at his home one afternoon. I knew him well. He had long served as the volunteer treasurer of the Red Cross, and we were also colleagues on the National Geographic board of trustees. I commented on how gratifying it was to see Harry Truman's reputation rising in the public mind.

"It will never go up in mine," said Bill gruffly.

"I'm surprised, Bill. Why not?"

"Well, you remember Jake Vardaman, don't you?"

"Yes, of course. He was my boss for a few months when he was naval aide before going to the Fed."

"At the Fed," said Martin with some emotion, "he was a disgrace. His conduct was childish, too. He would arrange for his secretary to break into a board meeting with the word that the White House was calling for Governor Vardaman. After this had happened a couple of times, I checked and found there had been no such calls. And he was unethical. He would pass word to friends of confidential decisions made at the Fed. This got so bad that I finally went to Truman and told him the situation—and that Vardaman had to go.

"The president just looked at me and said, 'Well, he was no good here at the White House. I had to do something with him, so I put him on the Fed's board.'"

Martin, to whom the Federal Reserve was sacred, was shocked at Truman's using it as a dumping ground for incompetents: "I lost all respect for Truman at that moment, and I've never felt any respect for him since!"

Although Truman appointed Clifford as naval aide to the president to succeed Vardaman, I figured it would only be a matter of weeks before the president resurrected the special counsel post and named Clifford to it. I said so to Clifford and was instantly cautioned to keep my mouth shut. "Watch and Wait" were our guidelines while domestic problems mushroomed.

Late on the afternoon of May 13, I took to my typewriter again. "John [Snyder] just came in," I recorded Clifford as saying, "to talk about the labor situation. It's just incredible! . . . Why, John actually said 'What would you think of having a careful review made of all labor legislation now on the books . . . and then some attempt made to work out a labor policy for the President?' I said, 'Why, John, do you mean to tell me that hasn't been done? Doesn't anybody know what the labor policy is?'"

And then Clifford stared at me in utter horror . . . and I looked back, just as amazed.

I continued my "eyes only" memo to myself by writing: "This is indeed the nadir, the complete bankruptcy of the administration, which after six weeks of a disastrous coal strike, finds the President's principal advisor on economic affairs wandering around the White House asking the Naval Aide if a study shouldn't be made to see if a 'policy' shouldn't be worked out!"

We were truly headed for a major crisis in late May with all coal mines shut down, coal then being the country's prime energy source. And a widespread railroad strike was imminent. Truman called an emergency meeting of the cabinet on May 24, asked Rosenman to come from New York, and told Clifford (still the naval aide) to attend. All except John Snyder urged Truman to take strong action and address the country by radio that night. Overruling his top reconversion adviser, Truman ordered his press secretary to schedule a 10:00 p.m. speech on all networks and told Clifford to write the speech—in a scant five hours! The president's strong stand against coal and rail unions won wide public acclaim and earned him the bitter opposition of organized labor. Many changes soon took place.

Chief Justice Harlan Stone died, and Truman nominated Treasury Secretary Fred Vinson to the post, replacing Vinson with John Snyder. A recent addition to the White House staff, John Steelman, would take over the reconversion responsibilities. Clifford's future? Hannegan of the Democratic National Committee for some time had been promoting Clifford for something other than naval aide, as he felt it essential that there be a counterweight to Snyder's conservatism. Hannegan, a fellow St. Louisan, had been coaching Clifford on the realities of Democratic politics. Clifford's wariness toward "liberal" policies evidenced the previous September was gone. He was becoming more "liberal" as his political education progressed. The tough antilabor tone of May 24 was a temporary deviation, needed to get Truman through an economic crisis.

Press Secretary Charles Ross also wanted Clifford in a more substantive position but spoke with caution, since he knew Truman instinctively shared much of Snyder's conservative approach to current issues. Truman responded as Hannegan and Ross hoped he would, and as Clifford and I were fervently praying he would. On June 27, the president appointed Clifford special counsel to the president, the job Sam Rosenman had held and the one Clifford hoped for. It would enhance his legal credentials when he returned to private life.

That job title was, however, highly misleading, as neither Rosenman nor Clifford had assigned legal duties of any sort. It had been dreamed up by Rosenman for himself when he resigned from the New York Supreme Court to spend full time during the war as a speech writer and adviser to Roosevelt. All legal advice to the White House at that time was provided by the Department of Justice, very different from later years when presidents have had sizable legal staffs at their beck and call in the White House.

Even before the appointment, Clifford had asked me to remain as his sole assistant, whatever his role might be. He did not want to be seen as a bureaucratic "empire builder," and I should remain in naval uniform. He wanted recognition as running a "one-man shop." It would add to his prestige and would play well in the press. On June 27, only Clifford's title changed, not mine, nor did my work change. Working solely for Clifford, I stayed in the role of "assistant to the naval aide to the president." (The new aide was Captain James Foskett USN, who was bemused by the strange ways of the White House.)

With Clifford beset by domestic political problems of many kinds, I was on my own when in early July—as I have written above—Truman asked Clifford for a list of agreements the Soviets had broken. I was convinced that Truman still failed to grasp the magnitude of the Soviet challenge. A mere list would serve no useful purpose. I determined to write a report on Soviet-American relations of the kind I thought the president should have. As a starter, I prepared letters for Clifford's signature to key government officials requesting their views and recommendations. He signed them without thought or question. With the replies in hand in late July, I began to compose a synthesis of the data. It was slow going. Clifford had left with Truman on a summer cruise on the *Williamsburg,* and I inherited the task of reviewing the stack of bills passed late in the congressional session and analyzing the recommendations of the Bureau of the Budget as to whether the president should sign or veto. Usually—but not always—I concurred with Budget. On occasion, I was in pretty deep water, as when I intervened and saved the day on a measure regarding the Foreign Service that the president decided to veto on Budget's recommendation. When the State Department persuaded me it was essential, on my appeal, the president signed it.

Along with congressional bills and the routine stuff that flooded Clifford's office, I worked on the Soviet report, sending Clifford drafts of the chapters as I had time to write them. With one I included a plaintive note that "it would cause me no pain at all to fly down" to Bermuda, where the ship then was, and deliver some papers in person. No sale!

When Clifford was back in town and had my completed draft of the Soviet report in hand, he at last turned his attention to it. His only reaction was that I might add a chapter asserting our full compliance with our agreements with the Soviets. When I could capture his attention five days later and objected that this would be self-serving and meaningless, he dropped the idea. I suggested that he ask George Kennan, now back in Washington from the embassy in Moscow where he had written the Long Telegram, to look it over. Kennan had no substantive suggestions. There were more delays, the most serious being Truman's and Clifford's preoccupation with the messy departure of Henry Wallace from the cabinet. (Wallace had been fired as secretary of commerce after delivering a speech regarded as too pro-Soviet and insisting on his right to continue speaking on foreign affairs, leading Secretary of State Byrnes to threaten resignation.) I had the report printed and bound in twenty copies. I hoped that the president would make judicious distribution of the "top-secret" volume.

Clifford gave the original to Truman on September 24. He told me, on coming out of the Oval Office, that the president was "startled and delighted at the appearance of the report . . . he would read it after dinner and would talk with Admiral Leahy in the morning."

This was my cue to take off for the admiral's small townhouse on Florida Avenue, next to the Cosmos Club, with his copy so that he would be prepared for the next day's talk. I had reviewed the final draft with him a week earlier and had consulted him throughout. I knew he was in total accord, except that, when I handed over the bound copy, he said, "It ought to come right out and say the Russians are sons of bitches!" He wrote a note for me to take to the office the next morning on his recommendations for distribution.

The next morning Clifford called me to his office as soon as he had returned from Truman's staff meeting. "The Boss doesn't want it known that there is such a report. He is very jittery in view of the Henry Wallace mess. Absolute secrecy is necessary," said Clifford. I passed the word to my contacts at State, where the report had been printed—there was no leak. Margaret Truman, in her biography of her father, gave a colorful account of his asking that all copies be given to him right away for safekeeping.

Was my work all in vain? I thought not. Until Truman read the report with its analysis of Soviet behavior and intentions, despite his irritation at broken agreements, he had continued his relaxed view of the USSR and continued talking about making a major loan to that country comparable to the huge emergency loan to Britain a few months earlier. No longer. His thoughts on Stalin and the Soviet regime hardened. He foresaw that strong counteractions might be necessary. Since the report presented the consensus of key figures in the Executive Branch, he now knew he could count on their support. He would need it in just five months.

The report remained top secret with most copies in Truman's safe until the late 1960s, when the veteran *New York Times* pooh-bah, Arthur Krock, approached Clifford for some anecdotes that would add spice to the memoirs he was writing. Clifford passed him his copy of my draft (the only copy of the text that he had). Krock printed it in toto as an appendix to *Memoirs*. Krock went overboard in his estimate of the report's significance and patted himself on the back for "discovering" it. He wrote that it "charted the postwar prospect with startling prescience in which the shape and thrust of Truman's subsequent great programs— the Greek-Turk [sic] aid legislation, the Marshall Plan, the North

Atlantic Treaty Alliance (including NATO) and what later became know as the 'Truman Doctrine'—were outlined."

Krock's book appeared in 1968 when Clifford was Lyndon Johnson's secretary of defense. He relished the publicity that followed Krock's lifting of the veil on the "Top Secret Clifford Report." Clifford was then in a struggle with Secretary of State Dean Rusk and with Johnson himself, trying to persuade them to reverse the failing U.S. policy in Vietnam. Publicity that portrayed him as long having been farsighted on foreign policy matters was the kind of laudatory attention he craved.

My role in writing the report did not surface until five years later. In Margaret Truman's biography of her father, she wrote that when he had asked Clifford for information on Russian-American relations, "Mr. Clifford passed the task along to his assistant, George Elsey, and Mr. Elsey spent most of the summer of 1946 writing it. . . . Mr. Elsey, who is now President of the American Red Cross, produced an immensely perceptive, enormously detailed document—a hundred pages in length—which was handed to my father over Clark Clifford's signature in September 1946." (Margaret, who had access to her father's files, stumbled as regards length—it was only seventy-nine pages.) Since she set out the facts, and my working papers in the Truman Library confirm authorship, the document has been generally described in the many books that refer to it as the "Clifford-Elsey Report." Richard Holbrooke, in ghostwriting Clifford's memoirs published in 1991 as *Counsel to the President,* sidestepped the authorship question by portraying it as a joint effort. The report is a good example of the old Washington adage: "No one signs a paper that he writes, nor does he write a paper that he signs."

Although I was still a White House social aide and still in uniform, working exclusively for Clifford meant that I no longer had the opportunities for intimate contact with President Truman that I had so enjoyed when substituting for Naval Aides Vardaman and Clifford on *Williamburg* weekend cruises down the Potomac River. The new naval aide, Foskett, invariably went himself. I had relished Truman's frank—sometimes blunt—assessment of the political figures in the news and his reminiscences of his own career. He loved to relive the machinations that had led to his nomination as vice president in 1944 and the wholly unexpected move to the White House. As for the White House: "I hate the God-damned place. It's terrible. I want to be back in the Senate."

This was a sentiment I heard often, spiced with stories of why the Senate had been a happier experience than he was now having.

From breakfast conversations when there were just the two of us, as his poker-playing guests were generally late risers, I learned of the wide range of his reading. His knowledge of ancient history would have done credit to a college professor, but he was, at times, embarrassingly ill informed on present-day personalities. He admitted that he had really "goofed" at a February press conference when he spoke of "President Eliot of Harvard" and referred to something Eliot had said "a day or two ago." This despite Eliot's having been dead for decades and his having met James Conant, the current Harvard president, on a number of occasions. "Facts about colleges, universities and their leaders do not stick with him because he has no frame of reference into which to fit them" was my note after one breakfast talk.

I sensed in these candid moments that he was essentially a conservative with little or no sympathy with organized labor and its leaders. He had been "pro-labor" in the Senate because it was Democratic Party policy, not because of his convictions. He knew, however, that the party could stay in power only if it kept labor happy, and he would sign or veto legislation as "Big Labor" demanded.

In the intimacy of the ship, his language was unguarded. The use of *nigger* was common, as were a variety of barnyard vulgarities. "Dirty stories," however, were not—at least, not from Truman himself. He would laugh if others told them, but his repertoire was confined to political anecdotes, scatological only if they involved a politician.

I was not to enjoy the president's hospitality on the *Williamsburg* again until he named me an administrative assistant in 1949.

Work with Clifford grew ever more fascinating because of the range of issues with which he dealt. Many picayune matters he handed me to deal with as I saw fit. Some of the big ones he handled himself, especially if they were political. Others involved us both, for example the postwar organization of the armed forces, a matter I had been following closely since 1945. We had lengthy talks with army and navy representatives and profited greatly from the seasoned judgment of experts from the Bureau of the Budget. It would be another year, however, before compromises could be reached.

Alleged "communist infiltration" of the federal government was a political hot potato in the summer of 1946. This issue was to reach white-hot intensity some years later with reckless charges by Senator Joe McCarthy, but it was already worrisome. Clifford delegated to me the job of shepherding through the bureaucracy a proposal to establish a commission on employee loyalty. Once again I was reminded of Truman's disdain (*loathing* would not be too strong a word) for J. Edgar Hoover, the well-publicized director of the Federal Bureau of Investigation. The president, Clifford said, did not want the bureau to have anything to do with investigating prospective federal employees whose jobs required security clearance. He wanted the Civil Service Commission to have the assignment. But when I went to meet with the three members of the commission, I ran into a stone wall. They had not the staff, the expertise, or the desire, and this they expressed with vehemence. Reluctantly, and with blunt language about Hoover, Truman acquiesced in another task for the director's "empire," signing the Executive Order on Employee Loyalty on November 25, 1946. I was to remain involved in one aspect or another of "loyalty issues" to the end of the administration in January 1953.

There was a lot of scribbling on speeches. Some were written from scratch; more often a draft came from a department or agency involved in an event. In September, for example, State sent us the draft of a speech for Truman to deliver at the opening session of the United Nations General Assembly. The assembly would be meeting in a building left over from the 1939-1940 World's Fair on Long Island, New York. As was always the case with something from State, we had to tone down the high-flown eloquence into language that sounded like Harry Truman. After the address, the president and Mrs. Truman held a reception for the delegates at the Waldorf-Astoria in midtown Manhattan. With other White House aides, I donned aiguillettes and white gloves and helped run the hundreds of guests through the receiving line, my last big affair as an aide.

The interests and the pleasures of the job in 1946 were to have permanent career impact. I couldn't bear to break away. With some pain, I turned down an invitation to be one of the first two recipients of the newly established Woodrow Wilson Fellowships at Princeton. (The other invitee, who did accept, was Bob Goheen, who had graduated one year behind me. In due course, he became president of the university.) I visited Cambridge and explained to my Harvard professors that it would be at least another year before I could return to complete the

Ph.D., whereupon one said: "If you don't come now, you never will."
He was to be proved correct. With special regret, I declined an offer for
a faculty appointment in the history department at Bryn Mawr. The department's chair was William Howard Taft's daughter, and she bluntly
said that White House experience was worth more than a degree—no
need to bother with a Ph.D.

As 1946 drew toward its end, politics began to overshadow all else.
The November midterm elections were a disaster for the Democrats.
The Eightieth Congress would be overwhelmingly Republican. It
would be uphill for Truman all the way. I reminded Clifford that, with
Sam Rosenman gone, the January '47 State of the Union message would
be his chore, one that he had overlooked. Rosenman had written earlier
messages based on his own grasp of the issues, but Clifford as yet had no
such command. I prepared letters to all members of the cabinet asking
for recommendations. He passed their replies to me. I felt comfortable
in handling foreign and defense matters but ill-equipped on such domestic issues as price controls, housing, and labor policies. We borrowed
a bright analyst from Budget. Between us, Jim Sundquist and I were
able to give Clifford in late December a pretty fair text.

I broke away from State of the Union work for a long weekend in
December with Mother and Dad in Oakmont: such weekends were increasingly rare. I must have spent considerable time talking to Dad
about the job and my future. Fifty years later, when disposing of Dad's
diaries, I found pasted on the December 31, 1946, page a single-spaced
typed account of the discussion. This was the only such record I ever
found. Dad wrote from his own arch-conservative perspective and put
his "spin" on many of my comments, for example that I was "positive
that the White House will continue the drive against the menace of
union leadership. The two things in the way of success are the Supreme
Court and the Executive Departments which have been loaded for thir-
teen years in favor not of labor but of unions." I would take issue with
his interpretation of some of my comments, but they reflect the views of
a man whose convictions were never in doubt.

Let Dad's diary entry be the conclusion of 1946.

When I returned to Washington from the Oakmont respite, the State
of the Union was top priority. Clifford checked the draft with various
cabinet members on matters of their concern. I went to the State
Department to review the foreign affairs section with Byrnes and

Undersecretary Dean Acheson. They were a prickly pair. Byrnes was vociferous in objecting to the positive remarks I had written about the United Nations. I caved in. There was no point in arguing. Byrnes would be succeeded in three weeks as secretary by General George Marshall.

I gave my foreign and military portions to Clifford, who fitted them into the domestic sections, which had passed cabinet scrutiny with only cursory changes. Clifford handed the text to Truman, who, a couple of days later, asked Clifford, Press Secretary Charley Ross, and me to join him in the Cabinet Room. He read the text aloud. Ross suggested a few editorial changes, and the president scratched in some words that fitted his speaking style and would make for easier reading. That was it! Nothing remotely resembling the elaborate staff work of later years as, for example, described by the *Wall Street Journal* in January 1999: "It's crunch-time at the White House. The elbows are out as cabinet secretaries, outside groups and their administration allies try to plead, lobby, badger and beg their way into what amounts to the Policy Wonk Super Bowl." Demonstration projects, poll numbers, focus groups, and media rollout plans had all preceded actual drafting, according to the *Journal.* We lived in a simpler—and happier—time, for which I am grateful.

(Another digression: I was amused many years later—2003 to be exact—when a fragment of a hitherto unknown Truman diary was discovered. On January 6, 1947, he had written, "Read my annual message. It was good if I do say so myself. Clark Clifford did most of the work. He's a nice boy and will go places.")

How critical 1947 was to be was soon apparent. In mid-February, the British government informed Washington that it could no longer provide military and financial support to Greece and Turkey. Frantic consultations followed, involving State, Defense, congressional leaders of both parties, and the president, of course. Conclusion? The United States should step up to the plate with whatever it would take to keep those two strategically located countries out of the Soviet orbit. Countless books and articles have been written on this decisive action; there is no need for me to recount it again.

Truman took this bold step on the advice, and with the strong support, of the new secretary of state, George Marshall, and Undersecretary Dean Acheson. Early drafts of the presidential address to Congress were written under the latter's direction, but, as was the case with nearly everything coming to us from State, extensive rewriting was needed.

With respect to State's proposed text, I quote a portion of a talk I gave in Washington in 1997 on the fiftieth anniversary of the famed "Truman Doctrine" address:

> I was worried by the absence of what today would be called a "sound bite." Where were the two or three sentences that would convey the essence of the president's policy? Where were the highly quotable words that the press and the public could grasp at once and know that this was a policy that went far beyond $400 million of assistance for Greece and Turkey? . . . I went back to State's final draft and focused on one unwieldy paragraph. The key thoughts were there, but they were buried in long sentences that would be hard for Truman to read and for listeners to grasp.
>
> I stripped out needless words. I broke the paragraph into three sentences and rephrased them. Each sentence was then set as a separate paragraph for emphasis. And each sentence then began with "I believe . . ."
>
> You know the result:
>
> "I believe that it must be the policy of the United States to support free peoples who are resisting attempted subjugation by armed minorities or by outside forces.
>
> "I believe that we must assist free peoples to work out their own destinies in their own way.
>
> "I believe that our help should be primarily through economic and financial aid which is essential to economic stabilization and orderly political processes."

As Clifford wrote in his memoirs years later: "These sentences, which George and I called 'the credo,' finally seemed to leap out at the listener."

I bore the reader with this detail because of the importance of the speech that forecast the basic foreign policy stance of the United States for the next half century and because no other sentences I have crafted are as widely quoted and as well remembered as "The Credo" of Harry Truman's address to Congress of March 12, 1947.

While Congress was digesting the implications of Truman's three bold sentences, economists at the State Department were working up another landmark proposal—massive economic aid to get Western Europe back on its feet. Marshall sprang the idea in rather opaque language in a commencement address at Harvard in June. The Marshall

Plan resulted. As Clifford and I watched with closest interest, State carried the ball with a strong assist from Secretary of Commerce Averell Harriman through the summer and autumn. It was December before a concrete proposal was ready for Congress. Thought to be too complex for a twenty- or thirty-minute address, it went to the Hill as a presidential message. On this document, as usual, I was a scribbler striving for clarity and clear expression, but I must be clear. The White House role—even the president's—was minimal in conceiving and executing the Marshall Plan. When partisan friends objected to the name, Truman's response was firm. "I don't mind it's being called the Marshall Plan," he said one afternoon in a Cabinet Room discussion. "It's all U.S. foreign policy and I'm responsible for that." That remained his position. In later years, he often said, "It wouldn't have gotten through Congress without Marshall's name and his leadership. He deserves the credit."

While I claim no credit of any sort with respect to the Marshall Plan, I do give myself a small pat on the back with respect to another foreign affairs matter of 1947. In the spring of the year, I noted a statement by the foreign minister of Brazil that the United States should take the initiative in coordinating Western Hemisphere defenses against communist activities. This was the pretext I had been looking for. I began heckling Clifford that the White House and State were so preoccupied with Europe that we were neglecting our Latin neighbors. When an inter-American conference was announced for August in Rio de Janeiro, I said Truman *must* attend. "Impossible," was Clifford's response. "The president and Mrs. Truman and Margaret are going up the Inland Passage to Alaska on the *Williamsburg*." My rejoinder, "That's a lousy idea."

I began a quiet campaign with friends at State to flood the White House with memos on the importance of the Rio Conference. One of my buddies prepared a note for Acheson's signature on the great impact Truman's attendance would have on inter-American relations. The result was that Truman did fly down, returning leisurely on the *Missouri* (so Mrs. T. and Margaret could have a summer cruise as he had promised them). Truman's participation was a huge success, and the Southern Hemisphere countries no longer felt neglected. Clifford was in the presidential party and had said I could go, too. I had had my nose to the grindstone for months without a break. I declined, with thanks, and loafed in Oakmont instead.

Thanks to public-spirited Republican leaders in the Eightieth Congress who put the national interest ahead of their partisan concerns, Truman's foreign policy proposals were receiving broad support. So were his proposals for reorganizing the national defense structure, culminating in the National Security Act of September 1947. This measure set up a separate air force (it had heretofore been part of the army). It, the Navy Department, and the War Department—now renamed Department of the Army—would be folded into a National Military Establishment under a secretary of defense. The act also established the Central Intelligence Agency and the National Security Council. This act was the result of a long, bitter struggle. The navy had fought a rearguard action, fearing army domination. Clifford had been in the thick of the fight almost from the day he had arrived at the White House two years earlier. His arm was twisted almost daily by the aggressive secretary of the navy, James Forrestal. When the bill was still in its formative stage, in late March 1947, Clifford had invited representatives of the army, army air force, and navy to his office to review the draft of the bill as it then stood. I had been intimately involved at every stage, being the liaison with experts on government organization in the Bureau of the Budget while Clifford had generally dealt with the secretaries of war and navy and senior officers. On this particular day, at the last minute, Clifford was given a crash assignment by Truman, and he left me in charge of the meeting. I was then, as a reader may remember, a commander in the U.S. Naval Reserve.

Facing me around a conference table were Lieutenant General Hoyt S. Vandenberg, U.S. Army Air Force, later to be NATO commander in chief and, still later, director of the CIA; Lieutenant General J. Lawton Collins, later to be chief of staff of the army; and Vice Admiral Forrest Sherman, later to be chief of naval operations. The atmosphere was strained. I made no effort to argue the case for the latest White House draft. I limited myself to pointing out the changes from the text the services had previously seen. After a few questions, the meeting adjourned. Vandenberg and Collins left politely. Sherman departed in a cold fury. The next morning, Forrestal phoned Clifford, who immediately relayed the content of the call to me.

The conversation went like this: "Clark, you're being damn rough on the navy."

"Why, Jim, what have I done?"

"Clark, you know damn well we don't like the way this unification crap is going. It's pretty bad when you put a Reserve three-striper in charge to cram a God-damn bill down the throat of a three-star admiral!"

Clifford, after reporting the call with all the oratorical skills he could muster, said with a grin: "Maybe you and I would be better off if you became a civilian." And so, in a matter of days, I shed the uniform I had worn since December 1941 and became a special assistant in the White House office. This was to make my work easier with government departments, and it also meant a raise in pay. As a commander, I received pay and various allowances of about $6,000 a year. The Civil Service job started at $7,100, and I would be eligible for overtime, which would be considerable. These figures represented solid middle-class incomes in 1947.

When Forrestal realized he had lost the fight to keep the navy as an independent department, he floated a new idea. He began circulating papers praising the British concept of cabinet government. Policy papers would be drafted by a cabinet secretariat, circulated in advance, and acted on at cabinet meetings. A secretary of the cabinet would control the agendas, manage discussion, and relay recommendations to the president. Forrestal leaked his idea to friends in the press, together with his proposal that Clifford be the cabinet secretary. All hell broke loose. John Steelman raged to Truman that if Clifford got the job, he would resign at once. I wrote that day, "This of course damn near kills the whole thing." Well, not quite.

When Clifford hinted to Forrestal that, if he would only stop bucking Truman, he could be the first secretary of defense, "Jim" calmed down. When he was appointed secretary as Clifford had come close to promising, Forrestal resurrected his cabinet secretariat idea. He tiptoed toward it, suggesting regular monthly cabinet luncheons, hosted by a different member each time. "The group needs a secretary who can take notes on agreements and decisions reached. He should come from the White House," Forrestal phoned Clifford, who promptly put up my name. "Do you think you can trust him?" Clifford was asked. "Oh, heavens, yes!"

Accordingly, I was invited to the Pentagon for a cabinet luncheon hosted by the secretary of defense. "I think you'll want to take a notebook along so you can record decisions and agreements," Clifford suggested. Nothing remotely resembling serious business came up, but some of the chatter was fascinating. Secretary of State Marshall, recalling his days as army chief of staff on the eve of World War II, reminisced about Roosevelt. "The president's greatest fault," said Marshall, "was his blindness to the need for a mobilization plan and his curious 'personal' handling of the situation, directing [Assistant Secretary of War] Louis Johnson *not* to talk with Secretary of War [Harry] Woodring on mobilization plans, and his willingness to listen to anguished pleas of [Secretary of Labor] Fanny Perkins, Henry Wallace, and others who feared 'military domination' and were alarmed at 'war mongering' by the War Department. This failure [by Roosevelt] to support the mobilization plan cost us many billions, many months, and inestimable lives."

Secretary of the Treasury John Snyder and Attorney General Tom Clark hosted the next two luncheons. I was pointedly not invited. Clifford said they were worthless bull sessions. Forrestal's idea was soon dead.

While relative harmony prevailed between the Democrats and the Republicans of the Eightieth Congress on key foreign policy and national defense issues, there was constant, open, and bitter warfare on domestic matters—price, housing, farm, and labor issues, among others. Truman opened a new battle front in June 1947 when he spoke at the Lincoln Memorial to the convention of the National Association for the Advancement of Colored People. Despite Franklin Roosevelt's vaunted concern for black Americans, he was never brave enough to antagonize southern Democrats by appearing before the NAACP.

Truman was different. He was outraged by the treatment of black soldiers on their return home from World War II service. Some—even while in uniform—were beaten, harassed, disfigured. In late 1946, he had appointed the Commission on Civil Rights, composed of eminent men and women—black and white—who were given the charge to "lay it on the line" and recommend actions to remedy the gross inequalities prevalent in our society. The commission was well into its work when Truman accepted the NAACP invitation, but a report was far from ready.

As usual, when an important speech appeared on the presidential calendar of future events, Clifford and I talked. Civil rights were not on Clifford's radar screen; he couldn't have cared less about the NAACP. "You take it," was the charge to me.

When faced with the preparation of a speech where I knew I needed help, I looked for an expert. I turned to Robert Carr, staff director of the commission, who was on leave from his job as a professor of political science at Dartmouth. Carr demurred when I called on him at the commission's temporary offices, rented from the American Security Bank on Fifteenth Street.

"Writing a speech for the president is outside my responsibility or authority."

"OK, that's probably so, but who knows more about what needs to be done and what needs to be said?" was my rejoinder.

We talked a bit, agreeing that a request to the head-in-the-sand Department of Justice for a draft of a speech would bring only mush. Carr was persuaded.

A few days later, I had an excellent paper that needed the barest fine-tuning. When examined more than a half century later, the text seems bland, but it was a shocker at the time. Such thoughts as "We cannot await the growth of a will to action in the slowest state or the most backward community" and "Our national government must show the way" brought huzzahs from minorities and liberals nationwide but angry howls from southern politicians who waved "states' rights" flags into tatters. When challenged, Truman said he was eager to get the commission's report. Clifford was worried. Had I led the president astray? I was delighted at the reaction and said we had to start thinking about the 1948 election.

And begin thinking we did. From midsummer on, we thought of every speech, every trip, and every appointment in terms of the next year's election, even though Truman had not said he would run. We just assumed it. Without permission, and with no mandate, Clifford began planning campaign strategy. Discretion—at times, deception—was necessary. Help came from an unexpected and very welcome source. Oscar "Jack" Ewing, administrator of the agency that managed Social Security and various welfare programs, was an ardent New Dealer. He was in close touch with other liberal men at the second or third level of their departments. Ewing held off-the-record dinner meetings in his apartment at the Wardman Park Hotel to discuss the issues they foresaw as dominating the 1948 campaign. Early on, Ewing invited Clifford to join the group. Its members were godsends for him, giving him a thorough grounding on many matters he had known little about. As the weeks went by and Clifford talked with me about '48, I sensed that he was turning from a cautious, prudent, quasi liberal into a flaming liberal— at least, for political purposes, if not in his heart. By the autumn of '47, he was saying (behind a closed door, of course) that Snyder, Steelman, and Attorney General Tom Clark were every bit as dangerous to Truman's chances the next year as were the Republicans.

Bolstered by his new companions, Clifford was the most ardent advocate for Truman calling Congress back into special session in late 1947 to pass a number on anti-inflation measures to combat skyrocketing prices. Truman's ten recommendations were virtually ignored. Instead of a ten-point program, his critics jeered, he got a "2 ½ point program" in a bill passed a few days before Christmas.

In those days, when any bill of significance arrived at the White House, the executive clerk—Maurice Latta—would pass it to Clifford to prepare a presidential statement to issue when the bill was signed or vetoed. If a president does not act within ten days after a bill's arrival, it is automatically vetoed, the so-called pocket veto. On the eighth day after the "2 ½ point" bill arrived, Latta walked into Clifford's office while he and I were drafting a strongly worded statement for Truman to issue the next morning blasting the Republican-controlled Congress for its "pitifully inadequate" response to the sufferings of American families caused by inflation.

"Mr. Clifford, can I please have the anti-inflation bill? I'm assembling all the papers the president is to sign tomorrow morning," said Latta.

Clifford shuffled through the mess on his desk.

"I don't have it."

Turning to me, "George, do you have it?"

"No, sir, I've never had it."

A kind of Keystone Kops escapade began. Within the hour, it was clear that the document with the signatures of the president pro tem of the Senate and the speaker of the House, attested by the secretary of the Senate, was nowhere to be found. This was a real crisis. The Press Office had announced that the president would act in the morning and issue a statement. The bill *had* to be signed. Truman could not be in the preposterous position of "pocket vetoing" an anti-inflation measure for which he had called Congress back into special session, no matter how inadequate he felt it to be.

Frantic phone calls were made: to the Government Printing Office to prepare on a crash basis a duplicate on the special heavy paper stock used only for "enrolled bills"; to the president pro tem of the Senate, Arthur Vandenberg, to warn him to stand by to sign the duplicate; and to the home of the speaker of the House, Joseph Martin, on Christmas vacation in Massachusetts. The speaker was not at home, and his maiden sister, with whom he lived, made it clear to the White House telephone operator that she would answer no questions as to his whereabouts.

It was now about 5:00 p.m.

What to do?

Send George Elsey to Massachusetts in search of the speaker!

A phone call to the Pentagon from the military aide revealed that the only plane available on an instant's notice was that of the chief of staff of the army, General Dwight Eisenhower. And so, at about six o'clock, off I went as the sole passenger on Ike's plane, flying with a grumpy crew who made their disappointment clear at being deprived of a holiday evening at home "for some damn fool political junket." Had it not been for the crew's displeasure, the flight would have been a joy. The East Coast was blanketed with snow. We flew very low, and the Christmas lights of every town sparkled brilliantly. With commercial airports closed, we landed at a Rhode Island State Police emergency field in Hillsgrove. A patrol car took me to the state line, where Massachusetts troopers escorted the Rhode Island car to Martin's house in North Attleboro.

I rang the doorbell. Startled at seeing two police cars at her curb, the speaker's sister opened the door a crack. I introduced myself as from the White House and said I needed to see the speaker. The door was flung open. Miss Martin's eyes sparkled; she rubbed her hands and asked breathlessly, "Has something happened to the president?"

To understand her excitement, one needs to remember that one of the first acts of the Eightieth Congress had been to provide that, in the absence of a vice president, the speaker of the House of Representatives was first in line to assume the presidency if anything happened to the incumbent. There being no vice president since Truman had succeeded Roosevelt, Miss Martin, for one fleeting moment, believed that her brother might be the president!

I explained to the crestfallen lady that Truman was fine and that I just needed the speaker's signature on an important document. In her disappointment, Miss Martin would provide no information: "He's out somewhere."

Massachusetts State Police had no trouble locating the speaker. Off we went to Dedham, where, at 11:01 p.m. in a high school auditorium before the Norfolk County Republican Club, Joe Martin signed my precious paper. At 3:45 a.m., I placed the substitute bill on Clifford's desk, weighing it down with paper weights in a V-for-Victory cluster, before walking home through the snow to my Nineteenth Street apartment.

The press the next day had some fun at the discomfiture of the White House. My quick trip was duly reported, and Dad noted sourly in his diary that I was "functioning as a messenger." What happened to the original? It had been before Clifford and me all day Sunday. I concluded that he had scooped it up with unread Sunday papers when we closed shop that day and it had ended up, unnoticed, in the trash at his house. I could think of no other possibility, but he reacted so angrily when I mentioned it that I never spoke of it again. The executive clerk, Latta, and his successor, Bill Hopkins, never again let an enrolled bill leave their office. From that day on, the staff was given only copies to work with.

It was an amusing close to an interesting year!

Chapter Seven

1948

Historians have declared the 1948 election to be the "political upset of the century." Truman beat the Republican nominee, Governor Thomas E. Dewey of New York, against all forecasts and seemingly against all odds. How did it happen? The Republicans had won control of the Senate and House in '46, had resoundingly rejected Truman's domestic agenda, although on a bipartisan basis accepting his major foreign policy proposals, and were confident the country was "ready for a change" after sixteen years of Democrats in the White House.

Truman's unforeseen victory in '48 was no accident. It resulted from thoughtful planning, bold actions, and an acute reading of the voters' minds. I was lucky in being able to play a role in the planning, in the actions, and in the campaign.

In November 1947, when Truman and Clifford were concentrating on getting anti-inflation measures through Congress, I was thinking about 1948. The 1947 State of the Union message had been not much more than a laundry list of recommendations. In my opinion, the 1948 message must be different. It was easier to get Clifford's attention with a memo than with conversation, so I wrote a paper often since quoted by writers who have plowed through my files in the Truman Library. The forthcoming State of the Union, I wrote, "must be controversial as Hell, must state the issues of the election, must draw the line sharply between Republicans and Democrats." Clifford gave me the green light to get started. (This single sentence kept popping up for years in political writings. In 1975, for example, the *Washington Post*'s chief political correspondent quoted my memo and urged President Gerald Ford to take it to heart if he was to have any chance in the 1976 election.)

We had an asset not with us a year earlier—Charles Murphy. A soft-spoken North Carolinian with years of congressional staff experience, Murphy was an administrative assistant to the president who had joined the staff some months earlier. Not only was he a better writer than Clifford, he was a dyed-in-the wool liberal, not a novice as was my boss. Together, Charley and I set to work. I concentrated on foreign and defense matters as I had a year earlier, while he took on domestic issues, which he knew instinctively how to present in the most favorable way. Between us, we composed a State of the Union speech that Clifford found no need to change. He passed it to Truman, whose edits were minimal—all this with time to spare. So relaxed was this year's pace that Truman even had time to read the full speech to the cabinet days before he went to the Hill.

At the Joint Session, Truman was received politely. Republicans sat on their hands while he read, in his flat, emotionless manner, his blueprint for 1948. Even the Democratic response was muted, but we on the staff were satisfied. A firm course was set with an eye on November. General Vaughan and I were on the porch outside the Oval Office when Truman returned from the Capitol. He waved us in, opened a desk drawer, and pulled out scotch and bourbon. As other staff members joined us, we drank to "Success in '48!" As we were drifting out, Truman drew me aside and told me of his pleasure at my work. I was astounded. I record this only because such comments from him were rare to nonexistent. It just wasn't his nature.

"Scotty" Reston, the usually perceptive political analyst of the *New York Times,* wrote a scathing critique. The address, he said, was no report on "the State of the Union." Reston missed the point. The address was a first draft of the Democratic Platform for the 1948 campaign. It was intended less for its immediate audience of senators and representatives than for those elements of the electorate whose support would be needed in November.

At Charley Murphy's urging, and with Truman's enthusiastic endorsement, we began planning a series of special messages to the second session of the Eightieth Congress that would expand on the issues that were, necessarily, only briefly discussed in the State of the Union. One message each week—"Hit 'em every Monday!"—became our working slogan.

As I have commented, Clifford had little interest in civil rights matters. As he, Murphy, and I were drawing up our list, I urged that the special message on civil rights be near the top, if not actually at the top. I wrote, "Truman and Democrats have everything to gain and nothing to lose from a forthright statement endorsing the findings of the Committee on Civil Rights," which had submitted its final report in late October. Clifford shrugged this off. "OK, George, but you'll have to be the one to do it."

While I had strong opinions, I lacked the legal knowledge to frame specific recommendations on such matters as voting rights. I knew it would be futile to ask for help from Justice, headed by a conservative attorney general from Texas, Tom Clark. The Civil Rights Commission staff had disbanded, and its staff director, Bob Carr, had returned to his faculty post at Dartmouth. I phoned him and asked if he could come back during the January exam break and prepare a special message to Congress. As he had when I'd asked him to do the NAACP speech, Carr hesitated—but only briefly. I put him up in a spare room in what is now called the Eisenhower Executive Office Building with plenty of pencils and yellow pads. In clear, sharp prose, Carr produced so admirable a draft that, with only a few editorial scratches, it went right to Truman's desk. I was elated. Clifford was indifferent. Murphy and Press Secretary Ross were nervous—they predicted a political firestorm from southern Democrats. Truman agreed with their forecast but was undeterred. The commission report had confirmed what he had long felt; it was time to lay it on the line in bold, clear terms. Thus, the landmark February 2, 1948, message to the Congress on civil rights.

Murphy and Ross were correct. All hell broke loose. Truman's legislative recommendations were dead on arrival, but the ground had been broken, the genie was out of the bottle, and the long tortuous struggle was under way, reaching a climax in Lyndon Johnson's administration when major civil rights legislation was passed. (Although, as I review this in 2005, one of Truman's recommendations—full voting rights for citizens of the District of Columbia—has not yet been granted.) In the weeks after February 2, as it became clear Congress would not act, I made a nuisance of myself by urging that the president act on his own where he had executive authority. He could end racial segregation in the armed forces and in the federal Civil Service. By the time executive orders had been drafted, the Democratic Party was in such turmoil that Murphy "put them on ice." The international situation had gravely worsened. It took all our attention.

In mid-March, the Soviets had brutally taken over Czechoslovakia. The only good to come out of this was congressional awareness that, unless the Marshall Plan was authorized at once and made effective promptly, Western European countries were likely to collapse in the face of Soviet pressures. With war clouds over Europe, we laid domestic matters aside and worked feverishly with State and Defense. Truman went back to the Hill, asking among other contentious things for a reinstitution of Selective Service. As if European problems weren't enough, Palestine became red hot. We of the staff hoped Truman had learned from the Henry Wallace fiasco of 1946 that he shouldn't try to handle highly complex foreign matters all by himself. As regards Palestine, he stubbornly told staff to keep "hands off." The results were unfortunate. Beset by worries on all sides, Truman forgot—or misunderstood—some of the papers coming to him from Secretary of State Marshall and "blew up," denouncing State Department "treachery" when our ambassador to the United Nations, Warren Austin, in an address at the United Nations, "reversed" U.S. policy, so Truman thought. In fact, as I quickly learned in delving into the record and querying White House and State staff, Truman had personally read and approved some days earlier the Austin speech, which outlined a plan for U.N. trusteeship of Palestine when the British mandate ended in May in lieu of partitioning the area into separate Jewish and Arab territories. He hadn't remembered? Or he hadn't understood? Whichever, it was another example of Truman's trying to juggle too many problems all by himself without allowing his staff to help.

State was so sensitive after Truman's blast that, a month later when Austin had to speak again at the United Nations, Undersecretary Robert Lovett called me at my apartment on a Sunday afternoon, had his secretary dictate to me a statement Austin was to make with respect to sending American troops to Palestine, and asked me for White House clearance. I went to the office, typed it up, and took it to the president in his second-floor study. With his "Approved, Harry S. Truman" in hand, I phoned the "OK" to the assistant secretary for U.N. affairs, Dean Rusk.

We continued to tiptoe on eggshells with regard to Palestine for a few more weeks with off-the-record meetings, memos written and rewritten, and long telephone conversations, all culminating in Truman's recognition of the new state of Israel in mid-May over the vociferous objection of Secretary of State Marshall. All this has been amply described in numerous books. Since I was little more than a sounding board for Clifford as he thought aloud and rehearsed the points he would make in meetings, there is no need for more here on the Palestine-Israel morass in which we found ourselves.

The European situation took another turn for the worse when the Soviets suddenly blocked all land access to Berlin. The city had been divided for administrative purposes into American, British, French, and Soviet zones. Berlin was deep inside that part of Germany controlled by the Soviets and, with all roads blocked by Soviet tanks, it looked as though Allied access was doomed and the city would be absorbed into the Soviet bloc. Rejecting an army general's advice to storm our way into Berlin, Truman decided we would supply the city by a massive airlift of food, coal, and all other necessities. This decision was applauded by all hands. As months went by and the airlift was a success, the president's stock began a slow recovery.

No matter what foreign crisis appeared on the horizon, we soon focused again on the November elections. The troubles over Palestine and the southern uproar over civil rights caused Clifford to muse with me as to whether Truman could even be nominated, let alone elected. Very privately, *very* privately, he wondered whether Truman was "deserving of four years more." However gloomy he was in intimate conversation, he put on a bold face publicly, especially on foreign affairs. The only way war can be averted, he told a major newspaper writer, was for the Soviet Union to conclude that "we are too strong to be beaten and too determined to be frightened," quoting, as he often did, my final words in the Soviet-American relations report.

In early June, Truman departed Washington for a long train trip through the upper Midwest to the Pacific coast, down to Los Angeles and home through the central states. Billed as a "nonpolitical" trip because the president was to receive an honorary degree from the University of California, the costs were borne by the president's congressionally supplied travel fund. The trip was blatantly political, and everyone knew it, but the Democratic National Committee was too strapped for funds to pay the bills as it should have. This trip and all the later ones before the election have been written about over and over; I'll mention only my roles in them.

Staying in Washington in June, my fellow stay-at-homes and I winced repeatedly at public relations gaffes reported by the press with embarrassing frequency. Chip Bohlen called from State in anguished tones. "Isn't there some way to stop the president from his careless remarks about Stalin and the Soviet Union?" Friends at the Democratic National Committee were wringing their hands at the news coverage. In retrospect, I'm glad television was in its infancy. Truman's "foot-in-mouth" disease could have been disastrous. When the party returned, Clifford, Murphy, and I were of one mind. The Democratic National Committee must quickly assemble a cluster of bright, energetic, and imaginative young men (in 1948, one didn't think of "young women") to research every city and every situation in which Truman would appear during the actual campaign scheduled to begin on Labor Day.

The committee came through. By September, it had hired Bill Batt, an aspiring politician from Philadelphia, and a half dozen researchers with sharp political instincts. Bill and his "boys" were to be of incalculable value throughout the autumn, but before we could put their work to use we had to jump the hurdle of the Democratic national convention in Philadelphia in July.

Truman faced some tough obstacles. Southern Democrats, steadily growing angrier over his civil rights message, threatened to leave the party. Many self-described "liberals" said Truman lacked the leadership skills to carry Franklin Roosevelt's policies forward. They wanted a sure winner and shouted it up for General Eisenhower, despite the fact that no one had the slightest idea of "Ike's" political philosophy—if, indeed, he had any. Henry Wallace, sulking, was an uncertain quantity. And there was the matter of the platform—could it be stretched to satisfy all the elements of the electorate Truman needed?

In theory, a party's platform is drafted by a committee of the national convention assembled to nominate the party's candidate for president. Not so in 1948. A draft of the platform came to us from the Democratic National Committee offices. After much rehashing by too many hands at the White House, the president gave me twenty copies to hand-carry to Philadelphia, where the Platform Committee, under the chairmanship of Senator Francis Myers of Pennsylvania, was assembled a few days in advance of the convention. I was warned that the senator's overlarge ego would not allow him to accept so important a document from a young White House "nobody." I gave my packet to the secretary of the Senate to pass to Myers and headed for the Thirtieth Street station for a train ride back to Washington. Myers's committee meekly accepted our draft, but the convention the following week did not. A furious fight erupted over the civil rights plank. When a revised plank as bold as Truman's February 2 message was adopted, conservative southerners in large numbers walked out to form the States Rights Party. J. Strom Thurmond, then governor of South Carolina and soon to be the nominee for president of the new party, was asked: "Why are you walking out? All Truman is doing is following the Roosevelt platform." "I know," Thurmond replied, "but that SOB Truman *means* it!"

While the quarrel over the platform was at white heat in Philadelphia, back at the White House we were concentrating on Truman's acceptance speech. The mood was upbeat. I wrote a note for myself about Truman's changed mood since the June trip to the west. Despite the flaws, he was confident he had succeeded in arousing the country to the reactionary policies of the "good-for-nothing, do-nothing Republican Eightieth Congress," words that now rolled off his tongue automatically. In June before the trip he had told me with deep feeling that he "dreaded" it. Now, as Judge Sam Rosenman (called back from New York to give us a hand), Charley Murphy, and I in shirtsleeves sat around the Cabinet Room table, shaping an outline for the speech, Truman walked in, chatted about our work, and said he was in "a fighting mood. I am all set to 'pour it on.'"

Truman was indeed in fighting trim as we rode the train to Philadelphia. He joked about how rough he was going to be on the Republican Congress but that he would never mention Dewey by name. His only worry? A gastrointestinal upset that he hoped wouldn't cause "an accident" when it came time to speak. We waited out long evening hours while tedious balloting for the vice president and the president dragged on. It was long after midnight when Truman was escorted to the rostrum. (In those days of television's infancy, no on had thought of scheduling events to capture the largest possible viewing audience.)

Truman brought the crowd to its feet when he announced that he was calling Congress back into special session in ten days. His purpose was clear. By asking for action on price controls and other anti-inflationary measures that he knew the Republican Congress would not pass, he would demonstrate that the moderate Republican nominees— Dewey of New York and Earl Warren of California—were not in control of their party. He had learned on the western trip that his verbal attacks on the Congress brought a warm response. The Republicans' failure to act on his "hit 'em every Monday" messages on raising the minimum wage, expanding Social Security, enacting a national health insurance program, providing more federal funds to the states for education, and other recommendations was clearly on record. These were moderate proposals that Dewey and Warren had generally endorsed. "They *say* they are for these things, now let them *prove* it" was Truman's challenge.

Despite little sleep by any of us, barely six hours after the acceptance speech we were back at it, plotting the charge to the special session. Truman ticked off the points he wanted emphasized. When someone mentioned "veterans' benefits," he rejected that with the intriguing remark that it would be "demagoguery." "I want no palpable demagoguery—just by inference!" He went on to laugh, "A demagogue is a member of the opposition who is getting the better of you!" He turned somber when legislation to relieve the crisis of the hundreds of thousands of persons displaced by the war was discussed. He spoke bitterly about the Jews. "Those God-damned Jews are never satisfied. They're always grabbing for more. We don't need them in November—to Hell with them. I'm not going to give them another thing!" I never knew what brought this outburst. It certainly was not an accurate expression of his real feelings, but it was in character. Whenever he felt unduly pressed, he would let off steam orally or on paper and then return to normal. This, to me, was an occasion to be regarded as another puff of steam.

The special session came and went in two weeks exactly as Truman had expected. All it did was authorize a loan to fund the proposed headquarters of the United Nations in New York City. But it had served the president's purpose. The Dewey-Warren moderate "New Look" for the Republican Party was nowhere to be seen.

When the southern Democrats who had walked out in Philadelphia formed the Dixiecrat Party, it was clear that the southern states were lost. I argued that "holding on to the South" no longer had any meaning and was no longer a valid reason to hold back on the executive orders banning racial discrimination in the federal Civil Service and the armed forces that had been "put on ice" in March. My colleagues agreed. I pulled the draft orders from the files and polished them with the expert help of Philleo Nash, an ardent civil rights activist. The president signed them with a flourish on July 26, the day the special session convened, another "in-your-face" gesture to the Congress, which had refused to respond to the February civil rights message.

Diverted little by the special session, Clifford, Murphy, and I concentrated on speeches for the campaign. While the president and other members of the staff, with generous input from the National Committee, planned the train trips that would cover the country (except the lost "Deep South"), we identified which issues were to be emphasized and where. Big cities would get prepared speeches intended for radio broadcast, delivered in an auditorium or ballpark before large audiences. Small towns would get informal, off-the-cuff remarks usually from the back platform of the president's railroad car. The big ones were to be drafted by a team Charley Murphy was assembling. The small-town stuff was to be mine. Here was where Bill Batt and his group were to prove their worth. They prepared a folder on each place the train would stop—facts on the place, names of local Democratic officials or candidates, suggestions as to a campaign issue that was "hot" locally. I would then develop an outline for Truman—not a written text, rather a series of topic sentences with two or three facts or phrases indented under each sentence so that he could speak knowledgeably, in a casual informal fashion, about the place, the key people, and a campaign issue of significance in that community.

Truman made a quick trip to Detroit on Labor Day, but the campaign effectively began on September 17 when we boarded, by coincidence, his seventeen-car campaign train. I was armed with briefcases filled with notes and outlines for the first few days with the promise that the daily pouch flown from Washington to wherever we might be would have more from Batt. So began what was to become famous as the "Whistle-Stop Campaign." The phrase had originated when Senator Robert Taft of Ohio derided Truman for stopping at every "whistle station" on his June trip to California. The words need an explanation for readers several decades later. In the 1940s, trains were still the principal means of intercity travel. Air travel was limited and expensive. Interstate highways were years in the future. A "whistle station" signified a town so small that a train would stop to discharge a passenger only if the train conductor signaled to the engineer that a stop was necessary. The engineer would acknowledge by a blast from the locomotive whistle. Senator Taft's comment was intended to be derogatory. Truman and the Democratic Committee saw an opportunity.

Telegrams flew out to the mayors of Los Angeles, San Francisco, and other sizable places visited on the June trip. Implying that Taft spoke for the Republicans, the mayors of San Francisco, Los Angeles, and other cities were asked if they thought of themselves as "whistle stops." The mayors were outraged! It was all good fun, but there was a point to it. Truman intended to emphasize small cities, towns, and rural communities throughout the campaign. Taft had handed him a useful political slogan.

In mid-August, Truman spelled out to two midwestern congressmen his intentions. They repeated his remarks to Drew Pearson, then one of the country's most widely read columnists (and a man whom Truman despised). Pearson quoted Truman as saying: "I'm going to make it a rip-snorting, back-platform campaign to what Taft calls all the whistle stops, but I call them the heart of America. When they count the whistle stops' votes, Taft may be in for a big surprise. I think the whistle stops will make the difference between victory and defeat." Unwittingly, through his column read all over the country with its focus on Taft, Pearson was helping Truman. The president's strategy was to ignore the moderate Republican candidates, Dewey and Warren, and fight the conservative ("reactionary" was his term) forces in that party. Truman, in effect, intended to campaign against Taft, the recognized leader of conservative Republicans nationwide. And that, indeed, was the pattern of the long September 17–October 2 swing around the country.

While Clifford worked over the text of "the big speech" of the day flown to us from Murphy, I labored over the notes for the back-platform talks, which, while seemingly impromptu and off-the-cuff, were anything but. No matter how many "whistle-stops" were scheduled for the day (and once we had fifteen), I varied the subjects so that Truman would be hitting on a different campaign issue at each stop. Knowing that Truman was highly quotable and that he would not be repeating himself, reporters would race from the press car to the rear of the train to hear his remarks. Scribbling a few sentences, reporters from big-city papers and the wire services such as Associated Press would hand their dispatches to a Western Union representative standing by for immediate relay to their home offices. Thus, there was a constant flow throughout the day of campaign oratory for radio and newspapers. This was in sharp contrast to Dewey's pattern. Confident of election, he paid little attention to small-city stops. He would repeat a few banalities in a friendly manner and be gone. Newsmen who alternated between the Truman and Dewey trains, spending two or three days on one before returning to the other, confided to me that they didn't bother to leave Dewey's press car to listen to his rear-platform remarks: "The governor just repeats himself and doesn't say anything anyway."

Sometimes I had to write a full text, not just notes, as I described in a September 23 letter to my parents just after the train had pulled away from Modesto, California, the Central Valley town where both had spent their childhood. (This was the only campaign letter I recall having had time to write.) An excerpt gives the flavor better than anything I can write six decades later:

> Yesterday was the worst day yet of the "Whistle Stop Campaign." I wrote a fifteen minute speech for Sacramento, only to have to discard it when the State Democratic Chairman said that there was a bitter intra-party fight on the subject in California, and that such a speech would cause him no end of trouble. . . . Of course, I had to write another speech. . . . In the meantime, the topic we had expected the President to discuss in Oakland was switched on us by the President himself. We met that emergency by a scissors and paste job hastily put together from speeches prepared for other cities. Clifford did most of that while . . . I went to work dictating partly from memory and partly from Washington notes the text of an "off-the-cuff" speech for the President to make from the steps of City Hall in San Francisco. . . . All of this was going on while we were stopping at the small towns and being plagued by the local politicos who board the train to ride for a few miles and who want to tell us exactly how to run things.

When we reached Washington on October 2, Truman had spoken 134 times and traveled 8,600 miles. There is no need to write about the later trips. They were "just more of the same." However, a few personal comments will illustrate the contrast between 1948 and modern times. Presidential security was naively simple. Each of us in the presidential party wore a blue lapel button with a white star throughout the campaign. This allowed us to pass through police lines no matter in what city. The train was freely approachable, and anyone with the blue button could invite a guest aboard without question, as I did with a cousin who dined with me on the train while riding from Kansas City to Topeka. Such freedom is unthinkable today.

I was also free to introduce friends to the Trumans. In Oklahoma City, for example, while Truman was at a ballpark for a "big" speech, I slipped off for a quick supper with a former Map Room colleague, Charley Berry, and his young bride. She was full of questions. Never having traveled overnight on a train, how did one manage? I said that one of the joys of stopping for a few hours in a large city was the opportunity for a bath at a hotel. The Berrys drove me to the station, arriving moments before the Trumans. I introduced them both. Charley's wife blurted out, "Mrs. Truman, have you had a bath?" Mrs. Truman looked quizzically at me, wondering what in the world I might have been saying about her. I blushed profusely. When I later explained and apologized for the kind of question one does not toss at a First Lady, she laughed heartily.

Despite Mrs. Truman's reserve in public, she was warmly human to those she knew. To me she was just like the members of my mother's chapter of PEO back home. I had no trouble relating to her. Years later, *Time* magazine writer Hugh Sidey wrote a short piece recalling the Truman '48 campaign by train and included this bit: "George Elsey . . . remembers the hard work, the sleepless night preparing speeches. . . . Once, when he took papers to Truman, who was dining with Bess, she looked up at Elsey and said, worried, 'You look peaked. Have you had anything to eat?' No, admitted Elsey, who had been just too busy for food. 'Here,' she said, pushing her piece of apple pie to him. 'You can eat this, and I shouldn't.' The *Ferdinand Magellan* with Harry Truman rolled on into history that night, fueled by apple pie."

Despite the pressures on him, Truman was similarly "human." In Colorado, one evening, I walked from my car to his with outlines for the next day's rear-platform talks. He asked if I had been looking at Pike's Peak. Dog-faced, I admitted I hadn't been aware we were near it. "Well, you must see it," and he took me out to the platform for a good look. We stayed out for a half hour in balmy weather while he talked about the mountains and the Royal Gorge through which we passed. His long association with the Old Trails Club seemed to have given him an encyclopedic knowledge of western geography.

While the work was hard, the warmth of Bess and Harry Truman made the trips enjoyable in a way that my "spies" said was in sharpest contrast to the tightly buttoned, stiff-lipped atmosphere of the Dewey train.

I learned other things from the reporters who divided their time between trains. They perceived Truman's crowds as growing steadily larger, while Dewey's were static—or shrinking. "Why?" I would press. The answers usually went something like this: "Dewey knows he has the election in the bag. He doesn't say anything. He doesn't want to upset anybody. Truman is putting on a big show. People may think he's going to lose, but he's free entertainment. He 'pours it on' the Republicans. When somebody out there in the crowd shouts, 'Give 'em Hell, Harry!' he shouts back, 'I'm just telling the truth about them and they think it's Hell!' And the crowds love it."

And so we went, down to the wire on November 2, 1948.

Every poll and every major newspaper forecast an overwhelming Dewey win. (Even Bess Truman, in a private conversation in the last week, conceded defeat.) Arthur Krock of the *Times,* widely regarded as one of the nation's shrewdest analysts, gave Truman 105 Electoral College votes "at most." In late October, he pressed Clifford for his estimate, which was 269, the slimmest margin over the 266 needed. Privately, Clifford confessed to me that he didn't believe his own count. But what did Harry Truman himself believe?

On October 13, while we were riding from Duluth, Minnesota, south to the Twin Cities, I was alone with Truman going over material for future whistle-stop talks. He interrupted and told me to start writing. He began rattling off the names of the forty-eight states (Alaska and Hawaii were still territories). Knowing by heart the number of electoral votes for each state, he told me where to put them on the sheet I marked in columns for Truman, Dewey, Wallace, Thurmond, and Doubtful.

When he'd finished, he asked, "George, how many do I have?"

Quickly adding, I answered, "340, Mr. President."

He smiled confidently. (In our haste, we had omitted Utah's four votes, but it scarcely mattered.)

When I showed my tabulation to Clifford (but to no one else), he shook his head in wonderment at Truman's delusion.

Truman was, in fact, too optimistic, receiving only 303 Electoral College votes, but even that was comfortably over the 266 needed. And my private session with Harry Truman on October 13 is why I always answer, when asked if Truman really thought he could win, "No, he did not *think* he would win, he *knew* he would win."

So much for what Truman, Mrs. Truman, Clark Clifford, and the press thought. What did I think? When asked, I've evaded, usually by saying I was certain the tide was running strongly in favor of Truman, but I wasn't certain that he'd be safely ashore by November 2. The fact is, I thought Truman would lose. I left the campaign party in Independence the Sunday evening before the Tuesday election for the long train ride back home to vote, Pennsylvania at that time having no provision for absentee balloting. On Monday, as a Baltimore and Ohio train puffed its way across Illinois, Indiana, and Ohio, I bought every paper available at each of the many stops. That evening, I filled out a chart torn from a magazine and could do no better than to give Truman 219 Electoral College votes to Dewey's 270 and Strom Thurmond's 42. So much for my analytical skills!

Why did Truman win? Some weeks after the election, I was invited to discuss the campaign with a political science class at Princeton. Unknown to me at the time, a student took down my words in shorthand, and a copy found its way to me years later.

What I said in forty minutes was concisely said by the "Sage of Baltimore," H. L. Mencken, in a few sentences: "Truman . . . assumed as a matter of course that the American people were just folks like himself. He thus wasted no high-falutin rhetoric upon them, but appealed directly to their self-interest. A politician trained in a harsh but realistic school, he naturally directed his gaudy promises to the groups that seemed to be most numerous, and the event proved that he was a smart mathematician."

In my opinion, the outcome of the 1948 election would likely have been different had television coverage been as broad as it was to be just four years later. In 1948, there were fewer than half a million TV sets in the country. This was the last election in which television played no measurable role, as I told a young Harvard senior, Albert Gore Jr., when he interviewed me in 1969 for his thesis, "Television and Presidential Elections." By 1952, there were 19 million sets in American homes. Had there been nationwide TV in 1948, Dewey's marvelous baritone, his polished manner, and his well-written speeches (even if they did not say much) would have contrasted favorably with Truman's folksiness. That went over well in face-to-face meetings but went over poorly when he stood before a newsreel camera or struggled with a prepared text. By 1952, TV made Truman's style obsolete. There would be no more whistle-stop tours. An era had ended. Had television blanketed the nation in

1948, Truman might well have been a president who only completed someone else's term and now be as forgotten as Gerald Ford, who is remembered primarily for filling in after Richard Nixon's resignation.

On November 3, I was happy for Truman and proud of my small role, which, to my surprise, in the next few weeks was recognized. A *Life* magazine summary of the campaign referred to "George Elsey, the 'whistle stop' and 'rear platform' expert who had the backbreaking job of preparing material for all save the major speeches." Press Secretary Charley Ross wrote a postelection article for the then popular weekly magazine *Collier's*. About the talks from the back platform of Truman's rail car, he said, "In the aggregate, these little speeches were perhaps more important than the major addresses. They got him close to the people." That, of course, was precisely their intent. And from Key West, Florida, where Truman and his senior staff went to convalesce and unwind, came a letter that I cherished. In warm tones, Clifford expressed appreciation for my work and mentioned that I would be joining the group the following week. I did, with a paper for Clifford summarizing the major items he and I needed to think about in preparation for the inauguration and that inevitable State of the Union address in January. No rest for the wicked!

Chapter Eight

"A Passion for Anonymity"

I had other things than vacation in mind when I joined the president and staff members in Key West in late November. Truman had told the cabinet three days after the election that he would lay out his domestic program in a written statement to the new Congress rather than deliver a State of the Union address in person. He would hit the high points of the domestic program in the January 20 Inaugural Address.

I felt this was preposterously wrong. I wrote Clifford, in Key West with Truman, saying of the inaugural: "No other occasion . . . offers the President so great an opportunity to speak to the entire world. His election . . . confirmed his role as the leader of the free peoples of the world . . . and I believe that his words on January 20 should match the dignity and responsibility of that role." He should at the inauguration, I continued, "set forth the broad principles that would guide our foreign policies for the next four years."

When I arrived in Key West and argued my case in person, Clifford was persuaded and said he would urge Truman to make foreign policy the subject on inauguration day. As to the State of the Union, I argued equally forcefully that a written message was a mistake. The president's prestige was at its highest. He should take advantage and appear in person. When my points were presented to him, the president agreed to the changes.

Now it was our job to "put up," not having meekly "shut up" when told Truman's wishes. Charley Murphy took the lead in preparing a State of the Union speech for January 5. He was given much help by David Lloyd, a new member of the staff, who had impressed us by his contributions to Bill Batt's shop during the campaign. While we were working on the speech one afternoon in the Cabinet Room, Truman walked in and said, in only half-joking tones, "If I run again, I'll pray I get beat." The remark symbolized to me the ambivalence about the job I had so often heard him express.

Sam Rosenman joined us near the end of writing the speech, pitching in with some wise suggestions. The bold, liberal themes of the campaign dominated the text, so much so that when Truman asked John Snyder what he though of a late draft, the secretary of the treasury swallowed hard and answered, "It carries out the president's campaign promises." Privately, he muttered to Rosenman: "It won't appeal to anybody outside the bottom third."

After the State of the Union, we had a few days' breather before hunkering down on the inaugural. One of the pressing issues for early consideration was a revision of the National Security Act of 1947. Forrestal had fought effectively to keep the authority of the secretary of defense limited, fearing loss of the navy's "autonomy." When given that job, he paid the price of his earlier success. He didn't have the power to manage the three military departments. The day after the State of the Union, Clifford and I, taking along an expert on government organization from the Bureau of the Budget, joined Forrestal for luncheon at the Pentagon to hear his views on what additional authority he needed. He was especially upset that the secretaries of the army, the navy, and the air force sat in the cabinet with him and acted as though they were his equals. Eisenhower, now retired from the army and president of Columbia University, joined us at Forrestal's invitation and spoke as I'm sure Forrestal hoped he would.

"You can't legislate unity," Ike said, according to my notes, "and you can't get unity so long as you have a bunch of people all thinking they are equal. If there's one thing I've had experience with, it's in making different people who think they're equal work together. Somebody has got to have authority and jurisdiction and 'court-martial' power over subordinates if effective 'unity' is to be accomplished. I did have that when I had two—or three—nationalities working under me. But you'll not get unity just by passing a law. You have got to produce a plan that the army, navy, and air force agree to before you try to get Congress to change the present law." Obvious advice, spoken by one who had learned it the hard way.

Forrestal was unusually quiet during our talk, but I failed to detect any sign of the mental illness that was to cause him to take his life in three months. As for working out "the plan" Ike spoke of, I was to have no part in it. I would be leaving the White House before the end of January, as will soon be explained.

Having made the pitch for an impressive foreign policy statement in the Inaugural Address, it was up to me to produce. Because of the significance of that speech—to me at least—I quote excerpts of a talk I gave at the U.S. Agency for International Development in 1999 on the fiftieth anniversary of the speech's delivery. The agency was dedicating the Point Four Conference Room. I had been invited to explain the origin of *Point Four* and its meaning.

In that innocent time before manufacturing a presidential speech became such a production, when Clifford or I wanted something on foreign affairs, we simply asked the State Department for a suitable draft. And so it was this time. In due course a draft arrived. It was well written. Indeed, it was eloquent, but I was disappointed. There wasn't anything new in it to excite the country or the world. The draft focused on three points. The first was continued support for the United Nations. Second, economic assistance for reconstruction, e.g., the Marshall Plan. Third, mutual military defense arrangements, soon to evolve into NATO. All well and good, but already well publicized. There was no imaginative new proposal that would capture attention, fire imaginations, and keep the momentum of American leadership in the postwar world.

Then, as manna from Heaven, came a telephone call from a man in the State Department whom I did not know. He explained that he had an idea for the Inaugural Address that he thought I should think about. His visit would have to be in strictest confidence.

My visitor was Ben Hardy. He was the author of the State Department draft, and he was bitterly disappointed that the bureaucracy above him had emasculated the paper. It had stripped out a broad proposal for technical assistance to developing countries. He laid out his thoughts to me. The United States, he said, had the knowledge and the experts to help these countries greatly improve their farming practices, the health of their people, their public works, and their educational systems—indeed, much of what was needed to bring them into the modern world. We had, Ben went on, understandably concentrated on Europe's needs for recovery, but the time was at hand to pay attention to the needs of the rest of the globe. And it would not be costly.

Why, I asked, had so imaginative an idea for technical assistance to the "Third World" (as we then called developing nations) been scuttled? . . . Ben gave the usual answers that one hears from a bureaucracy when suddenly confronted with a new idea. He was told that staff work hadn't been done, budgets not worked out, not the time, not the place to float an untested pipe dream, much work would have to be done before the idea would be ready for the president—if ever, and so on and so forth . . .

Ben Hardy . . . was running the risk of losing his job by making an end run to the White House. I promised that his secret would be safe with me. And so, with Ben's help, Harry Truman's Inaugural Address took on an exciting new look. To the three points of U.N., Marshall Plan, and NATO came a Fourth Point. It was a call for a bold new program for making the benefits of our scientific advances and industrial progress available for the improvement and growth of the underdeveloped areas of the world.

When the expanded draft was laid before the president, his enthusiasm for the "Bold New Program" was immediate, as I was confident it would be. He embraced it wholeheartedly. When he was told that State and the Bureau of the Budget had not yet done any staff work, he laughed and said, "I'll announce it and then they can catch up with me!"

The Inaugural Address's Point Four was greeted with acclamation around the world. . . .

Harry Truman was enormously proud of Point Four. In his memoirs, he wrote more enthusiastically about the accomplishments of the program than he wrote about any of the other foreign initiatives of his administration.

I, too, was proud to have been the intermediary for an exciting new phase of American foreign policy. Other similarly idealistic programs emerged in later administrations—Eisenhower's Food for Peace and Kennedy's Peace Corps are examples. Sadly, we have been proved naive. The valiant efforts of thousands of American men and women have all too often been lost in the turbulence of wars and revolutions in countries not ready—or willing—to accept the hand of "the Great Satan," as the United States is too often portrayed. But each president has tried, and I believe future presidents will continue to try, whatever the obstacles at the time may be.

As I said above, I would be leaving the White House when the inauguration was behind us. Clifford and I had had many long talks about our futures, almost from our first association. They had been more focused as the '48 election approached. I had turned down the opportunity to be director of the Roosevelt Library in Hyde Park, New York, in the spring of the year, not wanting to miss the excitement of a presidential race. If Truman was to lose—as almost everyone expected—I said I would return to active naval duty to assist Morison on his history of naval operations in World War II, staying at that until a suitable civilian job opportunity appeared. I had so promised Morison. When the unexpected happened and Truman won, I felt honor-bound to spend six months or so on the Normandy invasion but told Morison I would not be available to assist on other volumes. Clifford and the president himself said they wanted me back at the White House as soon as I could return.

Whether Clifford would be there then was an open question. He told me he was going broke on his government salary (less than half his prewar earnings as a St. Louis lawyer). Only a cabinet position would persuade him to stay in federal service. He would like to be attorney general, but Tom Clark was staying on. Forrestal, for a variety of reasons, was likely to leave as secretary of defense, and Clifford would take that post if it was offered, but it looked as though the nod would go to Louis Johnson, to whom Truman felt indebted. Johnson had been finance chairman for the '48 campaign, and he would be rewarded for his efforts by getting a job he yearned for. When Clifford had told Truman he would have to leave, he said Truman suggested that he be undersecretary of state, working with Dean Acheson, who would take over as secretary of state, replacing the ailing General Marshall. Clifford confessed that he felt "terribly let down" at Truman's indifference to his financial plight and his failure to express any appreciation for his work. (I shared his dismay that Truman was not profuse in gratitude, but, as I have written, that failure to express appreciation was in character.) Did I think he should accept the undersecretaryship? "Good God, no!" was my reply. Unlike Marshall, who let his undersecretary, Bob Lovett, run the department, Acheson would be a "hands-on" manager.

Rather despondent, Clifford sought out Acheson, telling him of

Truman's offer, that he would decline it, and that he would leave government to resume law practice. Acheson, Clifford told me the next day, was "shocked beyond words" that he would be leaving. Acheson went on to say that the poor caliber of the presidential staff so troubled him that he was not sure he wanted to be secretary of state if Clifford was not at the White House.

And so, with all these uncertainties, I cleaned out my desk, pulled my uniforms out of the closet, and prepared to return to Morison's office in Main Navy on Constitution Avenue. Clifford assured me he would welcome me back with enthusiasm—that is, if he was still there—and President Truman said he would have a job for me as soon as I came back.

Throughout the spring and into the summer of 1949, I worked diligently assembling and examining the voluminous records on the 1944 invasion of Normandy that had accumulated in the Office of Naval History and in the less-than-perfect files scattered throughout the Navy Department. British, Canadian, French, and German papers augmented the reports of our own naval and army units involved in the landings. I organized files and wrote some preliminary sketches that Morison and a retired rear admiral, with extensive work of their own, would later turn into volume 11 of *The History of United States Naval Operations in World War II.*

Ties with friends at the White House remained close. I joined them frequently—for example, at the ceremonies formally establishing the North Atlantic Treaty Organization, better known as NATO. My ties were perhaps closer than was prudent. I was startled to read in late May in a Washington newspaper (there were four in those days): "Rumor has George Elsey, a former right hand to Presidential Assistant Clark Clifford, scheduled for a job as administrative assistant to the President once he concludes his current tour of active duty as a Navy commander. An excellent choice, too, it's reported."

This was disconcerting; in fact, it was highly upsetting. Truman hated rumors or leaks involving the White House. Sometimes proposed appointments were not made because of leaks, usually assumed to have come from the prospective appointee. I most certainly was not the source, nor could I imagine who might have been. If such an appointment was in the offing, there was a potential embarrassment. I was still a registered Republican in Oakmont. The town was overwhelmingly

Republican. Local officials such as members of the council and the school board were effectively elected in the party primaries. Wanting to have a voice in local affairs, I'd kept my Republican registration. But what would gossipy columnists write and how would Truman react if this became public? To avoid a problem, during a May '49 visit to Mother and Dad, I quietly switched the party affiliation, keeping my voting address in Oakmont because residents of the District of Columbia had no voting rights in national elections. No one was the wiser, except Clifford, who was amused at my concerns.

By the way, what was an "administrative assistant to the president," the position mentioned in the rumor? The title dated from 1939 when Congress authorized the president to appoint up to six aides with that title to help him manage the increasingly complex federal government. At a June 1939 press conference when he announced the first appointees, Franklin Roosevelt wisecracked that they were men "with a passion for anonymity." Newsmen gathered around his desk in the Oval Office hooted with laughter. Such a breed was rare in New Deal Washington and unknown around the White House. The phrase was remembered, however, and successive administrative assistants took their cue from it. They quietly took on whatever task Roosevelt—and later Truman—assigned, avoided the limelight, and shunned publicity. However innocuous the title and silly the descriptive phrase, in the days when the White House staff was incredibly small by later standards, holders of those positions had considerable prestige and authority. When they spoke, it was assumed they were speaking for the president. Their status was given a boost in late 1949 when their salaries jumped above the top Civil Service grade.

(Since Truman's time, the White House staff has grown enormously. A slew of elegant titles permeates a sizable bureaucracy. "Administrative assistant" seems too modest for men and women who are anything but, and the title has vanished, forgotten except by scholars of long-gone administrations.)

A week after the disturbing leak—disturbing to me if to no one else—Clifford phoned. "I had a talk with the Boss yesterday. He began talking about his papers and whether he should plan a library such as FDR's. He has you in mind. I told him you had progressed to the point where you ought to be an administrative assistant, responsible directly to him." While the promotion and direct tie to the president would be welcome, I knew that if I was to return, there would be much more to do than plan the disposition of papers reflecting a long career in the public eye. In early July, Clifford phoned again. Truman would name me, he said, administrative assistant on August 15.

Clifford's interest in my promotion was not entirely altruistic. He would soon leave government and had stayed at Truman's strong appeal months beyond the deadline he had set. Now he said his departure in early 1950 was definite. He would set himself up in law practice in Washington, and he would count on me to help him stay in touch with White House goings-on. The higher my status, the better I could do so. In the remaining years of the administration, we kept in close contact, closer than would today be considered proper.

Sworn in as scheduled, I was assigned spacious rooms adjacent to other administrative assistants in the ornate State-War-Navy building. An old-timer told me that my suite had been the office of Major Dwight Eisenhower in the early 1930s when he had been an aide to Chief of Staff Douglas MacArthur. Adding to the aura, I placed framed reproductions of the official portraits of Roosevelt and Truman with their autographs on the mantel of the great marble fireplace and settled in.

My appointment as administrative assistant made the newspapers nationwide. Recognition in Washington, New York, and hometown Pittsburgh papers was to be expected but—to my surprise—friends and relatives forwarded clippings, usually with a photograph, from major cities across the country. Some, like Shreveport, Louisiana, were not so "major." The *Washington Post* embarrassed itself by using the likeness of a former congressman over my name, correcting itself the next day. The *San Francisco Examiner* stretched for a local angle when it headlined its story: "California man gets Presidential Post"—quite a stretch, since I'd left the state when only seven months old!

Radio newscasters also dutifully reported my appointment. In a chatty commentary, Frank Bourgholtzer of NBC pointed out that, at thirty-one years, I was the youngest man "in the president's inner circle." He accurately summarized my earlier duties at the White House, but he was far off the mark when he described me as "rangy and athletic." Rangy, perhaps; athletic, definitely not. He apparently had drawn his conclusion from an episode some months before. "In Key West, Florida, last November," he said, "Elsey and Dr. Wallace Graham [Truman's physician] relaxed by scaling the high wall of an old fort—

barefooted. At dinner that night, the president's daughter, Margaret, refused to believe they were capable of the feat, so the next day, George and the doctor had to repeat the stunt while Margaret watched."

The next two years were enjoyable. As an administrative assistant, I attended the president's morning staff meetings, thus resuming the daily direct contacts I'd had with him in Map Room days. I also resumed weekends on the *Williamsburg* and joined him and the other staff members on the November and March "working vacations" at the Little White House in Key West, Florida. Now I was a full-fledged member of the presidential party, joining in the poker games and the friendly talk of the dinner table. Both on the ship and in Key West, Truman was totally relaxed, given to reminiscences of his political life and pungent observations on past and present political figures. The Senate invariably figured in the talk. "I work harder than any two senators put together; some just work at the publicity they can get." He often quoted Woodrow Wilson's remark that "senators don't have brains. They just have knots on their heads to keep their bodies from unraveling." But he had enjoyed the place, and "I wish I was still there" was a common remark. "Trumanisms," my term for colorful and characteristic remarks, popped up frequently. I give as an example just one of dozens. Annoyed on reading a criticism by a prominent religious figure who referred to his Pendergast associations, he quipped: "There are more Madams in Heaven than preachers and more political bosses in Heaven than political reformers!"

Truman was totally relaxed in Key West. His luncheon and dinner anecdotes were sometimes serious, sometimes funny, and always revealing of the man. I noted a remark on the evening of December 14, 1949, when we had just returned from a formal, rather stiff naval reception. "I don't like," he said, "to go to formal parties. When we're in Washington the Madam is always trying to get me to dress up and go, but what I like to do best is get off some place with a gang of men and tell dirty stories and play poker."

The interest of this quip is that, as I have mentioned before, Truman did not himself tell off-color stories. He would roar at those told by others, but his own stories invariably related to politics, politicians, and historical figures. I never understood the origin of the popular perception that his language was vulgar and obscene, because it surely wasn't. He was especially watchful of his language in the presence of women. If he let a "damn" slip out when a woman was in the room, he would immediately apologize to her. True, he used barnyard phrases at times, but this was to be expected from a man who had spent many years on a farm. It seemed only natural for him to say of a congressional critic, "He's just pulling on a hind teat." Anyone who had ever milked a cow—or tried to—caught the meaning at once.

As for poker, indeed he loved the game. He thought it not seemly to play it in the White House, as Warren Harding had so loved to do, but Key West and the *Williamsburg* were perfect sites. There were games every afternoon after his nap and every evening after dinner. I was included when promoted to administrative assistant. Nervous at first in the presence of veteran experts, I soon found my stride. When I left the president's personal staff, I checked my records of wins and losses and found my net loss for the many, many games was $12.00. Not bad for so many hours of pleasant company!

As for the morning staff meetings, whether in Washington or Key West, I found them unchanged from Clifford's 1945 description of them: "This is no policy making body. It's just a collection of not-too-well-informed men, each one interested only in his own job." There was no hierarchy. Truman was his own chief of staff. Each member reported directly to him and carried out the duties assigned him by the Boss. I was expected to resume working with Clifford and Charley Murphy on speeches and messages to Congress and to take on a new task close to the president's heart. He had begun thinking—as had all presidents before him—of his legacy. In January, as I was leaving for the navy, he had called me into his office to say that he wanted me to return to help him with his papers and plans for a library. Ray Stannard Baker, he said, had done a "fine job" in editing Woodrow Wilson's papers. "I'd like to see that sort of thing with mine." Now that I was back, he wanted me to figure out the best way for his papers to be published as well as where they and all "the junk" he had accumulated could be preserved and eventually made available to the public.

As for editing and publishing the presidential papers, I turned at once to my good friend Wayne Grover, archivist of the United States. Grover and I agreed that Baker had done well by Wilson, and Sam Rosenman's edition of the Franklin Roosevelt papers was excellent, but there was always the question of objectivity when papers were edited by a friend or close associate. Grover and I thought it preferable that

Truman's and future presidents' papers be official publications of the United States government. The National Archives with its skilled staff could handle the job easily, Grover said. He was optimistic. Legislation authorizing this new function was passed in the first year of the Eisenhower administration, but political pressures put the publication of Ike's papers ahead of Truman's. The Truman volumes did not appear for some years.

I take some pride in having helped set the precedent that presidential papers be regarded not as personal memorabilia to be treated as family or friends thought cast the best light on their man but as official public records.

More pressing than the question of the publication of Truman's official papers was that of where they, his prepresidential records, and all "the junk" that had come his way should be housed. Truman decided that he would follow Franklin Roosevelt's example and build a combination museum, archival storage facility, and research library. Where? On the Truman family farm in Grandview, Missouri. This would be built, as Roosevelt's had been, with privately raised funds and then donated to the United States government. Truman asked an architect whose work he admired, Ed Neild of Shreveport, Louisiana, to make preliminary drawings for such a building. When the president gave the plans to me to review, I saw at once that Neild had greatly underestimated the space that would be needed. I went back to Grover and asked him to lend us staff to survey the volume of the prepresidential papers and the probable volume of White House records by the end of Truman's term, as well as all the gifts and other artifacts—many of considerable value—and calculate the space necessary to house all of it. Furthermore, and this was sensitive since Truman regarded Neild so highly, I thought the architectural design was prosaic without the character befitting a presidential commemorative building. I suggested to Truman that a replica of the Oval Office be incorporated into the plan. He could do FDR one better, as the Roosevelt Library at Hyde Park had no element that conveyed the impressive dignity of the White House. This appealed to Truman at once, and the order was given to include the Oval Office as the library-museum's centerpiece. Most subsequent presidential libraries have replicas of the Oval Office—my unacknowledged contribution to the bunch of them (although the idea would certainly have occurred to somebody fairly early).

Cruises on the *Williamsburg* sometimes produced surprises. After luncheon one day, the president drew a sketch of the family homestead, now being farmed by his brother Vivian and his sons. He marked where he wanted the library/museum built. He would need his brother's consent. Would I go out to Grandview and talk to Vivian? On the way, I should stop in Columbia and see the president of the University of Missouri, who had been after him to put the building on his campus. This would be a courtesy call. Truman had neither an association with nor an interest in the university, but he had to be polite.

The stop in Columbia gave me the chance to see a friend from graduate days at Harvard. David Pinckney, now a professor of history, told me quietly that university officials knew there was no chance of corralling the presidential library but felt they had to make the offer as a courtesy to a president from his home state. My visit with the university president satisfied the niceties, and that was that.

Brother Vivian Truman was harder to deal with. He met me at Kansas City's Union Station and drove first to the "Little White House" in Independence. Wouldn't I like to see the place? He didn't have a key, but he was sure we could get one from Mrs. Truman's sister-in-law, who lived around the corner. Knowing very well Mrs. Truman's sense of privacy, I declined his offer. One thing I didn't need was her wrath had she heard Vivian and I had paid an uninvited visit to *her* house.

(Digression: Vivian Truman seemed much disappointed at my declining to see the house that had been built by Mrs. Truman's grandfather and was known locally as the Wallace House. I knew that relations between Mrs. Truman's relatives and the president's were nonexistent. Was it possible, I wondered, that Vivian's disappointment was due to his never having been in the house and his hopes that my visit would give him the opportunity to see the inside of a place to which he had never been invited?)

Vivian and I went to the farm and tramped around, I with the president's sketch in my hand. When we reached the grassy knoll the president had selected as the library site, with its sweeping vistas of rich farmland, Vivian snorted. "Ain't no use wasting good farmland on any ole dang library! Put it over there!" And he pointed to a swampy area some distance away alongside a railroad track. I had not been sent to negotiate. I sought out Vivian's son Harry, who had spent a couple of nights with me in the staff billet at Potsdam six years earlier. The visit ended pleasantly with a gossipy drive back to Kansas City.

When I reported his brother's reaction to the president and allowed as how he had a problem, he laughed. "Vivian's as stubborn as I am, but we'll work it out." Fortunately, the city of Independence came to the rescue by offering parkland close to the city's center and the Wallace House. The Truman farm in Grandview, with or without brother Vivian's approval, would have been a woefully inconvenient location.

Until I transferred to Averell Harriman's staff in December 1951 (as I shall recount in due course), I stayed in close touch with the archives and the plans for the library. David Lloyd, somewhat reluctantly, then took over from me.

While extricating myself from planning the library and the publication of Truman's presidential papers, I wound up my last involvement with documents from the Roosevelt administration. Truman had been reluctant to release the Roosevelt Map Room files of Roosevelt-Churchill-Stalin-Chiang correspondence and similar sensitive materials. As long as they were at the White House (in my personal custody), they were safe from unfriendly congressional fishing expeditions looking for juicy bits to bolster Republican cries that FDR had sold out to Stalin. I felt the time had come to turn over all Roosevelt-era materials to the archivist for transfer to the Roosevelt Library in Hyde Park. There was no need for Truman to be accused of hiding Roosevelt's "sellouts." Somewhat nervously, Truman agreed, and I was able to clear the safes in my office of the last vestiges of Franklin D. Roosevelt.

As I have said, I was expected on returning from the temporary navy duty in August '49 to resume work on speeches and messages. I found that a significant change had occurred in my few months away. Charles Murphy was taking the lead in speechwriting. Clifford's focus was on his soon-to-be-established law practice. Murphy was a better and swifter writer. With a pen and a pad of yellow paper, he could turn out a solid draft of a presidential speech in a couple of hours. Nor did he share Clifford's pretense that every speech from his office was solely his own product. Early in the second term Murphy had assembled a first-rate team of young assistants to whom he gave generous credit. He had plucked David Lloyd when Batt's team disbanded after the '48 election, and he had drawn David Bell and Richard Neustadt from the Bureau of the Budget. (Bell was to become John Kennedy's first director of the budget, later administrator of the foreign aid program and ultimately a Harvard professor. Neustadt was to become a professor at Columbia and then Harvard, where he attained fame as the academic expert on the presidency. Lloyd, the most versatile, died much too young while representing the Truman Library in Washington. Somewhat later, Kenneth Hechler, whose political science class I had addressed at Princeton just after the '48 election, joined "Murphy's speech factory." Ken later served nine terms as a congressman from West Virginia.)

Speeches, messages to Congress, veto statements, and the like under Murphy were prepared in an orderly and timely manner, in contrast to the scramble that had prevailed under Clifford, who, with me as his only assistant, had trouble keeping up with the load. It was a pleasure to work with Charley Murphy and his group, all of whom I knew and liked.

Truman made a swing through the upper Midwest and on to the West Coast in May 1950. The speeches and the "whistle-stops" were so well prepared—and so far in advance—that I joked to Murphy that I felt as though we were on Dewey's train in '48—except, of course, Truman had something to say!

There were occasional exceptions to the team approach, and one I remember well because of its lasting effect. The afternoon following our return from the May trip, the amiable—and very tired—Charley Ross called me to his press secretary's office. Having just returned from lots of speech-making, we had no stomach for more. But, said Ross, the president had been invited to a ceremony the next day at the Library of Congress, where he would be presented with the first volume of *The Papers of Thomas Jefferson,* being published by Princeton. "You're a Princetonian and something of a historian. How about working up some notes the Boss can use tomorrow?"

Just as tired as Ross, maybe more so, I went home, crawled into bed with paper and pencil, and scrawled out a text. My secretary deciphered the scrawl the next morning. I took it to Ross after the morning staff meeting. He read it quickly and led me back into the Oval Office, saying to Truman as we entered: "I suggest you read what George has written. Instead of 'off-the-cuff,' give it as a short address. I'll release it to the press." The president read it aloud, grinned an OK, and soon we were off to the Library of Congress.

What had I written? Not long before our West Coast trip, Archivist Grover had mentioned in one of our friendly luncheons that a committee for which he was responsible was about to be eliminated by the General Services Administration, under which the archives had recently been placed in a governmental reorganization. The committee, known as the National Historical Publications Commission, advised on the government's policies with respect to encouraging and supporting research and publications relating to American history. Recalling Grover's remark about the prospective demise of the commission, after appropriate mention of the importance of publishing Jefferson's writings, I had Truman announce that he was asking the National Historical Publications Commission to consult with scholars in various fields of history and report on what should be done to make available the writings of men and women "whose contributions to our history are inadequately represented by published works." With such a statement by Truman, all talk of killing the commission vanished.

To make certain that he was taken seriously, Truman named me as a member of the commission. Its preliminary report was submitted one year later. The White House release accepting it noted that Truman's charge to the commission had "received a very favorable response . . . economists, sociologists, and historians who work in fields other than that of past politicians welcomed especially the idea of paying attention to captains of industry and labor, inventors, scientists, educators, religious leaders, editors, writers and architects."

Murphy, Bell, Lloyd, Hechler, and others teased me no end that I had proposed some sort of relief program for unemployed historians. Perhaps so, but in the more than half century since Truman's Library of Congress speech, the commission (renamed the National Historical Publications and Records Commission) has sponsored and assisted in the funding of hundreds of scholarly works of American life and history. Of the scores of speeches I had a hand in during the Truman years, this is the only one I wrote from scratch that was delivered exactly as written. I am proud of what it has accomplished.

Because I had been so involved since the outset of the Truman administration in foreign policy speeches and messages to Congress, I cared deeply about how the press interpreted—and the public understood—the international issues facing the nation. We had failed, it seemed to me, to produce a coherent description of our foreign policies in an easily readable, readily understandable form for wide public distribution. Within weeks of returning to the White House, I began talks with friends in the State Department. Bureaucracy being bureaucracy, and the subjects being complex, it was not until the following summer that a draft of an eighty-page pamphlet entitled *Our Foreign Policy* was hand carried from State for my review. A foreword by the president was included. I took the galleys to discuss with the president on a September weekend *Williamsburg* cruise down the Potomac River. When I explained how this had come about and the intended purpose, Truman—who to that moment had known nothing of it—headed for his cabin and started reading. He was back in two hours. "It's a damn good job, but I have some changes. I don't like this sentence," he said. "It says 'three times in recent years we have been forced to sacrifice peace . . . to preserve the independence and freedom that we value even more highly.' We haven't 'sacrificed peace,' we got into Korea to *preserve* peace. Tone that down."

Marginal comments abounded: "So-called communism is a fake and a delusion." A sentence saying that Soviet leaders had marked China for the same subservient status as the Eastern European satellites evoked this: "China has a moral code and cannot take the immoral so-called Communist road." Annoyed at seeing "Communist," Truman wrote, "Change all capital letters in communist and communism to *lower case*." He added "H.S.T." to emphasize this feeling!

In a paragraph on atomic energy, Truman blacked out a reference to Bernard Baruch, whom he denounced to me as a "show-off" eager to take credit for the work of others whenever he could get away with it. This salty remark came as he handed the galleys back. Realizing that these and other off-the-cuff-reactions might need second thoughts, he said I should work it all out with State as we deemed best. That was easily done.

Public response to the pamphlet was gratifying. Within three months of its issue, more than four hundred thousand copies were in circulation. Press, radio, and magazine comments were largely positive, although, as was to be expected, there was some sniping at "Truman propaganda." Demand was steady. An updated 1952 edition also brought favorable reactions. This was another project that I found highly satisfying.

Having come to know James Webb well when he was budget director in Truman's first term, my relations with him as undersecretary of state in the second term continued warm (when Clifford had declined that post, Truman switched Webb from Budget to State). Knowing well my role in getting "Point Four" into the Inaugural Address, Webb counted on me to keep this new foreign aid program under State's control. I found his eloquent arguments unpersuasive. I felt that the Economic Cooperation Agency, manager of the Marshall Plan, had the experience and a better chance of enticing funds from Congress than did State. Nevertheless, we remained friends. He would invite me from time to time for a quiet luncheon in his office to review the Washington scene. He spoke freely. One day in February 1950, for example, he said he was convinced we were "dropping behind" in the Cold War, that Secretary of Defense Louis Johnson was a "real SOB with whom officials at State found it impossible to work," that almost as difficult was John Snyder at Treasury, whose "shocking narrowness" blinded him to serious international economic problems. Even Charles Brannan, the bright young secretary of agriculture, who had been a major asset in the '48 campaign, was "nearly impossible to deal with." Pointedly, Webb bemoaned Truman's "politics as usual" approach to problems. Aiming directly at me and my White House associates, Webb said we were all "concerned with trivia." (Webb was right.) That was not the happiest of our tête-à-têtes, but we continued to get along well.

A month later, when Webb's boss, Dean Acheson, was off on another unproductive conference in Europe, Truman invited Webb down to Key West for a general review of State Department matters. Webb asked Truman if I could sit in on the discussion and take notes for him. Most of the talk concerned prospective appointments to various department and ambassadorial posts. One Truman remark I recorded is interesting as showing that even the firmest of Truman's decisions could sometimes be changed. "The President stated under no circumstances would he consider appointing John Foster Dulles to be ambassador to negotiate the Japanese Peace Treaty—or to *any* other position at *any* time." He had to eat those words some months later when, to win Republican support for the Korean conflict, he named Dulles to negotiate that treaty.

When the talk turned to foreign affairs, Webb declared "Indochina to be one of the most important problems we face." Webb asked Truman if it "could be handled in the same general manner as Greece and Turkey," to which the president shot back: "Absolutely not. The instability of the French government requires a different approach." He told Webb to be "most careful" but gave no further guidance, and the conversation moved on to other topics.

Webb had supported Forrestal's abortive effort to develop a cabinet secretariat, an effort that had gone nowhere. In his new post at State, Webb tried a new approach to achieving better interdepartmental coordination. He proposed that the undersecretaries meet monthly, with formal agendas of topics for discussion and records kept of decisions reached. Webb thought that by lowering the profile from cabinet to subcabinet level, he might succeed where Forrestal had failed. Keeping himself in the background (not easy for him to do), Webb persuaded Secretary of Commerce Charles Sawyer to host a "little cabinet" dinner in May 1950, with me invited as "guest of honor." My presence would reassure the president, and anyone else at the White House, that the undersecretaries were up to no mischief and not straying from administration policies. Webb's initiative also failed. The outbreak of the Korean conflict a month later doomed such idealistic schemes.

As an administrative assistant, I was expected to take on any task given by the Boss. Assignments were many and varied. One of the more unusual was his request that I prepare the annual "Fitness Report" for his naval aide, Rear Admiral Robert Dennison, whom Truman had first met when Dennison commanded the *Missouri* bringing the Trumans home from the Rio de Janeiro conference in September 1947. The navy requires a report on each officer each year from his superior officer. Here was I, a Naval Reserve commander on inactive duty, evaluating one of the regular navy's rising stars. (Dennison was to become a four-star admiral and commander in chief of the Atlantic Fleet during the Cuban missile crisis of the Kennedy administration.) Truman's request to me was not as far-fetched as it might seem. I was better equipped than anyone at the White House save Truman himself to write about Dennison's abilities. During the bitter conflict in late 1949 between the navy's top brass and their counterparts in the newly independent air force, at Dennison's request I had worked with him in preparing statements that became the basis for the testimony of the chief of naval operations before Congress (another unusual role for a reserve commander).

I had also worked smoothly with Dennison when we helped Truman extricate himself from a public relations blunder. In one of his intemperate letters, he had written a congressman some scathing comments about the marines. ("They have a propaganda machine equal to Stalin's" was one of the choice sentences.) I was in the Oval Office on another matter in midafternoon on September 5, 1950, soon after the early edition of the *Evening Star* hit the street with the text of the letter and some vigorous reactions. "You navy people," Truman said, "will have to get me out of this one. It looks as if I'm in trouble again." He leaned back in his chair and laughed heartily. He seemed to think the matter was something of a joke, not to be taken seriously. I was not so sure.

After talking with Charley Ross and Dennison, at the latter's request, I drafted a letter from the president to the commandant of the marine corps. The commandant was invited to the White House, and Truman handed the letter to him in person with appropriate apologies. He followed up the next morning by going with the commandant to a gathering of marine corps veterans where he wowed the crowd with an extemporaneous talk. All was forgiven.

The marine episode was typical. Any problem, large or small, involving the navy or the marines and the White House brought Dennison and me together in friendly partnership.

As an administrative assistant, I was, from time to time, the target of attention from a senator or congressman who was seeking a back-door approach to the president when he couldn't get through the front. I never responded to an invitation from the Hill without checking with Charley Murphy and reporting to him afterward. As an example of such congressional contacts, I'll cite Hubert Humphrey, the junior Minnesota senator. Humphrey's habit of using a thousand words when one hundred would suffice irritated Truman. Unable to get an Oval Office appointment he greatly wanted in the summer of 1951, Humphrey invited me to lunch with him in his office. At the time, Republicans were harping on "crime and corruption." Humphrey poured out his heart on how damaging to Truman and the Democrats in general were the attacks. He felt the president must "make a new pledge of cleanliness in the government" in a great speech. The perfect locale? The Minnesota State Fair! He would introduce the president!

Another senator, Brian McMahon of Connecticut, fed me excellent steaks quite often in his office. Each time he was in a stew about some aspect of the nation's atomic energy program. Murphy thought I should accept the invitations, although we knew the senator was wasting his breath—and his steaks. Only the president set atomic energy policy, and he was not interested in McMahon's worries. He was happy to let his staff hear the senator's whistles in the wind.

One senator with whom we understandably had no relations was

Joseph McCarthy, Republican of Wisconsin. Wildly charging communist infiltration of the federal government, McCarthy made headlines day after day, week after week, in reckless attacks on civil servants, past and present, throughout the second term. Conservative Republicans jumped on the McCarthy bandwagon. Senator Karl Mundt of North Dakota and Congressman Richard Nixon drafted a bill to tighten internal security. So stringent were its provisions that Truman said it smacked of "police state tactics. We've got to protect the Bill of Rights," he told Charley Murphy and me in July 1950. "Jesus Christ, that's what we're fighting for." A connection between Mundt-Nixon and the month-old conflict in Korea was not exactly clear. What was clear was Truman's determination to object to legislation that, in his view, curtailed personal liberties. Congress quickly overrode his veto. There seemed to be no stopping the McCarthy juggernaut, nor that of Richard Nixon, the young Californian fast building a reputation based on "getting the Reds out of government."

In a tactic that, in retrospect, was inexcusable, I prevailed upon a friendly journalist with an "inside" to marine corps headquarters to obtain the personnel file on McCarthy's wartime service in the corps so that it could be scrutinized by a staff member of the Democratic National Committee. McCarthy was boasting flamboyantly about his combat record; Democrats wanted to puncture his balloon. No setting straight of the record, however, slowed down McCarthy's diatribes against Secretary of State Acheson or the "cookie-pushing pinkos" in State. He even smeared General George Marshall. McCarthy's downfall did not come until the Eisenhower administration when his Republican Senate colleagues, having no need to belabor the White House, joined Democrats and censured him. He drank himself to death after having done vast harm to countless loyal men and women.

McCarthy's charge of communists in the government was just one of the issues that made Truman's second term painful. Alleged organized crime throughout the country and corruption in the administration were additional Republican shibboleths hurled at the president, as Hubert Humphrey had so emotionally stated to me. Senate hearings and the incessant yammering of Senator Estes Kefauver of Tennessee led to the widespread impression that the Truman administration was "soft" on organized criminal activity. There was little the staff could do to counter the belief that the president was indifferent. His well-known disdain for J. Edgar Hoover, the longtime director of the FBI, didn't help. Hoover had a near godlike image in the public mind, and he reciprocated Truman's disdain in spades. I knew that Admiral Sidney Souers, former executive secretary of the National Security Council, had a close relationship with Hoover. I sought out Souers and asked if he could think of ways to improve the Truman-Hoover relationship, hopefully to the point that Hoover could be prevailed upon to make some public statements praising Truman's strong efforts to fight crime. (A real long shot!) Souers suggested that he and I call on Hoover and ask how the White House could be helpful to him personally and to the FBI in general. Hoover was easy to flatter, said Souers. He and I saw the director in his spacious suite at the Department of Justice in mid-September 1950. Hoover seemed surprised—and pleased—at our visit. In two weeks, Souers and I had nine recommendations for actions to enhance the FBI, every one of which—no surprise—would involve substantially more money for the bureau. The centerpiece of the wish list was a proposal for an "FBI academy," which could become "the West Point of Law Enforcement." I duly reported our visit and Hoover's wishes to the president and asked permission to work with the attorney general in preparing necessary legislation and budget estimates. My effort was futile. Truman would have nothing to do with Edgar Hoover's "empire building."

"Crime" plagued Truman to the end of the term. So did "corruption" in the government. Unfortunately, there was a real basis for the accusations of skullduggery, especially in the Internal Revenue Service. We on the staff watched with dismay as the president tussled with one painful exposure after another. Souers, remaining close to Hoover, passed to me the name of one well-placed Treasury employee whom the FBI had determined was "fixing" income tax cases. He thought I knew him well enough to warn him to "lay off." I steered clear, knowing his ties to the White House were closer than Souers suspected. (Some years later, Truman's appointment secretary, Matthew J. Connelly, served a prison term for his involvement in such matters.)

Chapter Nine

Korea

The last few pages may portray a business-as-usual atmosphere throughout the second term. However, things were anything but usual from June 25, 1950, onward. Routine staff work continued, but the conflict between North Korea and South Korea overshadowed all else for the rest of Truman's time in the White House.

When Dean Acheson that day phoned Truman, just beginning a short vacation in Independence, to report that North Korean forces were moving south in great strength, the president determined to return to Washington, assemble his advisers, and ascertain how we could support South Korea. When I asked him a short time later how he had made the decision, he said he'd made up his mind to oppose communist aggression "years earlier." The situation, he said, "was like Greece and Turkey in 1947 and Berlin in 1948. The only decision I made was to tell the military to take whatever steps were necessary to meet the situation, and I had made that decision a long time before. All I really had to do was to tell them to get moving."

Truman's knee-jerk reaction was understandable, but in one critical sense it was a mistake. He made no effort to nail down congressional support as he had in 1947 for Greece and 1948 for Berlin. Members of both parties initially applauded Truman's stand against the North Korean invasion, universally believed to be supported by the Soviet Union. However, that support soon diminished. Ill-trained and weakly armed American troops, moving from soft occupation duty in Japan to bitter conflict, suffered heavy casualties. With Congress not on record as being in support of the military intervention, as things got rough Republicans—and anyone else opposed to our involvement in an Asian war—became harsh critics.

In a Bastille Day conversation with the president, I remarked that drafts of congressional resolutions endorsing United States resistance to the North Korean aggression had been kicking around the White House for some time. He said he had never heard of them. "I certainly never would have asked for anything. It was none of Congress's business. If Congress wanted to do it on its own initiative, that would have been all right with me, but I just did what was in my power, and there was no need for any congressional resolution."

This was Truman at his feistiest, but he was dreadfully wrong. And we of the staff had served him poorly by not pressing for a full discussion of the pros and cons of seeking congressional involvement in the opening days of the conflict. It was soon too late. We had "Truman's War" to deal with.

As the situation turned sour in Korea, I was encouraged by the return to Washington of Averell Harriman. I had long admired him, being first acquainted with him during his Map Room visits when home from his World War II post as ambassador to the Soviet Union. I got to know him better when he became secretary of commerce in 1947. He was a vigorous participant in the shaping of the Marshall Plan. In late '47 as plan legislation was being drafted, he invited Clifford and me for a talk on how the plan could be administered most effectively. In what I was to learn was typical Harriman style, the talk went on . . . and on . . . and on . . . We moved to Harvey's, a well-known restaurant a half block from the Mayflower Hotel. Harriman kept right on expounding—and expanding—his ideas. We were the last to leave Harvey's and did so only when the head waiter said he had to lock up.

Having thus known of Harriman's ability to look at complex questions deeply and thoroughly, I was pleased when Truman told us in an early June 1950 staff meeting that he would bring Harriman home in August from Paris, where he was serving as the European administrator of Marshall Plan operations. Truman needed top-flight help. Louis Johnson, Forrestal's replacement as secretary of defense, was causing huge problems. Johnson loathed Acheson and despised anyone associated with the State Department. He was infuriated that State had produced a study (NSC-68) calling for major strengthening of U.S. defenses when Johnson was determined to cut the Pentagon budget to the bone. He had his eye on the Democratic presidential nomination in 1952 and was going to portray himself as a dollar-saving strong man who could whip the military into shape. Truman, torn between his respect and affection for Dean Acheson and his gratitude for Louis Johnson's fundraising that had kept the '48 whistle-stop campaign afloat, was turning to Harriman as mediator. I wrote the White House press release announcing Harriman's forthcoming return to Washington in mumbo-jumbo bureaucratese saying that "Mr. Harriman's long experience in international affairs will be of great value to the President in the development of Government-wide policies relating to our international responsibilities." This vagueness was intended to allay any suspicions on Johnson's part that Harriman's homecoming was a threat to his status.

When the Korean crisis burst on us just nine days after the Harriman announcement, Truman ordered him home at once. Harriman had been a friend of Acheson's since their days at Yale. From his first hour in Washington, Harriman found Johnson's behavior with respect to his cabinet colleague intolerable. Johnson's attacks on Acheson grew ever more vituperous. When Johnson went so far as to tell Harriman he would see to his appointment as secretary of state if he would join in forcing Acheson out, Harriman had had enough. He went to Truman with a litany of Johnson misdeeds, concluding with a report of the crude effort to bribe him into betraying Acheson. That did it.

I was sitting with Press Secretary Ross in his office in early September working on some routine matter when Truman walked in. I jumped up to leave, but the president motioned me to sit down, saying, "Elsey, you should hear this." He told us he had just ended a session with Johnson in the Oval Office. He poured his heart out on his long association with "Lou." He owed so much to him. But disloyalty could not be forgiven. "When he came in," Truman said, "I had a letter of resignation ready. I handed him a pen and told him to sign it. He broke down and cried. I waited and said, 'Lou, you've got to sign.' And that's that. Charley, work up a press release."

Truman already had General Marshall's consent to return to the Pentagon as Johnson's successor. Harriman, Acheson, and all of us on the White House staff who had been privy to the mess were vastly relieved.

In addition to helping Truman resolve a nasty intracabinet fight, Harriman had other valuable attributes. His estimate as to how far the Soviets might go in backing the North Korean assault on the South, based on his firsthand associations with Stalin and other top communist leaders, was of great value to State Department and Defense officials.

And, as chance would have it, he was on a first-name basis with prickly General Douglas MacArthur, commander of all American forces in the Far East. As a rich New York polo-playing socialite in the 1920s, Harriman had often entertained MacArthur at the great Harriman estate a few miles up the Hudson River from West Point when MacArthur was commandant there. Now, when MacArthur's mercurial bursts of ego and his penchant for grandiose statements about the military situation in Korea—not always accurate—were raising Washington blood pressures to dangerous heights, it was good to have someone close at hand who had long known him.

When Americans troops were forced to the tip of the Korean peninsula and there was worried talk of "an American Dunkirk," Truman sent Harriman to MacArthur's Tokyo headquarters for a firsthand assessment. Trusting Harriman completely, in contrast to his contempt for the "youngsters in Washington," MacArthur outlined his plan for an audacious amphibious landing at Inchon on the west coast of Korea that would catch the North Koreans off-guard, endanger their supply lines, and force their retreat. Harriman returned an enthusiastic endorser of the general's plans.

MacArthur's success at Inchon in September raised his self-confidence to new heights. He was itching to overrun all of North Korea and take on China if she entered the fight. His public statements and the increasing uncertainty in the Pentagon as to whether he would obey orders to exercise restraint worried Truman greatly.

One afternoon in early October on a Potomac River cruise on the *Williamsburg,* Truman mused that he wished he could talk to MacArthur face-to-face. The general had turned down all invitations to come to Washington since the end of World War II. (In fact, he had not been in the United States since 1936.) It didn't seem right to order him back with the situation in Korea so precarious. I reminded the president that Roosevelt had met MacArthur and Nimitz, the two senior commanders in the Pacific, at Pearl Harbor in the summer of 1944 for a review of war strategy. Truman seemed to have forgotten this. Someone asked, "Why don't you go out as FDR did?" Charley Murphy, in later years, credited me with proposing the trip, but my recollection is that it was David Bell's question. No matter whose idea it was, a lively discussion ensued as to the pros and cons of a quick Truman visit to the Pacific. His conclusion, "I'll go!"

On Tuesday, October 10, I left for Honolulu with Secret Service agents to arrange for Truman's stopovers en route to and from Wake Island in the western Pacific. MacArthur had balked at flying any farther from his headquarters in Tokyo than Wake, a decision that forced the president to fly three times as far as the general. I welcomed the Honolulu assignment. I could see my former ONI and Map Room boss Bill Mott, now on the staff of Admiral Arthur Radford, commander in chief of the Pacific. I found Bill in a sweat. Radford had not been invited to join the president for the meeting at Wake. Bill argued that the president's ignoring the commander in chief of the Pacific was bad for the navy's prestige. Could I do something?

Still a loyal Naval Reserve officer, although an inactive one, I responded as Bill hoped I would. When Truman arrived, I briefed him on Honolulu arrangements. Also, I recommended that Admiral Radford be added to the list of Wake conferees. "The commander in chief of the Pacific needs to know what will be expected of him as regards future operations in and around Korea," was my pitch. I wasn't sure what Truman's reaction might be, since Radford had been a leader in what had been called the "revolt of the admirals" a year earlier, protesting Truman budget cuts. But Truman's mind was focused on MacArthur, and he answered off-handedly, "Add him to the list." The admiral, whose houseguest I was, was embarrassingly grateful to me then and in future years when he was chief of naval operations and, later still, chairman of the Joint Chiefs.

I had a more delicate assignment as regards the president himself. Before I left Washington, he told me to make sure none of that "damned Hawaiian nonsense" was inflicted on him. No one was to hang a lei around his neck, and no grass-skirted girls were to be photographed giving him welcoming kisses. When I told the governor of Truman's instructions, he was horrified. The president's refusal to accept a traditional Hawaiian greeting would be widely resented. I worked out a compromise. When Truman arrived at the navy's official guesthouse, Mrs. Radford could be photographed putting a lei on him, *without kisses.* Not every assignment of an administrative assistant to the president related to weighty national affairs!

Although Truman was restless and eager to get out to Wake Island for his meeting with MacArthur, he spent the better part of a day sightseeing on Oahu. As we approached the Pali, the great cliff above

Honolulu, the weather looked threatening. I bet the president one dollar that it would not rain. I lost. Later, we made another weather bet. This time he lost, and I pocketed a dollar bill endorsed "Harry S. Truman, won & lost, 10/14/50."

So much has been written about the Truman-MacArthur meeting on Wake Island on October 15, 1950, that I'll pass over it. Truman was euphoric when he returned to Honolulu. Mistakenly, he was convinced that he and MacArthur saw eye to eye on policy. That was the heart of his radio report to the nation, drafted hastily in Honolulu by Assistant Secretary of State for Far Eastern Affairs Dean Rusk and worked over by Charley Murphy and me on the flight to San Francisco. There the president's radio address was delivered before an enthusiastic audience from the stage of the opera house where he had witnessed the signing of the United Nations Charter five years earlier.

The San Francisco report on Wake was to be the high-water mark of the second term. All went downhill thereafter. The news from Korea grew steadily more ominous. Chinese troops were massing for entry into the fray. MacArthur pooh-poohed the warnings and drove his army northward toward the Yalu River, the Korean-Chinese border. Despite warnings from countries such as India and intercepts of Chinese military radio traffic that indicated China was poised for action, MacArthur continued his bombastic statements, which were increasingly out of line with United States and United Nations policies.

November 1950 was a grim month. As warned by friendly Asian countries, as feared by State and Defense officials, but as declared impossible by MacArthur, Chinese forces poured into North Korea. Once again, American and South Korean troops were in retreat, this time in the worst of winter conditions. In an early December press conference, Truman carelessly and foolishly answered a series of questions in such a way as to give the impression that the use of atomic weapons in Korea was under consideration and, to make matters worse, that MacArthur had the authority to use them. My fellow staff members and I, sitting on either side of the presidential lectern in the ornate Treaty Room of the State-War-Navy building across West Executive Avenue from the White House, were sweating blood by the end of the conference. When the session ended with the traditional "Thank you, Mr. President," Ross took me by the arm and asked me to join him in his office to consider the crisis we were sure to be in. Within minutes, State and Defense press

officers were apoplectically phoning. Ross asked them to draft a statement "clarifying" our policy as regards atomic weapons and dictate it to
him as soon as possible. Dean Acheson sent his personal recommendation by messenger. Ross and I consolidated the suggestions, and he took
our draft into the Oval Office. He emerged in minutes, minus his usual
smile.

Despite the "clarification," Truman's press conference words provoked worldwide astonishment and outrage in many capitals. Prime
Minister Clement Attlee, prodded by the House of Commons, announced that he would fly to Washington. When he arrived, Truman
assured him, as the State Department had assured other governments
through our ambassadors, that the use of atomic weapons was not under
consideration and that only the president, not any military man in the
field, had the authority to order their use.

Truman took Attlee, Acheson, and many other VIPs for a luncheon
cruise on the *Williamsburg*. When it was over, I rode with Ross back to
the White House. He was relaxed and cheerful, feeling the worst of this
storm was over. I had scarcely reached my office when the phone rang.
Ross had collapsed at his desk and was dead of a heart attack. Truman
was shattered at the loss of his boyhood friend and stalwart adviser. We
of the staff felt Ross's loss more and more as the administration stumbled
through its last two years without his wise counsel and restraining hand.

The assistant secretary of state for public affairs, Edward Barrett, and
I had become good friends. We spoke frequently about the dangers of
MacArthur's pronouncements. The Sunday afternoon before Ross's
death, as we were both upset by the latest from Tokyo, Barrett came to
the White House. We realized that a direct order from Washington to
MacArthur to "Shut up!" was not feasible. And so, as good bureaucrats,
we composed a broad presidential order requiring that all public statements on foreign and military policy be approved before issuance by the
appropriate authority in Washington. In order that it not appear to be
directed at MacArthur—although, of course, it was—the directive was
addressed to members of the cabinet, heads of defense agencies, and all
ambassadors and military commanders overseas. The next day, Barrett
cleared the draft with Acheson, and I checked it with Murphy and Ross.
I took it into the Oval Office. "Get it out!" was Truman's immediate response. Two days later, cables from the Pentagon went to twenty-five
military commands worldwide.

Ed Barrett's and my hopes that this would rein in MacArthur were not realized. He continued to speak his mind, especially to politicians and journalists opposed to the administration. But the existence of a written presidential directive that MacArthur flagrantly ignored was to have some significance a few months later, as I shall explain in due course.

As the military situation in Korea darkened, with the Chinese forcing MacArthur's troops to retreat for the second time deep into South Korea, so did the economic situation at home grow darker. Prices were shooting up. Defense production was chaotic. Executive branch agencies squabbled furiously. At a cabinet meeting in late December, Truman announced that he was establishing the Defense Production Agency under Charles Wilson, head of the General Electric Corporation. He was going to ask Congress for authority to set wages and prices. "I had hoped not to do this, but the emergency forces it," my notes read. "We're faced with the real thing. I've worked ever since I became president to prevent this. I haven't made as ominous an announcement to the cabinet since I became president."

Truman asked the secretary of state to speak. "The best guess we have as to Soviet intentions," Acheson said, "is Chinese propaganda. They say everything we are doing to strengthen ourselves and Japan and Germany and Western Europe is 'provocation of World War III.' We interpret this as not a bluff. They can push us into war at any moment. We must conduct ourselves on this assumption. Our plans and our promises can no longer be enough to reassure anybody here or abroad. Our only salvation is vast—vast—increase in military power. We are still only spending on the military what we did a year ago. Something colossal must be done. We are at a very critical moment."

Secretary of the Treasury John Snyder was next in cabinet rank. He had no comment, no surprise to me. He saved his opinions whenever he had any, which was not often, for the president personally.

Truman asked Secretary of Defense Marshall, next in cabinet rank, for his views. Apparently feeling that Acheson had covered the international situation sufficiently, Marshall concentrated on the need for increased military appropriations. He reported that congressional opinion supported economic controls and that he was hearing much talk on the Hill of "full mobilization" as in World War II.

Harriman, sitting in as a presidential staff member, was the only optimist. "I still believe," he said, "there is a possibility war can be averted, but we must build up our military strength, and we must keep the Allied governments with us."

Vice President Barkley wanted to know if our Allies knew the seriousness of the situation. When Truman said they did not, Barkley asked, "Can't they be told?" Marshall was firm. They could not be told; we had no confidence in the security of anything we said to them.

The cabinet meeting ended in a fashion typical of government officials in trouble—with complaints about the press. Secretary of Labor Maurice Tobin's remark was typical: "The morale of the people is at low ebb. I blame it on the U.S. press. In World War I and World War II we had wonderful press. Now all we have are cry-baby stories."

In this somber atmosphere, Truman prepared to receive several foreign visitors in the next few weeks. The first to arrive, in early January, was Prime Minister René Pleven of France. I sat in on Acheson's briefing session with the president. The French would want to know, the secretary of state predicted, how fast we could build up our contribution to the NATO forces. They were deeply worried about growing Soviet strength. They would also want to know American views on rearming West Germany. According to my notes of the Oval Office briefing, Acheson did not expect Pleven to ask for anything for his own country. He could not have been more wrong.

France, unlike Great Britain and the Netherlands, was determined to reestablish its pre–World War II dominance over its former Asian colonies, even though they were now nominally independent. The Indochinese were seething for genuine, full independence, egged on by Soviet and Chinese communists. French troops in Indochina were barely hanging on. In three long sessions over two full days, Pleven and his crew asked for substantial military and economic help. Without American support in Indochina, Pleven said, France would be unable to do what was expected of it in NATO. With NATO still in its formative stage and the Soviet threat in Europe keeping Acheson, Marshall, and the American Chiefs of Staff on the anxious seat, the French bluff—if that's what it was—worked. By the end of the Pleven visit, my eighty-eight-page transcript of the talks reveals, our team had made a complete turnaround. What had been a cool "You know that we have our hands full in Korea" turned into a warm "We'll do all we can to help you." Truman seemed to have forgotten the skepticism about the French in

Indochina that he had so forcefully expressed to Undersecretary of State Jim Webb in Key West the previous March.

No American sitting in on the Truman-Pleven talks could possibly have foreseen how this commitment to involve the United States in Indochina would haunt the nation for decades to come.

With troubles at home and abroad, Truman hunkered down and worked harder than ever at his desk. The public saw little evidence of his leadership. Trips were rare. Speeches were few. Korean War news and problems in the economy took the headlines. The contrast with the how the president is perceived today is remarkable. The current president, as I write this a half century after the Korean conflict ended, is "big news" every day. A large White House staff is expert at keeping the president front and center of all government activity. News releases from all departments are coordinated to support and emphasize the president's policies. Presidential flights to cities throughout the nation are frequent. It's a rare day without a presidential appearance on the television news programs. By today's standards, our efforts to bolster Truman's image were primitive—and largely ineffective.

In late January 1951, I wrote a two-page memorandum to Special Counsel Charles Murphy, with copies to other colleagues, proposing that the president make several trips to military posts and defense plants around the country, speaking in his effective off-the-cuff manner to troops and workers. All that came of this was a short trip to nearby Aberdeen, Maryland, to see new army ordnance developments. Good news stories and good film shots for the weekly newsreels at neighborhood theaters resulted, but there were no more sallies from a beleaguered White House. Such a trip was "gimmickry" to Truman, and he would have no more of it.

As public support for the Korean conflict continued to erode, Ed Barrett at State and I continued our huddles. Ed proposed that we arrange for a friendly senator to ask the president why we were staying in Korea. Truman would reply with an eloquent statement, explaining that, if not checked, communist aggression would endanger Japan and all of East Asia as well as undermining confidence in Western Europe. We had the statement ready. "No," said Truman. This would be another "gimmick," and he would have no part of it.

Although such an arranged exchange of letters between the president and a friendly senator was "phony" to Truman, MacArthur in Tokyo had no such qualms. In response to an inspired cable from the Republican speaker of the House, Joe Martin, the general replied in a grandiloquent statement that was at sharp variance with our national foreign policy to keep the war limited to Korea. Martin released the exchange in a speech to the House of Representatives on April 5. Harriman and General Omar Bradley, chairman of the Joint Chiefs of Staff, urged Truman to fire MacArthur forthwith. Acheson and Marshall advised prudence, but a day later all four returned recommending that MacArthur be relieved of his commands. Truman, now greatly perturbed, consulted Chief Justice Vinson, who told him that this was a constitutional matter—the authority of the president as commander in chief was at stake.

Our morning staff meeting on Tuesday, April 10, was the most striking in my memory. Violating custom, I took notes. The president began: "So the staff won't have to read it in the papers, I'm going to tell you now that I fired MacArthur yesterday. Frank Pace [secretary of the army] is in Japan or Korea—I don't know exactly where—he is going to tell him. I'd kind of like to announce it myself."

Turning to Joe Short, Ross's successor as press secretary, "Joe, do we have a press conference on Thursday?"

"Yes, Mr. President. It's an afternoon one at four o'clock."

"Well, I'm afraid it won't hold that long. I'd like to do it myself, though." Referring to Merriman Smith, dean of the White House correspondents, who had once broken an arm while racing to a phone to report on an earlier Truman press conference, he added, "I'd like to see Smitty break a leg getting out of here. Wouldn't they all run!"

As laughter subsided, I asked, "Mr. President, which job did you fire him from, or was it all of them?" (MacArthur had multiple assignments from the United States and the United Nations.)

Truman: "All four of them. And I'm putting [General Matthew] Ridgway in all of those jobs. I've wanted to do it for six months. I guess I should have before this."

(The "six months" was an overstatement; in mid-October, Truman was still basking in the glow of the Wake Island meeting. Ridgway was the field commander in Korea. MacArthur remained in his sumptuous quarters in Tokyo except for quick photo opportunities in Korea.)

The air force aide, Major General Bob Landry, asked, "Does this involve other countries?"

The response was brusque. "No, I have all the authority. The United Nations made me its agent. So all the authority is in the president of the United States. I don't have to consult any other country. But I will tell them."

The naval aide, Rear Admiral Dennison, cheerily remarked, "They'll like it. There will be dancing in the streets."

Someone asked, "Will he retire?"

Truman: "So far as I'm concerned, he's already retired. He has no more right to all those stars than I do. He never commanded more than a division."

(Again, Truman was overstating. In his pique at MacArthur, he was remembering only his World War I service and ignoring his role as chief of staff of the army in the 1930s and his World War II command in the Pacific.)

I had another question: "Does Frank Pace know this?"

Truman's answer: "No, not yet," evoked much laughter. "The reason I'm having Pace tell him is because Ridgway can't leave the front."

Without resolving when and how a public announcement would be made, we moved on to other subjects.

When Pace was located in Taegu, Korea, he was directed to fly at once to Tokyo and deliver in person the presidential order relieving MacArthur of all his duties. The message was sent through the State Department, using diplomatic codes, at General Marshall's suggestion. He knew that the bombshell news would surely leak if sent through the army's system.

Communication glitches delayed delivery of Pace's instructions, but an unwelcome intrusion overtook the Pace plan. Officers on evening duty at the Pentagon were shaken by a rumor that the *Chicago Tribune* was about to break the story that MacArthur was going to ask to be relieved of his responsibilities because of restrictions imposed on him by Washington. Army Chief of Staff Omar Bradley, Dean Rusk from State, Averell Harriman, and Joe Short quickly gathered at Blair House, where Truman was living while the White House was being rebuilt. "They caught me in my pajamas," Truman told me the next day. "I authorized Bradley to send an urgent wire directly to MacArthur. And I told Joe Short to announce MacArthur's release and Ridgway's appointment right away. I wasn't going to let the SOB resign on me. I wanted to *fire* him!"

By the time White House reporters had been tracked down and assembled in Short's West Wing office, it was 1:00 a.m., Wednesday, April
11 (and early afternoon the same date in Tokyo). Short read a terse statement that flashed around the world so quickly it reached Tokyo before
Bradley's wire to MacArthur. MacArthur learned his fate from the press
rather than from an official message from Washington. That Mac-
Arthur was fired "in the dead of night" and that he was not given the
courtesy of an official notice before the public announcement added
more logs on the fires of criticism that soon raged around Truman. It
did not help his mood—or that of the staff—when we learned that the
Chicago Tribune rumor was false. There was no truth in the story that
MacArthur was planning to resign, and hence no need for the awkward
method of his dismissal.

MacArthur was the only subject at the Wednesday staff meeting.
Truman let loose. "MacArthur's going to be regarded as a worse double-
crosser than McClellan, who got in touch with minority leaders in the
Senate. He worked with the minority to undercut the administration
when there was a war on." (Truman later told me he had dug into the
history books to refresh his memory of Abraham Lincoln's problems
with General George McClellan and Polk's with General Winfield Scott
during the Mexican War.)

With generous help from State and Defense, our White House group
led by Charley Murphy spent the day writing a radio address for
Truman to deliver at 10:30 that evening stating in simple language why
we were fighting in Korea, why the war must be limited to Korea and
not extended as MacArthur had been so publicly urging, and why it had
been necessary to replace him. We worked under such pressure that we
neglected to name his successor. As I noted in my file of the speech, "At
10:23 p.m. Averell Harriman arrived in Matt Connelly's office [next to
the Oval Office] and asked me if there were any references to General
Ridgway in the president's speech. Startled, I confessed there was none.
Harriman and I hastily composed a sentence, and I took it into the Oval
Office. It was then about 10:26. The president was just closing his notebook, having been reading the speech aloud to himself. There wasn't
time to type the new sentence. I paper-clipped my longhand to his text
at the right place, just as he was ready to go on the air."

(In talking with one of George Bush's speechwriters in October 2001
about presidential speech preparation "then and now," I showed him

my notes on the April 11, 1951, radio address. He was dumbfounded at the contrast between our "primitive" practices and the massive machinery involved in preparing a modern White House television production.)

Although I had no intimation of it at the time, MacArthur's dismissal was to have a profound effect on my future. When I returned to my apartment late Thursday, April 19, the day after MacArthur's tumultuous welcome in Washington, I found an accumulation of "urgent" messages from Anthony Leviero. "Tony" was the well-respected White House correspondent of the *New York Times.* We were on friendly terms. When I returned his calls about 11:00 p.m., he said, "Thanks, but when I couldn't reach you, I called [Assistant to the President] John Steelman. He'll talk to the president on the matter I was calling you about. Please check with him in the morning."

At the end of the next day's staff meeting, Steelman asked me to remain. He told the president that Leviero wanted to do a story for the *Times* on the Wake Island meeting that would show how wrong MacArthur had been when he had told the president that the Chinese would not enter the war, as well as how false his assurances had been that American troops would start coming home by Christmas 1950. Steelman urged the president to let Leviero have the record of the Wake Island talks; it would take the wind out of MacArthur's sails. The general was being idolized by Republicans, and he didn't deserve to be.

Turning to me, the president asked, "You have a copy of those minutes, don't you?"

"Yes, Sir."

"Well, go ahead and let Tony have his story."

"What about Joe Short?" I asked, knowing how sensitive the press secretary was when any staff member other than himself dealt with the press.

"Don't tell Joe now," was the reply. "He'll find out later."

I called Leviero and asked him to come to my office. When he arrived, I handed him a set of the Wake Island minutes as directed. Viewed in retrospect, this was as gross an error on my part as can be imagined. Although told by Truman not to inform the press secretary, I should have consulted Harriman or Special Counsel Murphy. They surely would have counseled the president to give thoughtful consideration as to how and when the substance of the Wake Island talks should be made public.

Leviero's story was a page-one sensation in the *New York Times* the next day. Republicans were outraged at what they regarded as a deceitful attack on their hero. Other newspapers squawked at the unfairness of the *Times* having an "exclusive." The State and Defense Departments nervously denied any knowledge of the "leak." Most outraged was Joe Short. While he could with perfect honesty tell the White House press corps he knew "nothing about it," he felt that the president, Steelman, and I had pulled a rug out from under him. He could not vent his wrath at the president or at Steelman (who outranked him in the White House hierarchy), and so I got the full blast of his anger. He was only slightly mollified when I said that, if he felt that I had acted unprofessionally, I would submit my resignation.

Over the weekend, I composed a letter of resignation, taking full responsibility for releasing the Wake Island minutes to a reporter and making no mention of Steelman's or Truman's involvement. When I slipped in to see the president Monday morning, he rejected the letter out of hand. About Short, he said, "Each fellow here has his own particular feelings about his job. . . . Some people are jealous about theirs. It's tough to be around here. This is a hard place to work. You're young. This is your education." Then these reassuring words: "I need you. You've got something I want." Truman then grew more personal in his remarks than at any other time in our association. He commented that he had had no sons. Did I have brothers and sisters? What were my marriage plans? This intimate talk ended when Matt Connelly, the appointment secretary, came in to say that the cabinet had assembled and was waiting for "the Boss." Nothing more was said about resignation—*then.*

MacArthur's rapturous welcome in the cities he visited on his return to the States was echoed by Republicans in the Congress. His address to a joint session inspired one member to say that this was the "voice of God!" But as congressional hearings on his dismissal dragged on, the aura dimmed. MacArthur's desire to extend the Korean War by taking on China was characterized by the chairman of the Joint Chiefs as "the wrong war, at the wrong place, at the wrong time, with the wrong enemy." This hit home. Calm was gradually restored. Thoughtful writers and television commentators reminded the country that the Constitution provides for civilian control of the military and that the president's title of commander in chief was not intended to be an idle phrase. When administration spokesmen were pressed to show when Mac-

Arthur had violated a written directive from the commander in chief, the only one that could be cited was the one requiring Washington clearance of public statements on foreign policy—a directive repeatedly ignored by the general. This was the directive Ed Barrett and I had drafted on a Sunday afternoon the preceding December!

On the whole, 1951 was a rough year for Truman. General Ridgway recovered most of the ground lost by MacArthur's faulty strategy, but the conflict settled into a costly stalemate. The war became increasingly unpopular. Truman's nerves were raw. He bridled at criticism that he earlier would have shrugged off. I was peppered with notes. One morning, after reading an editorial in a New York paper, he scratched out on twenty-two sheets of a White House memo pad a scathing letter to the publisher. Although the editorial included favorable comments, such as "in these perilous hours, the President's qualities have served the country well," a few unfavorable phrases set him off. He was upset by the statement that "he had accepted mediocrity and tolerated unworthiness" and by this: "In domestic affairs, Mr. Truman has seldom shown rocklike qualities." The president's twenty-two pages of rebuttal were handed to me with instructions to check for possible errors in names and dates. I was to bring them back and discuss.

When I returned to the Oval Office, I said with a grin, "The names and dates are all OK, but there is one problem."

"What's that?"

"You have addressed the letter to the publisher of the *New York Times*. The editorial comes from the *New York Herald Tribune!*"

"The hell I did! Well, forget it. I won't send anything. But hang on to those pages. They might come in handy some day."

And hang on to them I have, to this day.

I was also able to stop other letters from being mailed that would have embarrassed the president. (I was not alone—all staff members were on the lookout for hastily written missives.) One that I held was a highly sarcastic letter to a New York congressman—a Republican, naturally. Truman was "congratulating" him for New York state troopers having arrested Truman's sister in a speed trap in the congressman's district and for having reported the arrest on the floor of the House of Representatives. Had Truman's letter been mailed, Kenneth Keating of New York's fortieth district would have had a field day quoting to the House its intemperate language.

Another letter I stopped was a six-page, longhand draft that Truman proposed sending to those members of Congress who had introduced a bill to repeal the tax-exempt status of the presidential expense allowance. Feeling sorry for himself—not Truman's usual frame of mind—he wrote that he was "harassed, misrepresented, and lied about," that he had "no future to look forward to," and that it cost him "$15,000 to $18,000 a year for the upkeep of the White House." He listed his taxes, wrote of his seventeen-hour-a-day workload, and concluded, "No president of a great corporation ever has to go to the poor house after retirement. Some demagogues would like to see that happen to the present occupant of the White House. He would do that rather than exploit for personal gain the greatest office in the world." The president's self-pitying letter deserved a quiet burial, which it got after I had an equally quiet talk with him.

But too many letters escaped staff review.

In the later months of 1951, I was drawn ever closer to Averell Harriman on matters relating to State and Defense. When he was attacked by congressional Republicans for having been at the Yalta Conference with Stalin in February 1945, where Roosevelt was alleged by Republicans to have "sold out" Eastern Europe to the communists, I worked with Harriman's able legal assistant, Theodore Tannenwald, in preparing a long explanation of what the Yalta agreements were—and were not. Harriman relied on it in his congressional testimony and then printed it for wide circulation. Harriman began to include me in luncheons and dinners in his rented, historic eighteenth-century mansion on Foxhall Road, regrettably torn down some years later and replaced by an exceedingly ugly German embassy residence.

By the autumn of 1951, Harriman was clearly the most important member of Truman's staff. He functioned in the role today called the national security adviser. He was convinced that the hugely successful Marshall Plan, scheduled to end in 1952, must be transformed and continued. It should be coordinated with the Pentagon's military assistance programs for friendly nations and also with the Point Four technical assistance activities. Reaching out to helpful Republicans and stalwart Democrats, Harriman oversaw the writing of an act that pulled everything together under the direction of a newly created cabinet-level post, the "director for mutual security." In effect, he had written his own job description. Truman nominated him, and he was easily confirmed in November.

I had followed this with close interest. I could go no further up the White House ladder. In any case, the administration would be ending in little more than one year, and I had the future to consider. Returning to Harvard to complete the Ph.D. had no allure. There seemed to be many possibilities in the expanding, challenging field of international development.

And I had another, most pressing reason to consider the future. The most important event in my life was impending. In mid-September, I had proposed marriage to Sally Bradley. Happily for me, she had accepted. My lonely bachelor days were soon to be over.

Sally was a fifth-generation Washingtonian—a rarity. A great-great-grandfather, Abraham Bradley, had been sent to Washington from Philadelphia in midyear 1800 by President John Adams to establish the "general post office" in anticipation of the federal government's move to the new capital city in November of that year. (The GPO was the forerunner of the Post Office Department now known as the United States Postal Service.) Bradley family members had been in Washington ever since, successfully and happily engaged in public and private affairs. Sally's father was a well-respected and well-connected attorney who had served in the Department of Justice during World War I. Sally, the youngest of four, had a brother and a sister who lived with their families in nearby Virginia, while another married sister and her family lived in Connecticut. Numerous cousins and family connections were scattered throughout the Washington area. One of my former Map Room colleagues had been a boyhood friend of one of Sally's brothers-in-law. His introduction of us led to my gradually being drawn into the lively doings of "the Bradley clan." I found the clan—and Sally in particular—sheer joy to be with.

Sally at the time was on the administrative staff of the Madeira School, a private girls' secondary school located on breathtakingly beautiful Virginia countryside overlooking the Potomac River. She had graduated from Madeira a few years earlier and attended George Washington University before dropping her studies to become a Red Cross volunteer during World War II. She was now back at Madeira assisting Miss Lucy Madeira, who had founded the school in 1906 and was an imposing, formidable presence.

My courtship of Sally had been much too slow. (It was the only time in my life when I was slow in coming to a major decision. I have no excuse and have always regretted my tardiness.)

Although lonely, my bachelor days had not been totally dull. My Map Room associates and, later, my White House colleagues had been generous in including me in social activities, and I had a large circle of Washington friends, but going home alone to the apartment at 1020 Nineteenth Street was a far cry from family life.

Only an occasional event from bachelor days sticks in my mind. In one, Mrs. Kermit Roosevelt, the lady who had failed to recognize Admiral Leahy at Hyde Park when he was the country's top-ranking military officer, included me in a wartime gathering of Roosevelts, Democrats and Republicans alike. I counted fourteen members of the Hyde Park and Oyster Bay clans assembled in her Willard Hotel suite, the one best known to the public being Anna Roosevelt Boettiger, FDR's daughter. Anna and her husband had left their home in Seattle to move into the White House so that Anna could provide companionship to her ailing father during her mother's frequent absences. The party was something to write home about—but only to my mother. Dad would have had apoplexy at my associating with such "riffraff." Amusing moments were many. I concluded my letter: "Later on in the evening some of the younger ones got into a violent argument about whether Roosevelts were better in groups or alone. It got hotter and hotter until Mrs. Kermit R. settled it by saying that so far as they themselves were concerned, they enjoyed other Roosevelts more when they were in large family groups but she was sure so far as the rest of the world was concerned, they were better taken in small doses, preferably one at a time. There was unanimous agreement on that with Anna leading the chorus."

Chapter Ten

Sally, Averell, and the Red Cross

Sally's father announced our engagement on Sunday, September 23. Note was taken by Washington, New York, and Pittsburgh papers and, of course, the *Advance-Leader* of Oakmont. A round of luncheons and dinners followed. The happy glow of time with Sally was interrupted by my seventh trip to Key West. On October 24, Admiral Dennison sent me a note saying that I was to fly on the president's plane on November 8. Two days after his note, Dennison asked me to join him for coffee following the morning staff meeting. I assumed it would be another problem of some sort involving the navy. Sure enough, the navy was involved, but not as I assumed. Dennison, uncomfortable and embarrassed, told me that orders were being processed for my return to active duty as historian for the United States fleet in the Mediterranean. I realized instantly what had happened. Joe Short's sniping at me, constant since the release of the Wake Island notes, had finally had results. Truman had asked Dennison to find a way to let me save face by returning to the navy in a suitable role.

I thanked Dennison and headed for Harriman's office. Two days later, on my first chance to see the president alone, I was able to report that Harriman had asked me to join him in his new role as director for mutual security. Truman smiled and said, "Just work it out with Bob Dennison so it doesn't appear the commander in chief is keeping a man out of uniform."

Harriman put me to work the next day without waiting for a formal transfer. He wanted an up-to-date report on Point Four, but primarily, he said, I was to be his general aide: "Tell me what I ought to be doing that I'm not." He closed a long conversation with: "Don't fight with other people and don't run interference for me. Let me do the fighting!"

On October 31, the president held a white-tie reception for Princess Elizabeth and the Duke of Edinburgh at Blair House. After the formal receiving line was over, Truman took me aside and asked if my situation was working out all right. I said it was and thanked him warmly for his interest. He wanted me, he said, to be on hand a few days later when Eisenhower was to report on his NATO assignment and to "take notes as usual."

On November 8, as Dennison had written, I flew with the president and other staff to Key West. I carried a duplicate letter of resignation as administrative assistant to the president in case the original had not been included in his to-do file. It had. On the tenth, Short—to his pleasure, I'm sure—released my letter and Truman's response. That afternoon, as he came down from an afternoon nap, the president spotted me and said, "I wrote you a letter yesterday and I meant every word of it. That was one I didn't need any help on." As we went out to the lawn, speaking softly because others were around, he said, "Now you just keep a stiff upper lip and everything will turn out all right. I know it will." I appreciated Truman's "little white lie," knowing that, despite his words, Charley Murphy had written the letter and Admiral Dennison's yeoman had typed it.

I phoned Sally to tell her the announcement of my job change might be in the next day's papers. Indeed it was—page one of the Sunday *New York Times* with a photograph. I had a sneaking feeling that Tony Leviero had something to do with the prominence of the *Times* story, an unspoken "thank-you" for the Wake Island story, which had garnered a Pulitzer Prize for the *Times*.

I excused myself from the presidential party and flew back to Washington. There was much to do. Sally had found a small cottage in McLean, Virginia. We hurriedly signed a year's lease before someone else took it, hoping that within the year we would find a suitable place to buy. And there were many loose ends at the White House involving plans for Truman's proposed library in Missouri, among other chores to complete.

Our wedding on December 15, 1951, was at the National Presbyterian Church, then just off Connecticut Avenue in downtown Washington. The handsome Romanesque edifice, long since demolished, was comfortably filled with Sally's large family of siblings, cousins, and in-laws; my parents from Oakmont; faithful Aunt Caryl from Chicago;

and loads of Sally's and my friends. Sally, her father, and her sister Barbara, matron of honor, arrived in a White House limousine kindly lent by one of the president's secretaries. Moments before they were due, my best man, Bob McMillen, said, "Something's up. It looks like the Secret Service is here." I went to a side window. Sure enough, a fire truck was there. Despite its impressive stone exterior, the church was essentially an old wooden building and a firetrap. Firemen were always on duty when the president was expected. I was flabbergasted. Truman was supposed to have left the evening before for a Potomac River cruise on the *Williamsburg*. He had given me his regrets. Yet here he was, coming down the aisle with Clark and Marny Clifford and my soon-to-be brother-in-law, Morton Freligh. His presence was a token of affection—or appreciation—for which I have been ever grateful.

Sally and I were off the next day for two blissful weeks in Bermuda. Then it was back to work in wet, chilly, Washington.

My work with Averell Harriman developed in an unexpected manner. Having been involved in various ways with the programs he was to administer as director for mutual security, I anticipated association with all of them, especially Point Four. It was not to be. I soon realized the political bug had bitten Harriman. He came right out with it on January 30, 1952, as we were flying in a small military plane to Stewart Field, an airport convenient to Hyde Park, New York. Harriman was to lay the presidential wreath at Franklin Roosevelt's grave in observance of the seventieth anniversary of Roosevelt's birth. Harriman confided that he had asked for the assignment because a large number of New York political figures would be there. He wanted to mingle so they could get to know him. Truman was not going to run again, he said, pledging me to secrecy. (This was no surprise to me. I had always believed it. In my memorandum to Clifford in November '48 relating to the January '49 Inaugural Address, I had referred to it as "Truman's only Inaugural.")

"The 1952 Democratic nomination will be wide open," Harriman said. "I'm going for it. What do you think?"

I was on the spot. I thought the idea ludicrous. Harriman had never run for any office. To the extent that he was known publicly—and it was a small extent—it was as our ambassador to Stalin during the war. That was no plus. He later had something to do with the Marshall Plan, but in most people's minds it wasn't clear what. More recently, he was seen as a troubleshooter for a president whose popularity was shrinking daily. Furthermore, while eloquent in private conversation, he was a lousy public speaker. A likely presidential candidate? Hardly. I do not recall how I answered his question, but I'm sure I pledged my support in any way that I could be helpful.

The next weeks were difficult. Sally and I were trying to get settled in the cottage while also looking for a house to buy. Harriman kept atrocious hours, thinking it normal to work until 7:00 p.m. or so and then saying, "Come to my house for dinner and we'll get this [whatever it was] wrapped up." He told me to find "a good public information man." I phoned William Paley, chairman of Columbia Broadcasting, and asked if Charles Collingwood, the CBS White House correspondent, could be given leave to join us. Collingwood fit the bill perfectly until Harriman's political aspirations became public knowledge and Charles had to return to his nonpolitical job. He remained a valued off-the-record adviser.

"Nobody in all these programs I'm supposed to be running," complained Harriman one day, "knows how to write a decent message to Congress. I'll have a hell of a time getting money this year without a strong message. Do something about it!" I phoned a former fellow graduate student, now on the Harvard faculty, Arthur Schlesinger Jr., and asked him to fly down. Arthur outdid himself. In short order, he wrote the most eloquent and persuasive message on the importance of the foreign aid programs that had yet been sent to Capitol Hill.

And so it went, doing what we could and calling for help when we needed it.

When Harriman went public with his political aspirations, my first task was to erect a "firewall" between his government office and the political office he opened a few blocks away. Anything that smacked of politics was picked up by a messenger from that office, handled there, or sent to the Harriman for President Committee in New York, chaired by Franklin Roosevelt Jr. As Harriman's campaigning for the nomination quickened, so did the pace of his government job. Congressional hearings on the aid programs were under way. Ted Tannenwald and I kept the shop running, meeting Harriman at the airport on his return from a campaign trip, riding with him to the Foxhall Road house, and working well into the night on government business.

Today, primary elections in key states effectively decide a party's nominee for president weeks—or even months—before the party's nominating convention. Not so in earlier years. The nominee was decided by the convention itself, after vigorous struggles and, usually, a number of ballots. Harriman assumed from the outset that he would have Truman's support. His belief was confirmed in a private meeting with Truman on Sunday, July 6. He returned to the office elated. If he truly had that support then, he surely did not have it later. The Republicans nominated General Dwight Eisenhower on July 11. Truman convened his shrewdest advisers, who were blunt. Harriman would not have the slightest chance against "Ike." Still, when the Democratic convention opened in Chicago on July 20, Harriman hoped there would be a deadlock among the other Democratic contenders and that he could, with Truman's backing, emerge as the consensus candidate. But on the twenty-third, Judge Sam Rosenman—still a trusted Truman confidant—asked me to phone Harriman in Chicago and deliver the bad news. Truman would do nothing to thwart the drive for the nomination of Adlai Stevenson and would actively support Stevenson if—as now expected—he got the nomination. He did.

Harriman's pace slackened not at all, despite his disappointment. Having been New York's "favorite son," he was counted on to carry the state for Stevenson. He spoke in every city of any size in New York, and he made swings through western states where his Union Pacific connections served him in good stead. (He had been chairman of that railroad for a number of years before the war.) There was no letup of official duties. Wherever he was, I could expect frequent phone calls. If he found it more convenient between campaign trips to spend a night or a weekend at his New York house, I would fly up with a bulging briefcase of paperwork. With luck, I could catch the 10:30 p.m. "sleeper" back to Washington. Otherwise, I stayed at whatever nearby hotel had a room. Mrs. Harriman—Marie—was rarely in evidence. She abhorred politics and politicians. She was gracious to me, however, and I enjoyed her put-downs of the pompous and her salty language. On one of my early visits, I'd asked where I might wash. "Go through the Library. The painting Winston Churchill gave Ave is on the left. Then look at the one Ike gave him, on the right. Painted 'by the numbers,' it'll make you want to piss!"

Eisenhower's election was, to me, a foregone conclusion. Harriman took off for his winter home in Hobe Sound, Florida, for a badly needed rest, but my phone continued to ring with questions and instructions.

He was soon back, offering promises of cooperation to the many Eisenhower appointees whom he had known for years. Indeed, Ike's cabinet, lampooned as "Nine Millionaires and a Plumber," had more of Harriman's longtime friends than did Truman's. When Harold Stassen, former Minnesota governor and unsuccessful candidate for the Republican presidential nomination, was named to succeed Harriman as director for mutual security, Harriman phoned him within the hour with congratulations and named me as the transition officer to ensure a smooth turnover.

January 20, 1953, was still weeks away, and there was much to do: reports to Congress, budget problems, and a NATO conference in Paris in December. Harriman took me to Paris, more as a gesture of appreciation than for anything I might contribute. At the official sessions, I was struck by how difficult it was for the American delegates from State and Defense to realize their day was over. Dean Acheson, ignoring his lameduck status, pontificated so much that I was embarrassed. From Paris, it was back to reality. I flew to Bermuda to join Sally, who was staying there with her sister Barbara and her family in my absence. Sally and I flew home after Christmas to the uncertainties of a new era in the country's and our lives.

My official ties with Harriman ended on inauguration day, but our personal ties continued. He asked me to stay with him while he contemplated his future. He was torn between returning to his prewar business interests, such as Union Pacific and Brown Brothers Harriman, a private bank serving the ultra rich, or rolling up his sleeves and making a run for the New York governorship in 1954. Either way, he would want me as his alter ego. By May, he had decided to make the political plunge. I had been dividing my time between Washington and New York. By May, I, too, had decided. New York was not to Sally's or my taste, particularly if life was to be centered on state politics. I told Harriman I appreciated his offer, but I would return to Washington.

"And do what?" he asked.

"I don't know," was my answer.

"Well, as you know, my brother Roland is head of the Red Cross. He says that the people at Red Cross headquarters are too ingrown, too set in their ways. He'd like to see some fresh blood—somebody who understands the federal government for one thing. Let's see Roland."

The three of us had lunch the next day at 59 Wall Street, the impressive home of Brown Brothers Harriman. By the time the meal was over, I had an offer to join the Red Cross at its national headquarters in Washington. Sally was even more pleased than I at the prospect of staying in Washington and of an association with the Red Cross. She was proud of her wartime service as a Red Cross nurse's aide and had a high regard for the organization—as did I.

The months with Averell Harriman had been fascinating. I had never before been associated with someone of great inherited wealth. He had homes in Manhattan, on Long Island, and in Florida and a ski chalet in Sun Valley, Idaho. All were beautifully furnished and maintained. The house on East Eighty-first Street, a half block from the Metropolitan Museum of Art, was itself a museum filled with paintings that were later to be prized possessions of the National Gallery in Washington. Harriman's personal library at Eighty-first Street intrigued me. The walls of books were arranged by the color of their bindings. A housekeeper or butler, influenced by the emphasis on decor to set off the paintings, had so arranged them. Not only did I find this amusing, I saw it as insight into Harriman's mind. He paid no attention to books. He learned by serious conversation, being a superb picker of other people's minds. Nothing seemed to please him more than an hour's good talk with a newsman from whom he could glean the current thoughts of political leaders and the mood of the public.

(An aside: Harriman won the New York governorship in 1954 but lost his bid for reelection in 1958 to another multimillionaire, Nelson Rockefeller. He had counted on victory that year, mistakenly believing it to be a sure thing that would lead to the Democratic nomination for president in 1960. With his political hopes shattered, Harriman moved to Washington "to be near things." Sally and I visited him from time to time in his Georgetown mansion. He congratulated me profusely when I was elected president of the Red Cross in 1970. He said he would take full credit. "After all," he asked, "wasn't I the one who suggested the Red Cross to you seventeen years ago?")

As agreed at the Brown Brothers Harriman luncheon, on June 15, 1953, I walked up the broad marble steps of the imposing Red Cross headquarters on Seventeenth Street facing the Ellipse south of the White House. As a starter, I was to be the assistant to the executive vice president, James Nicholson. "Nick," as he was universally known, had been with the Red Cross since World War I. Roland Harriman, bearing the title of president, was a volunteer appointed by the president of the United States. Nick was the day-to-day manager running the shop. Harriman was busy at the Bank, at the Union Pacific Railroad where he had succeeded his brother Averell as chairman, and in many other corporate and charitable activities. He had decided he had too much to do to remain as Red Cross president. He would remain the titular head of the organization, taking the title of chairman. A full-time salaried officer should be president. How Nicholson would fare if such a change took place was not clear, but Nick hoped he would be president.

Within a week of my arrival, I flew with Nick to Worcester, Massachusetts, to see Red Cross disaster teams helping the city recover from one of New England's rare tornadoes. (I had earlier seen the Red Cross in action when I'd flown with Truman in 1950 to review relief efforts for the victims of a four-state Midwest flood.) Barely back from Worcester, Nick and I had our shots and headed for the Far East. The Korean War truce had been signed. Nick wanted to hear from military commanders in the field what Red Cross services they expected for our troops who would be remaining in Japan, Korea, and Okinawa. Thanks to its services for soldiers, sailors, and marines in World War II and the Korean conflict, the Red Cross had prestige and stature scarcely conceivable today by those who know only its everyday programs at home. We were warmly received not only by military leaders but also by our ambassadors in Tokyo and Seoul. Syngman Rhee, president of South Korea, honored the Red Cross at a dinner at the Blue House, Korea's equivalent of the White House. We, of course, paid our respects to the Korean and Japanese Red Cross Societies, the president of the latter being a cousin of Emperor Hirohito.

We reviewed plans for the teams of young women who would soon begin traveling in mobile vans to provide the traditional coffee and doughnuts, movies, and simple recreational activities for the troops having the tedious duty of supporting South Korean forces along the DMZ, the Demilitarized Zone dividing North and South Korea. The leader of this program was to be Marie-Louise Van Vechten, who in later years was known to Sally, the children, and me as the beloved "Metzi." (She remains a close friend in 2005.)

Traveling throughout on military orders, Nick and I returned to San Francisco, where we parted company. He flew to visit Roland Harriman at the latter's cattle ranch in Idaho, where the Harrimans were vacationing. I was eager to join Sally, who had spent the weeks of my absence with her sister Barbara in Bermuda. Nick arrived at headquarters a few days later in a somber mood. Harriman had told him he would not be president.

A day or so later, Harriman phoned me. He had two candidates in mind for the presidency. Both had served in the Truman administration, and he wanted my opinion. Either would be splendid was my response. At the meeting of the board of governors of the Red Cross in November, Harriman presented his reorganization plan, which was warmly received. Harriman became chairman, and Ellsworth Bunker was elected president. Bunker, a former New York businessman, had been Truman's ambassador to Argentina and, later, Italy. Nicholson remained executive vice president. He bore his disappointment stoically.

With the many uncertainties of the past months behind us, Sally and I bought a house under construction in an attractive new neighborhood in northwest Washington less than a mile from her parents' former home and prepared for the arrival of our first child. (The address was 4747 Berkeley Terrace, later renumbered 4751.)

I soon moved from Nick's office to become executive assistant to Bunker. When he left in December 1956 to be Eisenhower's ambassador to India, I continued as executive assistant to the new president, General Alfred Gruenther, who had just retired as commanding general of NATO. I got along well with this four-star general widely known for an explosive temper and a stern impatience with staff. Gruenther promoted me to vice president with responsibility for international services, safety and nursing services, and a cluster of administrative offices. There is no need to dwell on these years in the detail that I have used in writing about White House experiences; they would have no interest for anyone. It's enough to say that I was always busy.

The memories of those years that most linger are of foreign travel, worth mentioning if only to demonstrate how different the international climate then was from that of today—and, incidentally, the slower pace of those years.

In May 1954, Nicholson and I, with Red Cross Counselor Harold Starr, sailed for England on the *Queen Mary,* much changed from the World War II troopship on which I had crossed ten years earlier. In England, we visited British Red Cross headquarters. The countess of Limerick, then its leader, briefed me on peculiarities of the meetings we were about to attend in Oslo, Norway. "You will learn, Mr. Elsey, that in many European countries the Red Cross is headed by the nobility or the senility—frequently the two combined."

After quick stops in Copenhagen, Helsinki, and Stockholm, meeting our counterparts in each place, we arrived in Oslo for a biennial meeting of the League of Red Cross and Red Crescent Societies. (Muslim countries use their religious symbol of the crescent.) Some fifty societies were on hand, seated in meetings according to the French spelling of their countries' names. Thus Etats-unis found itself next to Espagne. I quickly found Lady Limerick's pungent observation to be true. Spain was represented solely by his excellency el duque de Hernani. The venerable duke was prone to naps. When it came time for a vote on a resolution, I would nudge him awake. He would sleepily ask "oui ou non?" I would tell him how we would vote. He would hold up Spain's name card accordingly and then drift back to sleep.

In 1954, the Cold War was at its coldest—except in our Oslo sessions. The Soviet Union's lively delegation sought us out at coffee and tea breaks. We were soon on a first-name basis. Had we been seen at home on such friendly terms, the FBI and the CIA would have put us on their suspect lists. A medical doctor in the Soviet group explained to Harold Starr that he was an expert on venereal diseases. "If I can be of service to you," he told Starr one day, "please let me know." We decided that if this was Soviet humor, we'd stick with the Yankee brand.

After we returned home, informal contacts with the Soviet Red Cross were kept open through correspondence, carefully worded in formal stilted phrases to avoid suspicion by government snoops—theirs or ours. By early 1956, the Cold War seemed to have thawed a bit. Bunker approached the State Department. How about, he asked, an exchange of visits between the American and Soviet Red Crosses? State, already thinking that cultural and educational exchanges might lead to better relations, agreed that the nonpolitical Red Cross was the ideal guinea pig. In June, Bunker, Nicholson, a member of the Red Cross Board of Governors, and I set off for the USSR. We were warmly received by our friends of Oslo days and given two weeks of strenuous sightseeing in Moscow, Kiev, Sukhumi on the Black Sea coast of Georgia, and Leningrad. We tramped through miles (or so it seemed) of hospital corridors, nursing schools, factory assembly lines, and collective farms being shown Red Cross volunteers at work. Bunker's diplomatic experience was evident. He skillfully avoided our being photographed in situations that might be embarrassing if shown in the States. McCarthyism still lingered. To the chagrin of our hosts, he sidestepped every effort to have us pay our respects at Stalin's tomb.

The American ambassador was "Chip" Bohlen, my friend from the wartime White House. Bohlen was cautiously optimistic that our trip might do some good. In a meeting in his office, we described the efforts the American Red Cross had been making since the end of the war eleven years earlier on behalf of citizens in our country seeking to learn the fate of relatives in the Soviet Union. Many, if not most, were presumed to have died, but the uncertainty of their fate was painful. We had sent thousands of inquiries to the Soviet Red Cross. Not a single one had been answered. We told Bohlen we had made an emotional pitch during this visit for some response but had no intimation of success.

However, soon after our return to Washington, the floodgates opened. Replies to our inquiries by the hundreds came week after week. It seemed that the Soviet Red Cross had looked into each of our inquiries through the years, but the results had been sequestered by government order. It took us months to find the current addresses of the Americans who had turned to us for help. Many had died without ever learning the fate of their kin. Why had the Soviet government belatedly allowed its Red Cross to answer us? When Bunker and I later read that American security personnel had discovered that the image of the Great Seal of the United States displayed so colorfully behind Bohlen's embassy desk had been "bugged" by the Soviets, we thought we might have the answer. Was it possible that our talk with Bohlen, overheard, had finally brought the matter to someone high enough in the Soviet hierarchy to recognize that brownie points could be earned by allowing the release of the searches for lost relatives?

On our flight home, Bunker told me to start planning for a reciprocal visit in September and that I should accompany the Soviet delegation. Planning was not easy. Many chapters, when I phoned, were adamant. "No Reds here!" Anticommunist feelings were running high, fueled by revelations of Soviet espionage in our country. Also, many cities were ruled off-limits by our government in retaliation for comparable restrictions in the USSR. My hope of showing off my Pittsburgh chapter was out. The head of the Soviet Red Cross was Dr. G. A. Miterev, who had served as Stalin's minister of health during the Second

World War. He was therefore particularly unwelcome to rabid communist haters. Miterev had told me in Moscow that he especially wanted to see Disneyland, then a novelty enjoying world publicity. I found it to be on the banned list. National security was obviously not involved. This was just cussedness on our part in response to some cussedness of theirs.

My greatest problem was in finding interpreters. Few Americans other than those in academia or government were fluent in Russian. I finally found a young couple, she of Russian descent and he a staff member of the Brookings Institution. Vera Garthof told me her family background and promised she would not reveal it to our Soviet guests.

As had our hosts in the USSR, we placed primary emphasis on showing our guests the services of the Red Cross with sightseeing tossed in as a bonus. Our visitors were astonished at the insignificant size of the White House contrasted with the palaces they knew, but they seemed impressed that the guards there knew me and addressed me as "commander." They were incredulous when told, "Yes, President Eisenhower is here in his White House office now." That the public could walk freely in the home of the president was nearly beyond their comprehension. (Alas, no longer.)

After Washington, we rarely spent time on the sights, although in Nashville we made the obligatory visit to Andrew Jackson's home, the Hermitage. Its name baffled Miterev. How could the name of that great palace in Leningrad be given to this simple country house?

To Miterev, Vera Garthof was just an interpreter doing a menial job. He treated her rudely, expecting her to help with his luggage. When we were delayed in leaving Nashville for St. Louis by bad weather, Miterev was at his crudest. Vera, pushed beyond her breaking point, suddenly lashed out at him. As she spoke, Miterev registered astonishment and his demeanor totally changed. At that moment, our plane was called. I handed my briefcase to Vera while I shuffled boarding passes. Miterev stormed up to me, seized my briefcase from Vera, and spouted stormy Russian in my face. Vera calmed him. We boarded the plane.

"Vera," I asked when we were seated. "What in heaven's name was that all about?"

"Mr. Elsey, I owe you an apology."

"Whatever for?"

"I promised you I would not tell anyone of my family background. When he became impossible, I told him who I was."

"Why did that shake him up so?"

"Because he was born a peasant on my grandfather's estate!"

From that moment, Vera Garthof was the honored member of our group. Miterev opened doors for her and saw that everyone—including me—treated her with the respect due her status. What a revelation! A peasant's reverence for a descendant of exiled Russian nobility had survived a half century of communism, even in one of Joseph Stalin's trusted lieutenants.

The Red Cross Chapter in St. Louis chartered a small excursion sidewheeler for a Mississippi River cruise. Factory smokestacks were everywhere visible. Miterev, reminding us—again—that he was a former minister of health, began a disquisition on the hazards of industrial pollution. He demanded of our surprised St. Louis hosts what their city was doing about it. This was 1956—a number of years before "clean air" was a hot topic in the United States. Our hosts were surprised by the question and embarrassed when not a single one knew of any efforts to cut down on factory emissions. Miterev had the better of us, knew it, and reveled in his superior position. Suddenly I was glad that we were not going to my hometown. Pittsburgh at that time richly deserved its nickname of the Smoky City. (Years later, after the collapse of the Soviet Union, we became aware that Miterev's boasts about his country's "clean air" efforts were wild exaggerations.) St. Louis, incidentally, was the only city on our itinerary where the FBI asked me to account for our activities.

We included visits to private homes at every stop, making a point of it because we had never been allowed inside a house in the USSR. We included a simple apartment in lower Manhattan, a farmhouse in the Midwest, and comfortable houses in the suburbs of several cities. We tipped off our hosts in advance that we wanted the visitors to see typical American homes. As the trip progressed, our guests realized ordinary citizens enjoyed comforts beyond their imaginations. They tried, without success, to hide their amazement. We were on guard not to gloat at American abundance.

Only in Chicago did my plans go awry. Leaders of the Red Cross in the Windy City, nervous at the publicity the Soviet group had been receiving elsewhere, asked me to limit our visit to a few hours on a Sunday and to avoid the press at all costs. Too many residents of the area were refugees from Eastern Europe or had relatives there, and demonstrations might occur. And so we crept away on the New York Central's premier train, the Twentieth Century Limited. Alas, the Century was no longer a great train. Beaten by airline competition, it was ill maintained and sadly worn. We had been treated much better on the Red Arrow from Moscow to Leningrad.

After a quick review of the New York chapter's excellent services and the obligatory visits to the Empire State Building and Radio City Music Hall, Vera Garthof and I—with great relief—said farewell to our guests at Idlewild (now known as the JFK Airport).

Our exchange of visits had gone smoothly overall. The State Department was pleased. The White House took note. The way seemed clear for the two governments to plan a variety of cultural and educational exchanges. All such thoughts ceased abruptly that autumn when the Hungarian people rose in rebellion against their Soviet masters. The rebellion was put down brutally. Hungarians by the tens of thousands fled westward, many making it to the United States. The American Red Cross manned refugee centers in Europe and receiving stations at home. Soviet-American relations went into a deep freeze. Our exchange was in vain—at least for a few years—except for those long-delayed reports on World War II lost relatives, which continued to come despite a colder Cold War.

Bunker left us at the end of 1956 to resume his diplomatic career as ambassador to India. My sorrow that he was leaving was tempered by knowing that we would meet the coming October when an international Red Cross conference would be held in New Delhi. Soon after his successor, General Gruenther, took over, the general asked me to arrange a summer trip to Europe. He wanted to become acquainted with the International Red Cross offices in Geneva, inspect Red Cross services for Hungarian refugees, and check on our work at army and air force bases in Germany, France, and England. He and I had a busy July that requires no mention other than that, at a U.S. Air Force base in England, I fell and fractured my right femur. X-rays showed the break to be at the exact site of a fracture thirty-nine years earlier when I was an infant. Gruenther flew home alone, leaving me in the hands of a capable surgeon who ultimately became surgeon general of the U.S. Air Force.

I was back home a month later getting around on crutches. Gruenther and I began planning for the New Delhi conference. He thoughtfully said that, since plans for a family vacation on Martha's Vineyard had been scrapped due to my accident, we might partially make up for it by Sally's going with us to India. This was unexpected and truly exciting. Gruenther intended an around-the-world jaunt—a travel agent's dream. The itinerary: San Francisco, Honolulu, Tokyo, Seoul, Hong Kong, Calcutta, New Delhi, Karachi, Baghdad, Istanbul, Jerusalem, Rome, London, and New York.

Sally and I, by now, had two children; Anne was nearly four years old, and Howard was two and a half. Mother and Dad jumped at the opportunity of having the children with them in Oakmont. Dad provided a generous check to cover Sally's expenses. Sally and I left with Gruenther for San Francisco at noon on October 10 on a nonstop eight-hour flight. I was now on a cane, and Sally was burdened with my overflowing briefcase of conference documents. This first portion of the trip, as well as succeeding ones, was slow by today's standards but was close to record breaking at the time. No flight was memorable except that, from Tokyo to New Delhi, a fellow passenger was Indira Gandhi. Soon to be India's prime minister, she was already a figure of international interest and drew press attention and admirers at each refueling stop.

Sally has her own memories of the five weeks we were away. She was on her own when Gruenther and I were in Korea and Okinawa, where "dependents" were not yet allowed. She explored Tokyo on foot, as she later explored New Delhi alone when the general and I were sitting through tedious conference sessions. Happily, the Indian Red Cross made the weekends interesting, even providing a special train to take us all to Agra to see the Taj Mahal. And Ambassador and Mrs. Bunker were gracious hosts at the embassy residence, where he and I gossiped about the political chicanery going on behind the scenes at the supposedly nonpolitical Red Cross meetings.

General Gruenther was well known to be on close personal terms with President Eisenhower. In each capital city, the American ambassador was eager for "face time" with him. This was fine with Sally and me, for we were free to do as we pleased. In Baghdad, for example, we wandered freely in the bazaars hoping to find just the right rug for our living room. We were blissfully unaware of danger and felt at ease in the crowds, I moving awkwardly on my cane. Just months later, Iraq blew up in bloody revolution. The king was ousted. Westerners were harassed, beaten, or worse. Several Americans were murdered and their bodies dragged through the streets. We had truly been innocents abroad.

Istanbul was made memorable by our call on the Turkish Red

Crescent. Sally was the only woman in evidence. It was obvious that our elderly hosts were uncomfortable. Although polite, their attitude was summed up by that line from the musical *My Fair Lady,* "I'd be equally as willing for a dentist to be drilling than to ever let a woman in my life!"

Gruenther's closeness to "Ike" especially affected our reception in Israel. The reddest of red carpets were rolled out. A government plane gave us an aerial survey of Israel. The prime minister's personal aide, Teddy Kollek, was our guide. (Kollek was later famous as a longtime mayor of Jerusalem.) Gruenther, Sally, and I were luncheon guests of Mrs. Chaim Weizman, widow of the first president of Israel. We privately likened the occasion, historically speaking, to lunching with Martha Washington at Mount Vernon. However, bringing the analogy to modern times, Mrs. Weizman's passionate interest in social welfare made us think of Eleanor Roosevelt. The Six Days' War was in the future, and most of Jerusalem was in Arab hands. We could only gaze from a distance at sites we would have liked to have seen. (Not until Howard and I were in Israel in 1979 could I stand on the Mount of Olives, see the Wailing Wall vestige of Solomon's Temple, and visit Bethlehem.)

Gruenther was growing restless and flew home from Rome. Sally sighed with relief. I was used to the general's impetuous demands, but she was not. She, ever after, had admiring respect for Grace Gruenther, who had endured autocratic manners and an outsize ego for decades. Sally now had an appreciation for the anecdote, perhaps apocryphal, that ran as follows: A Red Cross volunteer gushed to Mrs. Gruenther at a reception, "It's wonderful to meet a great man with a little touch of modesty," to which Mrs. G. bluntly replied, "You're damned right. He has the littlest touch of modesty of any man God ever made!"

On our own at last, Sally and I went to London, where we had a great time shopping for gifts for Anne and Howard and other family members, adding to the collection accumulated along the way. One afternoon, while in a taxi going to meet Sally, I spotted a rug in a window of Harrods, London's famous department store. Better than any we had seen in Baghdad, it was just what we had been looking for. This rich red afghan has ever since been in our living room. It now shows its age, but we love it and the memories it evokes of adventures in countries now changed beyond recognition.

Sally's sister Barbara joined her on the drive to Oakmont to retrieve Anne and Howard. My mother cherished the weeks they were with her and kept in her purse until her death four years later a photograph Dad took of the children in the little red bathrobes bought to keep them warm in Pittsburgh's autumn chill. I had limped far enough on my cane and awaited them at home.

I made many other foreign trips. Quick runs to Geneva for league meetings became routine. Only one deserves mention. In the late 1950s (the exact date escapes me), the American Red Cross replaced older methods of artificial respiration with the mouth-to-mouth technique. Knowing that this superior method of saving lives was unknown to most Red Cross and Red Crescent Societies, I took an expert with me to a Geneva session. We staged a show-and-tell, with a lecture, film, and live demonstration. I handed out copies of our new teaching materials. We were received skeptically. Such "unsanitary" personal contact was unacceptable, especially if the victim and the rescuer were of opposite genders. However, in a surprisingly short time, the "American method" was widely accepted. Once again, the American Red Cross had led the way.

A conclave of league members, the first since New Delhi, was held in Athens in late 1959. We were given an especially warm welcome in recognition that the Truman Doctrine had spared Greece the fate of Yugoslavia and Bulgaria, its Soviet-dominated neighbors. Queen Frederika and her daughter Sophia, who was to become queen of Spain, received us cordially at the Royal Palace. Greek Red Cross members were marvelous hosts, ensuring that we saw the country's most famous sights. I was particularly moved by a visit to Delphi and its Temple of Apollo, whose motto, *Gnothi Sauton*—Know Thyself—had been my personal motto since college days. For me the small building was the holy of holies.

In his time at NATO, Gruenther had naturally regarded Soviets as "the enemy." Through Red Cross meetings, he had come to know Soviet delegates as "friendly colleagues." He invited Miterev to come to the States in 1961 for a second visit. I was to be the escort as before. Three physicians were in the delegation, and I focused the itinerary on medical matters. Our guests were impressed that in Rochester, Minnesota, our host was Dr. Charles Mayo of the Mayo Clinic. The clinic's reputation was well known in the Soviet Union. Service rivalry surfaced when Gruenther vetoed my plan to include the Naval Medical Center in Bethesda, Maryland, on the schedule. "No, scratch that. Make it Walter Reed!" (I should have known better than to put anything to do with the navy in front of a general for his approval.)

On this second visit, Miterev was, as before, voluble on all subjects, especially if he thought he could prove Soviet superiority as he had in St. Louis on the "clean air" issue. He had heard much about high taxes in the United States. He wanted me to understand how much better off Soviet citizens were than Americans. "I pay 14 percent in income tax but no other tax. Other people pay less if they earn less. I pay 1 percent to my union, and I pay 3 percent to the party—that can be as low as 1 percent, depending on your salary. Now isn't that a lot better than your system of high income taxes?" he wanted to know. When not expounding on Soviet superiority, Miterev had questions—more than on his first visit. He had read that President Kennedy was a Catholic. "Could this be true?" When I assured him it was, he shook his head in amazement. It was beyond him that an American president could believe in a religion. And so it went, wherever we were, comments and questions and judgments: "The streets are cleaner in San Francisco than in most of your cities."

Our Soviet visitors had scarcely returned home when it was time to prepare for another biennial league meeting. This was to be in Prague in late September 1961. I found the meeting atmosphere very different from that of Oslo, New Delhi, Athens, or Geneva. The league was meeting for the first time behind the Iron Curtain. Although the Czechs had never risen in revolt as had their Hungarian neighbors, they seemed restless, nervous, and resentful of their communist government tightly controlled by Moscow. Soldiers were everywhere. We Americans were quartered in a hotel next to an army barracks and sensed that we were under surveillance at all times.

The fact that I had resigned as vice president of the American Red Cross, as I shall shortly explain, made the Prague meeting special for me. I was saying farewell to friends from every continent whom I did not expect to see again. Miterev, on being told by Gruenther that I would be joining "a big capitalist corporation," lectured me in a paternal manner on the importance of humanitarian service. He sounded as though he meant it. Perhaps he did, but coming from one of Stalin's trusted associates, I found his sentiments not whole credible.

When the Prague meeting adjourned, it was back to Washington to empty my desk at the Red Cross and prepare for a new chapter in Sally's and my lives.

Chapter Eleven

Pullman and the Pentagon

Some weeks before the Prague meeting, Clark Clifford had asked me to come to his office. I had no inkling of the reason but was sure it had nothing to do with the new Kennedy administration. I had told him, while he was advising Kennedy in the interval between the November 1960 election and the January inaugural, that I could see nothing in government that could equal my experiences with Roosevelt and Truman. Unlike some of our former colleagues, I had no interest in a job with JFK.

When I arrived and we had chatted about the Kennedy team, Clifford said, "I'm not trying to change your mind. This is very different." He explained that one of his clients was an industrial conglomerate, Pullman Incorporated. This was a much diversified descendant of the original sleeping car company. One of the Pullman subsidiaries was the M. W. Kellogg Company, which he doubted I'd ever heard of. I replied that, to the contrary, I knew it well. My father had been a consultant to the Kellogg unit that built the plant in Oak Ridge, Tennessee, that produced uranium for the atomic bomb dropped on Hiroshima.

Clifford said that Pullman had no Washington representative. One was badly needed, by Kellogg in particular. Kellogg's foreign engineering and construction activities were growing at a rapid rate. Pullman was looking for someone who knew how to deal with State, Commerce, embassies, and the various agencies that provided funds for international projects. Would I be interested? It took no time for me to throw my hat into the ring. A challenging entry into the business world under Clifford's auspices seemed a great opportunity.

Clifford made a date for me with Kellogg's New York office two weeks hence when I would have completed some speaking engagements in the Midwest. In a Milwaukee television studio on a July Sunday afternoon, I had an urgent call from Washington. Would I call my father in Pittsburgh at once? I did so as soon as the TV interview was over. My mother had collapsed—cause unknown—and was in a Pittsburgh hospital. When I got there, Dad said it appeared to be a heart involvement. I stayed through Tuesday before going on to Washington, expecting to return to Pittsburgh the next weekend. Thursday morning, Dad called to say my mother had died during the night. An autopsy disclosed a ruptured aorta.

The New York interview was postponed until I had helped Dad settle down. When I was able to keep the appointment, an understanding was easily reached. I would open a Washington office in Kellogg's name, but it would serve all divisions of the sprawling Pullman family.

When I told General Gruenther that I would resign from the Red Cross on September 15, he snorted, "Impossible. I'm counting on you to be with me at the Prague meetings." Gruenther was a hard man to say no to. Thus, it was not until mid-October that I moved into a comfortable office at 1616 H Street, conveniently close to Clifford's office and from which almost any government agency I might be dealing with could be reached in a few minutes' walk.

The job was fascinating because I never knew what was coming next. I sometimes found myself on the opposite side of a position I had espoused while in the government. Example: The Commerce Department was exceedingly strict in controlling the release of up-to-the-minute technology. Commerce, supported by the Pentagon, was fearful that the Soviet Union could benefit by analyzing the latest American know-how. This made it difficult for Kellogg to compete with foreign engineering companies on oil refinery or petrochemical projects overseas. While I had been with Harriman in '51 and '52, I, too, had been a hardliner on export controls. Now I was summoning Kellogg's most eloquent engineers to go with me to Commerce to argue why a project—such as an oil refinery in southern Germany—would involve no security risks. Over time, I was proud that, although designs were sometimes modified to meet government concerns, no export license I sought was denied. Delayed often, yes. Denied, never.

Another matter that consumed much time and energy related to civil rights. While at the White House, I had pressed for federal leadership in the struggle for equal treatment for all Americans regardless of race. Now I was finding how difficult and complex this was. One of Pullman's freight car construction plants was in Bessemer, Alabama. The Feds were impatient with the company's slowness in integrating fully every facility on the property. We were not, the watchdog agency said, promoting blacks fast enough to make their weekly earnings equivalent to those paid to whites. Every measure demanded by the government was bitterly opposed by the steelworkers union. Pullman was in the middle. To guide us through the conflict in a legally responsible way, I worked hand-in-glove with lawyers in Clifford's office who specialized in civil rights matters. When the time came to leave Pullman, I estimated that I had spent more time on such problems than on any other subject.

I enjoyed the Pullman years with their frequent trips to Kellogg in New York, Pullman corporate offices in Chicago, and an engineering subsidiary in Pittsburgh. The Chicago visits gave the welcome opportunity to keep up with Aunt Caryl, and I always managed the Pittsburgh schedule so as to have an overnight with Dad in Oakmont. Aside from these personal aspects, the opportunity to interact with business leaders, to experience competition in the private sector, and to be the facilitator of company-government relationships provided intellectual stimulus very different from anything I had earlier done.

These years were good for Sally, too. With the children in school she now had time of her own. She yearned to be "doing something." I then learned for the first time why she had resigned her position at Madeira School when we became engaged. "Dad told me then," she now said, "George won't want you to be working." I was stunned. That sentiment reflected a long-gone era; my sentiments were wholly different. After expressing dismay that she had not told me this years earlier, I encouraged her to jump at the chance just offered her to return to the administrative staff at Madeira. This she did. For the next quarter century she was involved in the school's affairs, acting for a time as director of admissions. When not on the staff, she was a volunteer. As such, she began the school's annual giving appeals to its alumnae.

Madeira was not enough. She returned to George Washington University to complete the studies she had interrupted for Red Cross work as World War II was approaching. She went on to graduate studies on educational testing techniques. When not up to her neck at Madeira, she tested students at public and private schools in the Washington area. Had her father been alive to see the pleasure she took in her work and my pride in all she was doing, he would I am sure have changed his mind about married women working.

We were both happily involved in work we much enjoyed. With legal issues aplenty to be addressed at Kellogg, antitrust among them, I kept in constant touch with Clifford. In 1966, he asked if I would reconsider a return to government. Lyndon Johnson had asked him to recommend a man for the White House staff. My reply was quick and undiplomatic. "Not on your life. Johnson's staff is already too big. Bloated, full of backbiters and self-promoters, it's a world away from what we knew with Truman." Clifford grinned. "You've read it right. Not only is the staff too big, Johnson treats his people abominably. They are just like logs on a fire to him. When one burns out, he tosses another into the flames. I asked you only because he said I must know some young people who know how to get things done. You'd be foolish to get involved."

That did not end our talks about LBJ, who regarded Clifford as a trusted friend and adviser. As months rolled by, when Clifford and I had finished the business of my visits, our conversation increasingly turned to Vietnam. By the autumn of 1967, we were saying frankly to each other—behind tightly closed doors—that Johnson's policy was a ghastly mistake. We had to close out the Vietnam tragedy. Clifford very much hoped for Dean Rusk's job as secretary of state, but if he couldn't have that, he'd settle for Robert McNamara's spot as secretary of defense. However, he confided, he could not possibly let Johnson know how he felt about Vietnam, or he'd have the chance of a snowball in hell of getting any job. He must continue being perceived as a hawk on Vietnam. God forbid that anyone think of him as a dove.

If he did get the job at either State or Defense, Clifford wanted to know if I would leave Pullman and join him. He would need a personal aide in whom he had total confidence. We would work together as we had at the White House. We would do our damnedest to get the country out of Vietnam. I answered "Yes" instantly. My earlier rejections of a return to government were irrelevant. I believed so passionately that Vietnam was a tragedy growing worse by the day that I would help in any way I could.

By December 1967, McNamara's doubts about Johnson's hard-line approach were an open secret. Rumors were afloat that Johnson was looking for a way to dump McNamara that wouldn't open a public debate on Vietnam policy. In January '68, the Tet Offensive shook the country. Communist forces overran Saigon, the capital of South Vietnam. In strictly military terms, it was a defeat for the North Vietnamese; their manpower losses were horrendous. But Tet was a public relations disaster for Johnson. That communist troops could rampage through South Vietnam almost at will, catching us by surprise, brought American policy into question as never before. Johnson announced that he was nominating McNamara to be president of the World Bank and naming Clifford to be secretary of defense. In all news stories, Clifford was portrayed as a true hawk on Vietnam. And so Johnson thought him to be.

Clifford's story for posterity is set forth in his memoirs, *Counsel to the President.* He writes there that he was dumbfounded on reaching the Pentagon to discover that the military had no effective plan to win the war and that, not until then, did he decide that the United States should begin to wind down its involvement. This is the story he began telling at the time, but, based on many conversations with him in 1967 and into 1968, I know otherwise. He had to encourage the White House and the media to believe him to be a hard-liner on Vietnam because it was the only way he could enter the Johnson administration and work from a position of power to bring about change in the nation's Asian policy. He stuck with this tale when he wrote the memoirs years later to avoid the charge that he had gained his cabinet seat by deceiving the president.

True to his word, Clifford called me in late February 1968, a few days before he was sworn in as secretary. "I've found the right spot. You will be the special assistant to the secretary and to the deputy secretary." The deputy was Paul Nitze, whom we both knew from the Truman years. Clifford said he would start my security clearance at once. White House and Civil Service clearance would also be needed because the job was at executive level V, so high that there were only fifteen at that level in the entire army, navy, air force, and Defense Departments with their million or more civilian employees.

"How soon can you cut your Pullman ties?" Clifford wanted to know. Arranging an indefinite leave of absence from Pullman was easy, but Clifford had overlooked the glacial pace at which executive-level appointments were processed. I was not sworn in until May 1. Much had happened since February. President Johnson had astonished the country by announcing at the end of March that he would not seek election in November. That did not affect my decision to join Clifford. We were still in Vietnam, and we had to get out. Clifford was determined to find a way.

Duties of the special assistant were whatever the secretary wanted them to be—nothing more, nothing less. My predecessors under McNamara had wide-ranging responsibilities, aided by a staff of military officers and senior Civil Service members. McNamara had given the post a high rating "so they could get things done." When my longtime friend Roger Pineau came by soon after I had settled in, he asked what my "assimilated rank" was.

"General," I answered.

"But what kind of general—brigadier or major?"

"General," I said again.

"My God," Roger exclaimed. "You mean you rank as a four-star general?"

"Yes."

We both found this amusing, and Roger enjoyed teasing me about it to the end of his long life. However meaningless this "assimilated rank" seemed to be in May, it proved its value in the coming months.

Since I was the only person, aside from his longtime personal secretary, whom Clifford brought into the Pentagon, there was considerable curiosity about my role. It remained a mystery to everyone but the two of us. Clifford told me he would let Nitze run the Pentagon. He would devote all his energy to pushing Johnson into negotiations to bring the war to some kind of conclusion. Johnson was determined to "nail the coonskin to the wall" in his remaining months in office. This, in Clifford's mind, was impossible and would mean a further tragic loss of lives—American and Vietnamese. Clifford named me as the contact man for White House matters and let the staff there know that I was the one to call about anything related to the Pentagon. Johnson's staff, Clifford told me, included some men of dubious character who regarded the Pentagon as a "cookie jar" from which they could pull services and favors for themselves and political friends. Now that they could see their time at the trough coming to an early end, we could expect the worst. My role? "Keep Johnson's crowd happy if you possibly can. I can't afford to have any of them complain to the Boss that I'm not cooperating. He would turn sour on me. I'm going to concentrate on just one thing. You know what that is. Give in only when you absolutely must."

The next months were disillusioning. As LBJ's people saw their days numbered, requests from them escalated. "The president wants . . ." "The president would like . . ." "The president has asked for . . ." These so-called presidential requests would have been news to Johnson if he had ever heard of them. I learned to say "No" in a dozen ways. My staff was adroit in its ability to provide convincing statements as to why such and such actions were not feasible, were illegal, or would backfire politically.

However, some requests did come from Johnson himself. He was thinking ahead to January 1969 when he would be just another former president. He was determined that he would get what Truman, "Ike," and—oh, yes—Mrs. Kennedy were getting. "What communications services could he expect from the Pentagon?" When I looked into this, I found Defense officials wary. The acting general counsel wrote me that "no communication services, as such," were furnished former presidents. But orally, he confided that Defense paid telephone bills for Truman and Eisenhower and for six lines for Jackie Kennedy. I reported to Clifford, "This information is 'extremely sensitive' but be careful, it's believed to be known at the White House."

Charles Murphy, my Truman colleague who was now an aide to Johnson, phoned at his boss's direction to ask if wives and widows of former presidents were entitled to care at military medical facilities. My "assimilated rank" of general was handy. Within twenty-four hours, the secretaries of the army, navy, and air force answered my query. Clifford was able to tell Johnson the next day that wives, widows, and minor children of former presidents were eligible for medical care at any military hospital or clinic. At my suggestion, to avoid LBJ's ire, Clifford did not tell him that they would be charged for whatever service they received.

Johnson wanted a lot more than future telephone bills and medical care provided by the military. He told Jim Rowley, head of the White House Secret Service detail, to direct the chairman of the Joint Chiefs of Staff to provide helicopters, crews, and maintenance people to be "instantly available" to Truman and Eisenhower. This was to set a precedent for the helicopter he would want at his Texas ranch after January

20, 1969. Rowley, whom I had known well in the Truman years, thought he'd better see me before "directing" the JCS chairman. I suggested he ask Truman's and Ike's views. Both promptly, politely, but forcefully rejected any thought of helicopters. This did not deter Johnson, although he was miffed at not having the precedent he sought. He personally phoned the air force chief of staff, who had no choice but to obey his commander in chief. Not only was a helicopter to be assigned to the Johnson ranch, but a Convair passenger plane would be transferred to the air force base at nearby Austin for Johnson's use after January 20.

My involvement with the Johnson White House was constant. Whereas some was due to LBJ whims, there were serious matters too. Anti-Vietnam sentiment in the summer of 1968 ran high. Johnson was vilified in many quarters, and the Democratic Party was charged with being "the war party." Trouble was expected at the Democratic convention in Chicago in July. Johnson was expected, and the protestors geared up. The secretary of the treasury, responsible for the Secret Service, called Clifford for help. This, too, came my way. My military assistants, who knew the Pentagon inside out, jumped at the challenge. When the convention drew near, my air force aide, Colonel James Murphy, flew to Chicago. Several times a day, he called to discuss troops and equipment to supplement Secret Service and state and local law enforcement personnel. Whatever he asked for, I was able to provide. That "assimilated rank" of general was mighty useful. Before the convention ended, we had provided armed helicopters to provide emergency evacuation from Chicago if needed, armored personnel carriers with troops trained in crowd control, some sixty "explosive ordnance personnel" who prowled the convention hall twenty-four hours a day, and several hundred military support staff. Johnson, wisely but untypically, decided not to attend. There was chaos in Chicago, but the military presence ensured no serious rioting. Still, the behavior of the war protestors was a disgrace. Convention delegates were jostled and insulted. Bags of urine and excrement were hurled at them. Fistfights were common. Vice President Hubert Humphrey rode through the storm and accepted the presidential nomination. When it was all over, the director of the Secret Service came to the Pentagon to thank us in person.

Throughout the summer and into the autumn, Clifford continued to urge Johnson and administration hardliners, Secretary of State Dean Rusk in particular, to engage in serious negotiations to bring the war to an end. Johnson seemed ambivalent, appearing to be for negotiations one day and against them the next. And international events, far beyond Clifford's ability to influence, worked against any progress. Richard Nixon won in November claiming he had a "secret plan to end the war." (He didn't, and it went on for six more tragic years.)

Nixon's election did not end Johnson's grasp for "freebies" and "goodies." Since George Washington's day, presidential papers had been regarded as the personal property of the president. Franklin Roosevelt was the first president to have a voluminous collection, having held office for twelve years, during which the activities of the presidency had expanded enormously. How were the Roosevelt papers to be evaluated for estate tax purposes? Family attorneys scrambled for a solution that would avoid a high tax on FDR's estate, which was considerably smaller than popularly supposed. An ingenious solution was found: a friendly Dutchess County, New York, judge was prevailed upon to rule that Roosevelt had made a "constructive gift" of his papers to the nation before he died. Therefore, no tax was owed. Roosevelt's heirs were the direct beneficiaries, but the indirect result was more significant. The precedent was set that presidential papers do indeed have monetary value. Future presidents could claim income tax credit by "giving" their papers to the government. Heirs could claim credit for any not given during a former president's lifetime. (Never mind that such papers had been produced by federal employees on government time at government expense!)

Johnson, never one to miss a trick, decided to enhance the size of his prospective "gift." All departments and agencies were ordered to return to the White House all communications they had received from the White House during Johnson's tenure. At the Pentagon, compliance with the order became my responsibility. For six weeks or so, files were searched and copies made for Defense, army, navy, and air force files so that the originals could be returned to the White House. In Johnson's last week in office army trucks, well guarded since so much of their loads consisted of highly classified documents, drove to the White House. They were not unloaded. Their presence on White House grounds was enough to make their contents "presidential property." No matter that White House files, containing copies of everything sent to the Pentagon, were already destined for the future LBJ Library, and our stuff was not needed for the historical record.

That was not the point. By enhancing the volume of the "personal property" that Johnson would be giving the federal government, the amount of tax credit he could claim would be grossly enlarged. I thought at the time that this was one more example of Lyndon Johnson's greediness at public expense. Before he was ready to make his "gift," however, he was thwarted by the Tax Reform Act enacted in December 1969, which denied such tax credits. Both Johnson and the newly installed Nixon sent lawyers to lobby against any change. Nixon attempted to make a gift while vigorous debate went on for months. Johnson decided against doing so at a cost, estimated the *Washington Post,* "of several million dollars to his heirs." (Under a federal law enacted in the Carter administration and taking effect on January 20, 1981, Reagan's inauguration day, records generated by the White House are now automatically property of the U.S. government.)

Whether Nixon or Humphrey won in November, transition was inevitable. In early September, Charley Murphy directed Clifford and all other cabinet officers to ensure that the new administration would be well informed of the issues they would face. As a matter of course, Clifford passed this to me. Transitions were no novelty at the Pentagon. All went smoothly. As soon as Nixon began designating his selections for Defense posts, we provided briefing books, began security clearances, and fielded such questions as "Can Defense nominees use military planes before January 20?" and "Can the Pentagon assign a suitable house at Fort Myer for Vice President Elect Spiro Agnew?" If my staff and I did not know the answers, we knew how to get them in a hurry. Clifford made sure that I became acquainted with each new appointee. The partisan rancor that had soured the campaign was absent at the Pentagon. Each side wanted brownie points for a smooth transition. I left on January 20 with such a warm relationship with Melvin Laird, Clifford's successor, with my own replacement, and with other new men that we stayed in touch long after.

There was a brief, happy interlude away from Washington in the final days of the campaign. In mid-October, Clifford attended a regularly scheduled NATO conference in Bonn, the capital of the Federal Republic (the western part) of the still-divided Germany. He was taking Marny Clifford, and he suggested that Sally come with me. I was stuck in formal sessions most of the time, but Sally and other wives were entertained royally with delightful sightseeing excursions. There was a one-day break in the conference. This gave us the chance to fly to Berlin and visit the infamous Berlin Wall built by the communists to prevent escapes to the West. Anne and Howard stayed in school dormitories until weekends, when Dad flew down from Pittsburgh and Anne was the cook.

Although Clifford left the Department of Defense without having succeeded in his effort to get us out of Vietnam, he won widespread respect for his efforts, beautifully expressed by Hugh Sidey in an article published in the December 27, 1968, issue of *Time*. As for me, I was honored to be awarded the Defense Medal for Distinguished Public Service. The citation was overdone, with sentences such as this: "Perceptive in the delineation of issues, attentive to detail, keen in judgment and prodigious in output, he has been a trusted and wise counselor and an inspirational associate." All I really did was let Clifford try out his ideas on me and then talk back as frankly as I had at the White House— which was just what he had said he wanted when he'd asked me nearly a year earlier if I would join him.

Many years later, when Clifford was in his early nineties, and willing to talk more candidly than ever, we reviewed the events of 1968. Time had not softened my dislike for Johnson. I said I thought Johnson wanted Nixon to beat Humphrey. In a variety of ways—some public, some private—he had aided the Nixon campaign. He had conspicuously invited Nixon to visit him at the Texas ranch while snubbing Humphrey. He had openly disavowed some of Humphrey's campaign statements. Clifford agreed. Johnson, he thought, had favored Nixon because he was a true hawk while Humphrey seemed to be for peace at any price. We agreed that Nixon would probably have won anyway, but Johnson's behavior was no help to Humphrey. "And," Clifford went on, "I've never in my life said this to anyone, but I'll say it to you now. If Hubert had been elected, he would have been 'Mr. Democrat.' With Nixon in the White House, Lyndon was still head of the Democratic Party. Remaining party head meant *everything* to him!"

Chapter Twelve

Capstone

My return to the Pullman offices at 1616 H Street on the day after Richard Nixon's Inauguration of January 20, 1969, seemed like "coming home," as did the check-ins at corporate offices in Chicago, at Kellogg in New York, and at Swindell-Dressler, the engineering division in Pittsburgh. A substantial salary increase soon thereafter meant the nine-month absence at the Pentagon had been no career impediment. However, my frame of mind was not the same. I expected that I might be a "short-timer" with Pullman, as I shall shortly explain.

Pullman was generous and allowed a three-week summer vacation in 1969, although I had been back a scant six months. Sally had so enjoyed our brief visit to Germany the previous October with the Cliffords that she was eager for more European adventures. One afternoon, she and the children slipped off and returned with tickets in hand and the news that we were going to Europe. Ninety sixty-nine was a great time for Americans to cross the Atlantic. European currencies were cheap. Our bible was Frommer's *Europe on $5 a Day.* That was a come-on. We spent a good deal more than that per person per day, but Europe was still unbelievably a bargain for anyone with American dollars.

Sally, Anne, and Howard have their own memories. I'll list only the itinerary; the details would fill another book. By air to Amsterdam. Barge and bus tours of Holland. A flight to Frankfort and a day's cruise on the Main and Rhine Rivers. A drive by rented car to Munich, with a side trip to the famed castle of Neuschwanstein, through a corner of Austria, and on to Venice, which lived up to its reputation, although it was beastly hot. Sally was the driver to Florence and on to Rome, with enough time in each city to take in the "must-see" places. Saying farewell to Rome and the little Renault, which we would have liked to take home, we flew to Geneva, where Red Cross friends gave us a warmer welcome than we deserved. Quick drop-ins at Paris, Brussels, and London rounded out the "eight countries in twenty-one days" whirlwind. Veteran travelers turn up their noses at such a schedule, but it was the right way to give the children a sense of Europe. We enjoyed every minute. Not even upset tummies in Italy spoiled the memories.

Now to explain the "short-timer" reference three paragraphs back.

While I was with Pullman in the 1960s, I kept up my contacts at Red Cross headquarters, although my volunteer involvement was primarily with the local Washington, D.C., chapter. Occasionally, I took on a headquarters task, for example when I flew to New York as a member of a Red Cross team attempting to negotiate a better relationship with the United Way movement. At the Pentagon in 1968, I sought to strengthen the ties of the Department of Defense with the American Red Cross and the International Committee of the Red Cross so that, together, we could be more effective on Vietnam prisoner of war matters. In midsummer 1968, my old friend John Wilson, who had succeeded Nicholson as executive vice president, came to my Pentagon office to ask if I could pry loose some land controlled by the military for the Hawaii chapter. It was about to be evicted from its longtime home in the former Royal Palace, which was to become a museum. I was able to start the ball rolling, but it was two years before the chapter had the land it needed.

Because we were staying in touch, it was no surprise when Wilson phoned around Labor Day and asked to see me again. While the call was no surprise, the purpose of his visit surely was. John said he would be sixty-four in April 1969. He would like to retire then. He had recommended to Roland Harriman, still the Red Cross chairman, that I succeed him as executive vice president and serve as such until the current president, General James Collins (who had followed Gruenther), retired at the end of September 1970. I would then move up to the presidency on October 1. Harriman, John said, had approved this plan.

I was stunned and asked for time to think it over. Sally was equally stunned. A few days later, I told Wilson that I was greatly honored and was much interested in becoming president. However, I did not want to fill his post as executive vice president for the year and a half interval between his and Collins's retirements for several reasons. First, I had promised Pullman I would be back in January 1969. Second, being heir apparent to Collins for so long a time would be awkward for us both. Third, I thought the executive vice president should be a long-time career staff member. There was a fourth and more significant reason. The presidential election was coming up. The president, whether Nixon or Humphrey, would be free to replace Harriman as chairman. The new chairman could pick whomever he chose as president and he—or she— would want his or her own executive vice president. Then where would I be?

John was disappointed with my answer. We let the matter ride until the November election was behind us. He and I flew to New York on November 13 to lunch with Roland Harriman in the same elegant dining room at Brown Brothers Harriman where I had first met him in 1953. Roland Harriman was as ardent a Republican as his brother Averell was a Democrat. Roland felt he had a good relationship with President-Elect Nixon. He was confident he would remain chairman of the Red Cross. We reviewed the situation. John Wilson agreed to remain one year longer than he had wished, not retiring until April 1970. Harriman would tell Collins that he would select me to be his successor on October 1, 1970, and that the executive vice presidency should be left open for me to fill.

Our luncheon ended with Harriman saying he was glad we "agreed in principle." I jokingly responded that I had often heard his banking partner, Robert Lovett, say when he was undersecretary of state, and later secretary of defense, that "agreeing in principle" was a polite way of saying the parties hadn't agreed at all! Harriman took the crack in good humor and, choosing different words, said the three of us were "of one mind."

I was back in New York three days after leaving the Pentagon on inauguration day 1969 to catch up on events at Kellogg. Midday, I lunched with Harriman again. Our November conversation was confirmed. He suggested that I attend an International Red Cross conference to be held in Istanbul in the autumn. I demurred. Another leave of absence from Pullman so soon would not be appropriate. With the Red Cross thus in a state of "watchful waiting," I plunged into a huge backlog of Pullman work, since the Washington office had been left open while I was at the Pentagon.

All went according to plan. Harriman nominated me, and the board of governors elected me president at the Red Cross annual convention in Chicago in June 1970. That the convention was in Chicago was a convenient coincidence. I was able then and there to bid farewell to many warm friends at Pullman, resigning as of June 30.

I moved back to the Red Cross in midsummer 1970 for a few weeks of overlap with General Collins, so that I could meet the new faces and grasp the changes that had taken place since my departure nine years earlier. I was to become president and chief executive officer on October 1 of an organization of more than 14,000 employees and about 2 million volunteers with an annual expenditure of $177 million. In addition to the headquarters in Washington, there were four regional offices known as "areas" and 3,400 chapters throughout the country. All of these statistics were to change greatly by the time I stepped down on January 1, 1983, on the eve of my sixty-fifth birthday, having served longer as president than any except the founder of the Red Cross, Clara Barton (1881-1904), and Judge John Barton Payne (1921-1935). Expenditures in my last year as president topped $722 million, and the number of employees had grown to 20,700, while volunteers—thanks in part, but only in part, to more precise counting—numbered just under 1.5 million.

Recounting these twelve years in any detail would be of interest only to a historian of the Red Cross and probably not even to him or her, and certainly not to a casual reader. I left an abundance of records in Red Cross archives—let them suffice. I'll comment only on four areas in which I like to think I made a substantial difference, bequeathing to my successor a stronger and more effective Red Cross than the one I inherited. When I stepped down as president, I believe the organization was (1) better governed, (2) more effectively managed, (3) more sharply focused on the nation's needs, and (4) more realistically financed.

First, governance.

The Red Cross proudly describes itself as an organization ruled by volunteers. In 1970, I found that to be true only in theory. Roland Harriman had been the "principal officer" (to use the phrase of the congressional charter) for twenty years. Forceful at first, he had settled into a comfortable routine of letting the paid staff at headquarters in Washington run the show. He lived in New York, and his Washington visits were few and brief. The fifty-member volunteer board of governors was quiescent. When I flew to New York to discuss the first meeting of the board for which I would be responsible, he told me there was no need for meetings of any board committees. "Just give the board next year's budget for approval and tell them what's been going on."

That was not my concept of the role of the body legally responsible for the organization. To Harriman's surprise, I proposed full agendas for each board committee. Throughout my tenure, I made sure that the board was presented at each meeting with substantive issues to discuss and decide—matters of personnel, finance, program, long-range planning—the gamut. No longer were board members merely informed—or perhaps not informed—of what staff at headquarters had decided. When meetings became worthwhile, attendance and participation picked up markedly.

Dr. Frank Stanton retired from his long-held post as president of Columbia Broadcasting System in April 1973 on reaching age sixty-five. He had a splendid public reputation and was mentioned as an excellent candidate for various federal positions. But he had managed to offend President Nixon, and he liked to repeat the story, told him by a Nixon associate. "I hate the SOB," was Nixon's comment when Stanton's name came up. "Roland Harriman wants to quit at Red Cross. I'll put Stanton there where he can't cause me any trouble!" And so, by presidential appointment pursuant to the federal charter, Stanton became Red Cross chairman, succeeding Harriman, in May 1973. He was superb in the post, throwing himself into every aspect of the organization. Although he continued to live in New York, he responded to my calls and would come to Washington at any time requested. Soon after his appointment, I proposed that I be permitted to arrange dinners for the board of governors and their spouses at their twice-a-year meetings in Washington. He and I would be cohosts. The purposes? To express our appreciation for the time and effort these volunteers devoted to Red Cross matters and, of greater importance, to meld the governors into a cohesive family, which was difficult when they met only in formal business sessions. Stanton was enthusiastic when I said I could arrange dinners in venues unique to Washington, such as the National Gallery of Art, the various Smithsonian museums, the Pentagon, and Clara Barton's house in nearby Glen Echo, Maryland.

Our dinners became a resounding success, serving their purposes so well that they have been continued by my successors. In October 1998, on the twenty-fifth anniversary of the first dinner, which had been held at the Stephen Decatur House on Lafayette Square facing the White House, President Elizabeth Dole invited Sally and me to dine with her current board. Dole asked me to explain the origin of the custom and to repeat a speech of mine that had become something of a Red Cross legend: "Triumph and Tragedy—Clara Barton and Mabel Boardman."

While the dinners by themselves may not make the Red Cross any "better governed," it is clear that the pattern I began of ensuring that the board of governors is fully and deeply engaged has resulted in sound governance by men and women who take their responsibilities seriously. So seriously that when one of my successors—Bernadine Healy—took actions displeasing to the majority of the members, her resignation as president was forced in September 2001 after less than two years in the job.

Second, management.

I draw a distinction between "governance" and "management." The former refers to the policy-setting board of governors of the Red Cross; the latter, to the paid professional staff that conducts the day-to-day affairs of the organization. Just as I like to believe that the Red Cross was better governed when I retired, so I like to believe that it was more effectively managed in 1982 than in 1970.

When I returned to the Red Cross in 1970, I was even more concerned than I had been on my first arrival in 1953 at the provincialism of the career staff leadership. The Second World War had ended twenty-five years earlier, the Korean conflict had intruded, and we were in the protracted agonies of Vietnam. Yet the top posts were still occupied by men, all older than I (then fifty-two), who seemed to live as though they were in the glory days of World War II when the Red Cross had the enthusiastic and generous support of the public, money had been no problem, and criticisms could be ignored. Only one of the four vice presidents and none of the four powerful area managers had any military experience. None had served in government or had business or industry experience. Their outlooks were narrowed still further by their being longtime veterans of "the national organization." They looked down on the chapters. There were no women and no minorities in the upper reaches of the staff pyramid.

How did I fit in? I was an "insider" of sorts in that I had been at headquarters from 1953 to 1961, but I had not truly "belonged." I had been imposed on the career staff by Harriman and then promoted by "outsiders" Bunker and Gruenther, successively occupying posts that longtimers felt belonged to them. From 1961 to 1970, I had distanced myself from the headquarters clique. As an active volunteer in the Washington, D.C., chapter, I had expressed views rather freely on national headquarters practices that I thought were unwise from a chapter point of view.

The culture of the Red Cross is best not assailed head-on. As the new president, I made changes cautiously—too cautiously, I later concluded. As a first step, I stated my philosophy to the management group at headquarters that the so-called national organization existed to support and guide chapters—not to "boss" them. To me, chapters were the source of volunteers and the units that provided most of the services to the American people. My approach was one that should always have been obvious, but in a way it was revolutionary. Even Roland Harriman was taken aback. When he remarked to me, soon after my first foray into the field, "I hope you gave the chapters hell," I responded, "Not at all. I went to see where national is falling down and how we can do better by the chapters!"

For the first several years, I managed without an executive vice president. I wanted direct "hands-on" control so that I could be sure that changes in policies, programs, and administrative practices were as I wanted them. As vacancies arose at management levels, I filled the positions with men and women who would bring fresh perspectives to headquarters. In due course, all vice presidents were strong executives who had demonstrated their abilities in chapters or "outside." (The vice president for health services came from the United States Public Health Service, and the vice president for finance had been a senior officer in a major insurance company.) By the time I stepped down as president, Bob Wick, the executive vice president, had been enticed from the Detroit chapter, where he had an outstanding record, women held vice presidential posts, a woman was an area manager, an African American man was manager of the prestigious eastern area, and an African American woman was the national director of personnel. Alas, chapters lagged behind headquarters. Local chapter boards still favored white males as their staff leaders, but in the national sector the pattern of "white males only" was gone forever. We had by 1982, I believed, a leadership group that could cope with the changes required in a fast-changing world.

Third, programs.

Improving governance and management enabled me more readily to make the changes I felt necessary in Red Cross activities. On returning to headquarters in 1970, I found that Services to the Armed Forces and Veterans, always shortened to SAF&V, commanded the largest single portion of the budget—about a third. SAF&V had changed almost not at all from World War II days, when military forces were overwhelmingly draftees with twenty-one dollars a month as their base pay. The War and Navy Departments had provided next to nothing at that time in the form of social services. The Red Cross had entered the breach, providing recreational activities, counseling, and communication and financial services. Although military pay now reflected civilian wages and supports of many kinds had been initiated by the army, navy, and air force, the Red Cross had barely adjusted to the changes and still maintained a large paid staff at military installations at home and over-seas. There was little I could do at first, with the nation bogged down in Vietnam. Not until the Paris Peace Accords were signed in 1973, end-ing open conflict in Vietnam, was it politically feasible to pare down SAF&V, reduce its staff, eliminate some programs, replace staff with volunteers where possible, and redirect the main emphasis of the Red Cross from services for the military to services in our communities. In my last year as president, expenditures for SAF&V had dropped from one-third to just under 10 percent of the total.

At the national convention in New Orleans in May 1973, I proposed the theme that I believed should guide our planning now that Vietnam was behind us. The Red Cross should commit its strengths to helping the American people: "*A*void avoidable emergencies, *P*repare for those that cannot be avoided, and *C*ope with crises when they occur." This "APC" formula that I put forth in New Orleans survives today in the official mission statement, with word changes, now reading "to help people prevent, prepare for and respond to emergencies." So embedded in Red Cross thinking is this concept that few, if any, volunteers or staff know of its origin in a New Orleans convention address long ago.

Disaster activities needed a complete overhaul. In the summer of 1970, before taking over as president from James Collins, at his sugges-tion I flew to Corpus Christi, Texas, to see how the Red Cross was help-ing victims of a major hurricane. I was impressed but also surprised. Scores of caseworkers were dealing with families in procedures that seemed not to have changed in decades. Policy required a detailed scrutiny of a family's predisaster living standard, its losses, and a calcu-lation of the financial assistance that would be required from the Red Cross to restore the family to its predisaster status. Chairman Harriman was still saying, as he had for years, that 85 percent of Red Cross disas-ter costs were incurred in rehabilitating families, with only 15 percent spent during the actual emergency.

It seemed to me that lots of things were wrong with policy and practice. Foremost, especially in the southern states, restoring a family to its predisaster status meant inevitably that whites were treated more generously than blacks or Hispanics. Second, little or no effort was made to guide victims to other sources of aid. Year by year, more and more federal monies were available for disaster sufferers—but only if applied for. Third, with inflation on the rise, rehabilitation costs were getting out of hand, and we soon would have to change our ways whether we wanted to or not.

I charged Robert Shea, the energetic vice president to whom Disaster Services reported, with overhauling the program. Under his firm hand, disaster policies were totally rewritten. Long-term rehabilitation became the rarest of exceptions. The focus would be on immediate emergency assistance of food, shelter, and clothing as needed, standardized for all disaster victims without regard for their predisaster living standard. All victims were to be informed of federal and state assistance programs and assisted in applying for them. Fundraising by chapters to meet to the extent possible the costs of disasters in their communities became mandatory. And, in a change of philosophy, the Red Cross would reach out to agencies such as the Salvation Army and church-related organizations to form partnerships when disasters occurred, rather than regarding them as unfriendly competitors, as had too long been the case.

Shea worked so quickly and effectively that the new procedures were largely in place when Hurricane Agnes slammed into a number of the eastern states in July 1972, causing—in the words of the National Weather Service—"the worst disaster in American history." More than 29,000 Red Cross volunteers responded, aiding more than 700,000 people. Agnes fundraising took a dramatic turn when Bob Hope, an entertainer with a superb reputation of public service, staged a money-raising telethon with a bevy of Hollywood stars. I toured some of the worst-hit cities in Pennsylvania with Hope, shared the shock he felt at seeing the wind and flood devastation, and was pleased with the effectiveness of the redesigned relief program.

In contrast to SAF&V's reduction and Disaster Services' narrowed scope, Blood Services grew explosively. This would have happened no matter who was president, but I went out of my way to make "Blood" my number-one priority in resources and personnel. I particularly encouraged the scientific research and development efforts of the professional staff, purchasing and outfitting laboratories in Bethesda, Maryland, near the campus of the National Institutes of Health. I approved pay levels for professionals that dismayed old-time Red Crossers. Internationally renowned Dr. Tibor Greenwalt, Blood Services director, was adept at anticipating regulatory actions by the Food and Drug Administration, which had legal oversight on all blood matters. "Tibi" was ready to adopt new tests and new procedures the moment they had FDA approval. When he retired, I was aided by a board of governors committee in enticing talented Lewellys Barker from the Public Health Service as the new director. With such men in charge, I had no need—which was good, since I lacked the ability—to be involved in the technical aspects of Blood Services.

My involvement with "Blood," aside from ensuring that it had all the resources it needed, was largely political. We seemed to be constantly at odds with the American Association of Blood Banks. The AABB in the 1970s included many commercial groups and even some hospitals that paid donors for their blood, in contrast to the Red Cross, which accepted only volunteer donations. Although it was statistically proven that blood from paid donors carried significant risks of hepatitis, sexually transmitted diseases, and other blood-borne illnesses because donors were apt to conceal their medical histories in their eagerness for cash, the AABB was loath to adopt a "volunteers only" policy. There were other differences between the Red Cross and the AABB, but that was the most significant. I was involved in many contentious meetings, none of them pleasant. Not until the Food and Drug Administration issued its National Blood Policy Statement having the force of law in 1978 did the AABB and the rest of the nation's blood banks follow the Red Cross policy of "volunteer donors only" for blood to be used in human transfusions.

Thanks to the Red Cross practice then in effect, that normal retirement was to take place when one reached age sixty-five, I did not have to face the complexities and the crises that AIDS posed for all institutions dealing with blood and blood products. I stepped down just weeks before the connection between blood and AIDS was established in 1983, thus unintentionally bequeathing an enormous headache to my successor, Richard Schubert.

Moving in 1970 to headquarters after eight years of involvement in the safety, health, and youth activities of the Washington, D.C. chapter, I was especially interested in ensuring that the Red Cross training courses offered by chapters to the public reflected the latest and best medical knowledge. All first aid, water safety, nursing, and related manuals and visual aids were reviewed in my first few months. Schedules were developed for their updating. As an example: staff worked with experts from the National Academy of Sciences and the American Heart Association to redesign our method of teaching cardiopulmonary resuscitation—CPR for short. Another example: after initially receiving bad advice from the National Academy, we incorporated into our teaching materials the Heimlich maneuver, the technique of helping a victim expel food or other objects on which he is choking. Revisions were not onetime exercises; all teaching materials were under constant scrutiny and revised as often as warranted.

When I stepped down as president, I was confident that the Red Cross was fulfilling its congressional charter obligations as regards service to the armed forces and disaster preparedness and relief. I was proud of our Blood Services, and I was comfortable with the quality of Red Cross courses and the broad array of services chapters were providing to their communities.

Fourth, finances.

I believe that the Red Cross was on a more realistic financial footing in 1982 than it had been in 1970. I look back with tight-lipped satisfaction on my financial management. It was not easy going. Throughout my twelve years, we were in an age of inflation. I commented to the board of governors near the end of my tenure that "the inflation rate in *every* year since I assumed my present responsibilities has been greater than in *any* year of my predecessors—Ambassador Bunker and Generals Gruenther and Collins." The consumer index rose to a peak of 13.3 in 1979, and the recessions of 1973-1975 and 1981-1982 were the worst since World War II.

One of my first acts in 1970 was to recommend that the board of governors establish a committee on members and funds. As first vice chairman of the Washington chapter, I had learned how difficult relations could be with a community fundraising organization with which we were—theoretically—a partner. I saw tough problems ahead and felt the board should analyze our relations with the newly named United Way. We needed a fundraising strategy of our own. To my amazement, career staff at headquarters was complacent. Board involvement was "unnecessary."

Some history is pertinent. The board of governors had decided in the mid-1950s to give up independent Red Cross fund campaigns and enter into "partnership" with the Community Funds and Councils (known from 1970 on as the United Way of America). Initially, the arrangement seemed to work. Red Cross chapters informed their local "partner" of their needs and their quota of the national Red Cross needs. The two groups joined forces for communitywide fundraising. But "partnership" had been forgotten by 1970. The United Way regarded the Red Cross as "just one more local agency." It resisted money being sent to Washington, regarding it as expensive "dues" to headquarters, not understanding—and not wanting to understand—the scope of the Red Cross's national programs. The result: more and more chapters were unable to remit their full quotas to Washington.

I overrode staff objections. A board committee on members and funds was established, and the board of governors was informed of growing problems in our relations with the United Way. Board members became directly involved in situation after situation where the Red Cross case had to be presented forcefully to ill-informed local United Way leaders. I met frequently with William Aramony, the hard-hitting executive of United Way's national headquarters. We met sometimes alone, at other times with executives of groups such as the Scouts and the "Y's" whose national needs were similarly ignored by local United Way offices. We protested vigorously at the increasing practice of the local United Ways of portraying themselves as providers of community services and ignoring the organizations that were the actual providers. Aramony's excuse that each local United Way was "independent" was belied by the influence and direction he had on their actions. Despite our sharp differences of opinion on many matters, I found Bill Aramony personally likable. I regretted that, some years after my retirement, his taste for high living led him to appropriate United Way funds for his personal use. A long prison term resulted.

Our problems with the United Way movement were more serious than its self-aggrandizement and its harmful guidance to the locals to "be sure the money you raise stays at home." Year by year, it was losing its focus on health and human services. Local United Ways were increasingly including a widening array of ethnic, racial, religious, and cultural groups. While yearly raising more money in total, that money was being divided among more and more organizations. Furthermore, yearly totals were not keeping pace with the inflation of the 1970s. In 1976, I was invited to meet with the long-range planning committee of the national United Way board of directors to testify on United Way's relations with the Red Cross and other large organizations. "Not good" was my succinct summary. I referred to the United Way's latest annual report showing that less in dollars of constant purchasing power had been raised that year than in the late 1960s. Thus, despite the heralded success of its campaigns, United Way was actually less successful year by year in meeting the needs of an increasingly complex society.

I believe the Red Cross was "more realistically" if not "more richly" financed when I stepped down as president because the illusion of "partnership" with the United Way had been replaced with an honest understanding of our financial situation. Ignoring United Way threats, at the Red Cross annual convention in Hartford, Connecticut, in 1977, on my recommendation, the board of governors authorized chapters to resume independent fundraising to supplement their steadily decreasing United Way allotments. We tightened the belt in all activities of the national sector. As noted above, SAF&V was much reduced and our response to disasters was sharply focused on immediate emergency assistance. The area offices in Alexandria, Atlanta, St. Louis, and San Francisco were slimmed down. Many of their duties were handed to the larger chapters, who became "mother hens" to their smaller neighbors. Blood Services became self-supporting through "cost recovery," and it now carried its share of chapter and national sector overhead. "Cost recovery" was also introduced into the health and safety programs. Courses were no longer free—fees were charged for texts, teaching materials, and a share of chapter overhead. We adopted the "total return" concept for the endowment fund rather than the "income only" practice that had prevailed since the fund's inception some sixty years earlier. Wherever possible, we "unbundled" such items as insurance, billing each chapter its precise share rather than lumping this and similar items into the national quota assigned each chapter annually.

All these and many other changes—some major, some minor—resulted in my being able to report to the board of governors in my last year as president that the national sector's proportion of the fund campaign goal would be the smallest since the First World War and the chapters' proportion the greatest. Chapters would be better able to make the Red Cross case to their local United Ways and had the best incentive yet to raise money themselves—the latter being the key to our future security.

Despite all our actions, in my final report to the board in October 1982, I was candid and reported the facts:

> If one but glances at the 1970 and 1982 annual reports, he will be impressed by the seeming rich growth of the American Red Cross over those twelve years. But a close look reveals that, whereas Blood Services have about nine times the revenue now as twelve years ago, all other activities of the Red Cross—chapter and national sectors combined—are supported by funds that have not even doubled in that period. Indeed, in terms of dollars of constant value, funding for all Red Cross services other than blood is substantially less than in 1970—a distressing one-fourth less. Increasing public support and revenue is, without question, a premier challenge for the Board and chapter and national management.

It was a challenge to which my successor, Richard Schubert, would vigorously respond.

Forgetting, with pleasure, the arduous chores of administration, I remember, with pleasure, some of the international experiences of the job. The first Red Cross overseas adventure—and in many ways the best because my family was with me—was the summer of 1972. I broke away from Hurricane Agnes relief and money-raising efforts to fly with Sally and Howard to Geneva, where Anne was enrolled for summer courses at the university. After glorious days of Swiss sightseeing, during which Howard and I were amateur climbers on the lower reaches of the Matterhorn, we moved on to Vienna and then to Belgrade. There I was back in harness, paying an official visit to the Yugoslav Red Cross on its invitation. The schedule included more hospitals, clinics, and children's nurseries than we cared to see, but these were offset by the flight to breathtaking Dubrovnik and a drive along the spectacular Dalmatian coast. The president of the Yugoslav society, our host, was a Croatian who liked to boast of his closeness to Tito, the communist dictator of the country. I sensed that he and I were not welcome in Serbian communities—a premonition of the ethnic hatreds that were to tear the country apart some years later.

From Belgrade we flew to Moscow as guests of the Soviet society. To a great extent, the Moscow and Leningrad visits were repeats of my 1956 trip, but the atmosphere was very different. We were subjected to no lectures on the perfection of the Soviet system as before, and we were free to move about as we wished, limited only by the language barrier. Helsinki, Stockholm, Copenhagen, and London completed the tour, with courtesy calls on each Red Cross and generous hospitality everywhere. Then home—to the renewed rigors of hurricane fundraising.

Five months after the combined vacation and goodwill European jaunt, I flew in the opposite direction to Saigon, capital of South Vietnam (now Ho Chi Minh City). The State Department had received a cable from my old boss Ellsworth Bunker, now our ambassador in Saigon. He had reason to believe that an American Red Cross official would be permitted to visit American prisoners of war being held by the North Vietnamese. I took off at once, although this meant that I would miss the important meeting of the board of governors at which Harriman had privately told me he would announce his decision to resign as chairman. For political reasons too complex to summarize here, my visit to North Vietnam to see American POWs and deliver relief parcels prepared by Red Cross volunteers never took place. Greatly disappointed, I flew home, reaching Washington for the closing hours of the board meeting. I gave an account of the frustrations of our embassy and our military leaders in dealing with the North Vietnamese, especially on POW matters. The only pleasure I had in the failure of the Saigon mission was that it enabled me to be back home when Harriman stunned the board by his announcement and to witness the outpouring of affection and admiration from board members for his devoted leadership of twenty-three years.

In the summer of 1973, I flew with Frank Stanton, our new chairman, to Teheran for an international Red Cross conference. This, like the New Delhi meeting of 1957, was attended by representatives of all governments that had signed the Geneva Conventions as well as all Red Cross and Red Crescent societies. Unlike Harriman, who had never attended an international conference (not even one as close as Toronto in 1952), Stanton was active in all the sessions, debating eloquently and winning friends worldwide by his warmth. There were no political fights, as there had been in Delhi, although delegates from the communist countries made their obligatory political remarks for the record. Delegates were awed by the lavish entertainments provided by the shah and staggered by the opulence of the palace of the shah's sister. We were shielded from contact with the elements of the population that were soon to expel the royal family and turn the country into a harshly ruled theocracy. At Teheran, I was appointed to the finance commission of the international league, an involvement that was to last for fourteen years, during which time I would make frequent trips to the league's headquarters in Geneva.

I was back in Belgrade in 1975, reluctantly, to participate in the First Red Cross and Red Crescent Conference to Promote Peace. While my counterparts in such countries as Canada, Japan, Great Britain, and the Scandinavian nations knew no good could come of it, we did not see how we could avoid attending. The conference was just as expected— much anti-Western chatter from Soviet bloc countries and venomous attacks on Israel by many of the Muslim delegates. Wordy resolutions of actions inappropriate for the Red Cross were passed, but "our side" succeeded in blocking most of the language offensive to our governments and our societies. The setting was ironic. Yugoslavia was portraying itself as the world's leading proponent of peace even as the country was beginning to come apart, as it did in the "ethnic cleansings" and the civil war of the 1980s and 1990s.

There were some small pleasures in the otherwise noisome atmosphere of the peace conference. The first Red Cross in the Balkans had been established in 1875 in the small kingdom of Montenegro, incorporated into Yugoslavia after World War I. To commemorate this centenary, delegates were flown to Cetinje, Montenegro's capital in its days of independence. As a boy, I had collected stamps of Montenegro. I was delighted to explore the historic places that I knew from stamps—the former monastery, for example, that had been printing books before Columbus discovered America. I was especially pleased to see in the former royal palace (a modest two-story frame building—this "kingdom" had been an isolated mountainous area of only a few hundred thousand residents) that the royal stamp collection on display was not as complete as mine!

Although each international meeting has its memories for me, there is no need to do more than mention some of them. Another international conference with government and Red Cross delegates was held in Bucharest in 1977. Nicholae Ceausescu was then Romania's harsh dictator, to be brutally executed by a mob a few years later. The country was under such tight control—as Iran had been four years earlier—that delegates were shielded from any signs of unrest. (In Baghdad in 1957, only when General Gruenther and I were having drinks with the Swiss manager of the hotel where we were staying and he told us that Iraq was seething and could explode at any time did I have intimations of problems.) In Bucharest, we were as oblivious to political unrest as we had been in Teheran and were to be in Manila in 1981.

An international conference in Manila in 1981 was my last as president. At lulls in the sessions, I had long talks with Jerome Holland, Stanton's successor as chairman, on the future of the Red Cross. Holland and I worked exceptionally well together. He was a great strapping fellow, an all-American on a winning Cornell football team in the late 1930s with a Ph.D. from Penn. He was president of Hampton Institute (now Hampton University) when President Nixon named him ambassador to Sweden in 1970. He had resigned as a member-at-large of the Red Cross Board of Governors on departing for Stockholm and had been reelected to the board on his return to the United States. When Frank Stanton had told me, to my dismay, that he would serve as chairman no longer than the two three-year terms allowed all other Red Cross board members, I had urged him to recommend Holland to the Carter White House as his successor. The appointment was promptly made despite Holland's public reputation as an ardent Republican.

Now, as Holland's first term as chairman was nearing its end, I asked Jack Currin, our general counsel, to sound out his contact in the Reagan White House on a second term for Holland. "No dice," was the reply. "No Carter appointees will be reappointed. Give us another name."

This I had no intention of doing. I felt it important that the first African American to be the Red Cross chairman not be dumped after what would seem to have been a mere token appointment. Some weeks went by without White House or Red Cross action. Holland's three-year term expired. The Red Cross was without a chairman as its annual convention was fast approaching. I told Currin to warn his White House contact that, when the convention opened in St. Louis without a chairman, he could be certain that word would spread that President Reagan had refused to reappoint Holland *because of his race*. Unpleasant news stories would surely result. That did it. Two days before twenty-five hundred delegates assembled, Holland was reappointed.

I had been running a real risk by taking the stand I did. Reagan could have appointed a crony and told him to "get rid of that fellow Elsey."

But my tactics had worked, to my great relief, and Holland continued as our leader until his death in 1985.

In our talks at breaks in the Manila conference, I reminded Holland that I would resign as president on reaching age sixty-five in February 1983. We needed to plan for my successor. I noted that Harriman had chosen Bunker, Gruenther (with a nudge from the White House), Collins, and me. I thought there should be a more formal way of choosing a president. "Brud" Holland agreed. We decided that he would name a committee of board members and announce it at the February 1982 board meeting, with the aim of having the name of a presidential candidate presented to the board for election in October 1982, the last board meeting before my retirement date. As far as I was concerned, the talks with Holland were the most important events at the Manila conference.

All went according to our agreed schedule. A board committee worked diligently and found the perfect new president in Richard Schubert, a former undersecretary of labor and recently president of Bethlehem Steel. Schubert had an outstanding record of volunteer involvement. I stepped down a few weeks early, on January 1, 1983, to let Dick take over.

My international work continued as chairman of the league's finance commission, a post I resigned at the international conference in Rio de Janeiro in 1987. My last trip to Geneva came two years later. I was invited to attend a special session where I was presented with the Henry Dunant Medal. This is the highest award of the Red Cross–Red Crescent movement, named for its Swiss founder. Someone tipped off the White House about the award. I was surprised—and much pleased—to receive a warm congratulatory letter from President George H. W. Bush.

No account of foreign adventures would be complete without mentioning that Red Cross visits went both ways. Just as I was a guest in many countries, so was I host to many visitors to our shores. Unlike the 1950s when I escorted visitors, from 1970 on Dorothy Taaffe and Joseph Carniglia, directors of international services, had the travel duty for visitors from nearly every continent.

Of all the improbable events in my life, my receiving the once bitterly hated Emperor Hirohito of Japan in my office must rank close to the top of the list. Hirohito—ranked in the minds of Americans of the World War II generation with Adolf Hitler as the very embodiment of evil—

and his empress paid a state visit to the United States in 1975. At the request of the empress, who was honorary president of the Japanese Red Cross, a visit to us was added to the itinerary proposed by the State Department. Much to-ing and fro-ing between State's protocol office and Dorothy Taaffe ensued. We were told, among copious instructions, that we must make no request of the emperor or empress.

The great day arrived. The imperial party was escorted to my office, where I had arranged a display of objects representing the long association of our two societies. I told Emperor Hirohito how proud we were of the great vase he had sent to the American Red Cross in recognition of our assistance after the Tokyo earthquake in 1923. When the interpreter finished translating my words, the emperor looked up at me and said, "Ah, so." An eloquent man he was not.

Turning to the empress, I addressed her as "madame president," not as "your imperial majesty." I asked her, as president, to honor us by signing our guest book. She smiled and did so, then handed the pen to the emperor and told him to sign also. When a protocol officer from State, after the visit, rebuked me for violating his instructions not to make any request of the emperor and empress, I blandly remarked that I had not asked the empress, I had asked the honorary president of the Japanese Red Cross. The officer left in a huff, thinking me impossible.

At my thirty-seventh and last meeting of the board of governors in October 1982, a resolution—embarrassing in its flowery prose—about my twelve years of service was read by the secretary. I recalled a quip of my greatly admired friend of World War II days, Fleet Admiral Leahy: "That would sound nice if set to music." I did not take seriously the sentiments of the board resolution, having written many such farewells for men and women retiring from military and federal service and from business and volunteer organizations. I knew better than to inhale such rarefied hot air. Still, it was pleasant to hear—even without music. And it was pleasant, too, when the board of governors designated me as president emeritus, an appreciated honor unprecedented in Red Cross history.

A few weeks later, my office colleagues surprised me with two bound volumes of letters from former board members, retired Red Cross staff, and leaders of foreign Red Cross and Red Crescent societies with whom I had worked, as well as from some longtime personal friends. Some letters came directly to me. None was more gratifying than the one from board member Hugh Chaplin, a physician and professor of medicine at Washington University in St. Louis. I have kept it. Among other sentences of fulsome praise, Hugh wrote, "I send you my special thanks for the clarity of your various communications, both formal and informal, and for the felicity of language and expression that has assured both understanding and esthetic pleasure." Winston Churchill has been quoted as saying that every minute of one of his speeches required one hour of work. I'll make no such claim, but I will say that each of my public addresses required much, much thought. Hugh's letter commenting on my speaking and prose style made me feel that the hours spent preparing speeches and reports were appreciated—at least by one hearer.

I was saddened that my father had died in my last months as president. I had looked forward to being able to spend more time with him than Red Cross duties had permitted. We had come to a friendly understanding on some political matters, and I cherished one of his last letters to me in which he concluded (after a blast at the country's "series of incompetent and dishonest presidents"): "The only truly honest president we have had is Truman who replaced the traitorous Roosevelt."

After stepping down as president on January 1, 1983, in addition to continuing to serve as finance chairman of the league, I became "consultant to the chairman" at Brud Holland's request. Holland's successor, George Moody—a Los Angeles banker and longtime Red Cross volunteer—asked me to remain in that role. Holland, later Moody, and Dick Schubert tossed various assignments my way and kept me comfortably busy until March 1, 1990, when—at age seventy-two—I felt it was time to give up the part-time post. Since then, as a retiree and volunteer, I have enjoyed speaking, writing, and consulting with current staff and volunteers when their interests send them in my direction.

In 2004, as I was completing this concatenation of memories, friends sent me copies of an announcement being circulated throughout the Red Cross of the retirement of a senior executive whom I very much respected. The announcement noted that Jack Campbell had come to the organization "when the legendary George Elsey was the President." I was bemused—and somewhat embarrassed—at the adjective, but concluded that it was probably better to be a "legend" than to be a "myth." To be so described is certification that I had been "real," even if many events in this account of an unplanned life seem to verge on the mythical.

Acknowledgments

I am deeply indebted to friends and former associates for suggestions and actions that greatly affected my life. The attentive reader of the preceding pages will understand my indebtedness to Samuel Eliot Morison, Richard Ballinger, James Charles Risk, William C. Mott, Fleet Admiral William D. Leahy, Clark M. Clifford, W. Averell Harriman and his brother E. Roland Harriman, John C. Wilson, and Harry S. Truman.

George Hartzog, then Director of the National Park Service, first suggested more than twenty years ago when he and I were serving on the Board of Directors of the White House Historical Association that I should write an account of my still unfinished career. Some years later, Robert Ferrell, Distinguished Professor of History at Indiana University and a fellow director of the Harry S. Truman Library Institute, repeated the Hartzog suggestion with the blunt comment, "It's time to stop talking and start writing." Bob had seen me in many TV interviews and thought I should tell my own story in my own way and not be at the mercy of television interrogators.

Belatedly following Bob's advice, in due course, I sent him a draft text of *An Unplanned Life.* He astonished me by forwarding it to Beverly Jarrett, Director and Editor-in-Chief of the University of Missouri Press, with the recommendation that she consider publication.

This to me was a startling thought. I had written with a primary readership of two in mind—my teenage grandsons Andrew and Brian Kranz—thinking that some day they might be curious as to what Grand-dad had been up to. A few computer printouts would do for other relatives.

Beverly Jarrett and her talented Managing Editor, Jane Lago, transformed the manuscript into this handsome volume. Although we have never met, through frequent telephone conversations and many letters, I have come to regard them as warm friends. I owe them much and am deeply grateful.

I am especially appreciative of the efforts of a former Red Cross associate, Bonnie Virch, who with infectious enthusiasm skillfully deciphered bad penmanship and poor typing to produce the clean text that attracted the attention of Bob Ferrell, Beverly Jarrett, and Jane Lago. Susan Fels has enhanced the book with her comprehensive index, and in preparing it she was a superb proofreader.

The book was written from memory refreshed by many contemporary notes, an occasional letter, a few newspaper clippings, and scattered photographs. Such errors as have escaped Bonnie's, Beverly's, and Jane's attention are my personal responsibility.

George McKee Elsey
Washington, D.C.
June 2005

Index